Global Environmental Governance and the
Accountability Trap

Earth System Governance

Frank Biermann and Oran R. Young, series editors

Related books from Institutional Dimensions of Global Environmental Change: A Core Research Project of the International Human Dimensions Programme on Global Environmental Change

Global Environmental Governance and the Accountability Trap

Edited by Susan Park and Teresa Kramarz

The MIT Press
Cambridge, Massachusetts
London, England

This book was set in Stone by Toppan Best-set Premedia Limited.

Library of Congress Cataloging-in-Publication Data

Names: Park, Susan, 1976- editor. | Kramarz, Teresa, editor.
Title: Global environmental governance and the accountability trap / edited by Susan Park and Teresa Kramarz.
Description: Cambridge, MA : The MIT Press, [2019] | Series: Earth system governance | Includes bibliographical references and index.
Identifiers: LCCN 2018028558| ISBN 9780262039062 (hardcover : alk. paper) | ISBN 9780262536233 (pbk. : alk. paper)
Subjects: LCSH: Environmental policy--International cooperation. | Environmental protection--International cooperation. | Globalization--Environmental aspects. | Environmental responsibility.
Classification: LCC GE170 .G5545 2019 | DDC 363.7/0526--dc23 LC record available at https://lccn.loc.gov/2018028558

Susan dedicates this book to Matthew, William and Christopher. Teresa dedicates this book to Tess, Tiago, Mateo and John.

Contents

Series Foreword

Humans now influence all biological and physical systems of the planet. Almost no species, land area, or part of the oceans has remained unaffected by the expansion of the human species. Recent scientific findings suggest that the entire earth system now operates outside the normal state exhibited over at least the past 500,000 years. Yet at the same time, it is apparent that the institutions, organizations, and mechanisms by which humans govern their relationship with the natural environment and global biogeochemical systems are utterly insufficient—and poorly understood. More fundamental and applied research is needed.

Such research is no easy undertaking. It must span the entire globe because only integrated global solutions can ensure a sustainable coevolution of biophysical and socioeconomic systems. But it must also draw on local experiences and insights. Research on earth system governance must be about places in all their diversity, yet seek to integrate place-based research within a global understanding of the myriad human interactions with the earth system. Eventually, the task is to develop integrated systems of governance, from the local to the global level, that ensure the sustainable development of the coupled socioecological system that the Earth has become.

The series Earth System Governance is designed to address this research challenge. Books in this series will pursue this challenge from a variety of disciplinary perspectives, at different levels of governance, and with a range of methods. Yet all will further one common aim: analyzing current systems of earth system governance with a view to increased understanding and possible improvements and reform. Books in this series will be of interest to the academic community but will also inform practitioners and at times contribute to policy debates.

This series is related to the long-term international research program "Earth System Governance Project."

Frank Biermann, Copernicus Institute of Sustainable Development, Utrecht University
Oran R. Young, Bren School, University of California, Santa Barbara

Earth System Governance Series Editors

Acknowledgments

This volume is the result of a wide and deep process of collaborative research that started in 2014 when we began working on a new research project on accountability in environmental politics. Coming from similar research backgrounds in environmental governance and international organizations, we found that accountability was often narrowly conceptualized, theorized, and practiced. We identified the need for a wider perspective that took into account diverse environmental issue areas, actors, and scales of governance. To this end, we decided to create a network to promote collaborative research on accountability and bring together scholars with intimate knowledge of key environmental regimes (air, water, forests, energy, and climate) along with scholars of global institutions (the United Nations Environment Programme, the World Bank, and the United Nations Framework Convention on Climate Change, among others) and of transnational actors developing rules for environmental governance. We raised funds and began organizing meetings for the network to meet on a regular basis through panels, workshops, and roundtables. These efforts brought together 46 senior and junior researchers from prestigious universities in developed and developing countries across Asia, Australia, the Caribbean, Europe, Latin America, and North America. During these meetings we began assessing the design, gaps, and potential for accountability across global environmental governance. These fruitful exchanges produced 13 original research articles in two special issues published in *Global Environmental Politics* in 2016 and *Review of Policy Research* in 2017.

In 2015, we became the Task Force on Accountability in Global Environmental Governance (AGEG) in the Earth System Governance project, which constitutes the largest research network of social scientists working on environmental governance. This institutional home has provided a platform to extend the reach of the network and nest it within a community of environmental scholars, so accountability can be functionally analyzed as a cross cutting issue. Our goal has been to develop the first global approach to mapping and understanding accountability in global environmental governance. With this edited volume we aim to establish a conceptual foundation and a baseline analysis of the practice of accountability across public, private, voluntary, and hybrid governance institutions in various environmental issue areas.

This book represents the culmination of a journey in which we had the good fortune to meet and work with extraordinary people and enjoy the generous support of several institutions. In addition to our collaborators in this volume, we are grateful for the intellectual inputs and encouragement from Steven Bernstein, Frank Biermann, Benjamin Cashore, Christopher Gore, Matthew Hoffmann, Michael Mason, Kate O'Neil, and Stacy VanDeveer. Institutions have also been important throughout this trajectory. The International Studies Association through its Venture Grants, the Sydney Environment Institute, the Australian Political Studies Association, the Munk School of Global Affairs, and the Earth System Governance project provided financial support that made our workshops and this book possible.

Finally, but most crucial to this enterprise, has been the support of our partners and children who gave up their time with us to allow for Skype calls at bizarre hours to accommodate time zone differences between Australia and Canada, long trips away from home, and jet lagged parents on return. For us, one of the greatest joys of this intellectual journey has been the pleasure of working together.

Acronyms

ACE—American Council on Education

ADP2—Ad Hoc Working Group on the Durban Platform for Enhanced Action

ARREST—Asia's Regional Response to Endangered Species Trafficking

ASTM—American Society of Testing Materials

BFAR—Bureau of Fisheries and Aquatic Resources

BIDS—Bad Ivory Database System

BRICS—Brazil, Russia, India, China and South Africa

CAB—Conformance Assessment Bodies

CDP—Carbon Disclosure Project

CB—Certification Bodies

cCR—carbon*n* Climate Registry

CDT—Cyanide Detection Test

CITES—Convention on the International Trade in Endangered Species of Wild Fauna and Flora

CLG—Corporate Leaders Group

COP—Conference of the Parties

CRAG—Carbon Action Rationing Group

CREST—Coral Reef Education for Students

CSO—Civil Society Organization

CSR—Compact of States and Regions

DRC—Democratic Republic of Congo

DETECT—Detection of Environmental Crime Training

EIA—Environmental Investigation Agency

ENGO—Environmental Nongovernment Organization

ERTs—Expert Review Teams

ETIS—Elephant Trade Information System

EU-TWIX—EU-Trade in Wildlife Information Exchange
FAO—Food and Agriculture Organization
FPIC—Free Prior and Informed Consent
FSC—Forest Stewardship Council
GEG—Global Environmental Governance
GEF—Global Environment Facility
GHG—Global Greenhouse Gas
GRI—Global Reporting Initiative
IAR—International Assessment and Review
ICA—International Consultation and Analysis
ICCA—International Council of Chemical Association
ICDP—Integrated Conservation and Development Projects
ICITAP—International Criminal Investigative Training Assistance Program
IEG—Independent Evaluation Group
IFAW—International Fund for Animal Welfare
IGO—Intergovernmental Organizations
IMA—International Marinelife Alliance
INGO—International NGOs
IO—International Organization
LDCs—Least-Developed Countries
LPAA—Lima-Paris Action Agenda
LMDC—Like-minded Developing Countries
L&G—Lean and Green
MAD—Multiple Accountability Disorder
MEA—Multilateral Environmental Agreement
MNC—Multinational Corporations
MSC—Marine Stewardship Council
NAZCA—Non-State Actor Zone on Climate Action
NDCs—Nationally Determined Contributions
NDFs—Non-Detriment Findings
NGO—Nongovernment Organization
PDC—Portfolio Decarbonization Coalition
PETA—People for the Ethical Treatment of Animals
PROTECT—Protected-Area Operational and Tactical Enforcement Conservation Training
QAG—Quality Assurance Group
RSB—Roundtable on Sustainable Biomaterials

SAD—Single Accountability Disorder
SBI—Subsidiary Body for Implementation
SE4ALL—Sustainable Energy for All
SIDS—Small Island Developing States
TAB—Technical Advisory Board
TAG—Technical Advisory Group
TNC—The Nature Conservancy
UNEP—United Nations Environment Programme
UNEP FI—The United Nations Environment Programme's Finance Initiative
UNEP FI PDC—UNEP Financial Initiative's Portfolio Decarbonization Coalition
UNGC—UN Global Compact
UNFCCC—United Nations Framework Convention on Climate Change
USAID—United States Agency for International Development
USEPA—United States Environmental Protection Agency
TBC—To Be Completed
WCO—World Customs Organization
WCS—Wildlife Conservation Society
WWF—World Wide Fund (for Nature)

I   Introduction

1 Identifying Multiple Accountabilities in Global Environmental Governance

Teresa Kramarz and Susan Park

Introduction

Global environmental governance (GEG) has burgeoned amid the ongoing deterioration of the environment. Problems with GEG are widely known: the system is fragmented with duplicated efforts, dispersed political authority, and weak regulatory influence. Blame is also directed at a culture of unaccountability (Najam and Halle 2010), where accountability is defined as when "some actors have the right to hold other actors to a set of standards, to judge whether they have filled their responsibilities in light of those standards, and to impose sanctions if they determine that those responsibilities have not been met" (Grant and Keohane 2005, 29). There have been attempts to address this culture of unaccountability: whether through greater transparency, the provision of justification and reasoning for governance decisions, or establishing monitoring and evaluation procedures. Arguably this has led to an accountability trap: those governing the global environment are increasingly reliant on accountability processes, such as verification, measurement, and compliance monitoring, to demonstrate that they are accountable for their decisions. Adherence to these processes are intended to improve governance, and by doing so, contribute to improving environmental outcomes. Yet it is unclear if and how the proliferation of accountability tools contributes to improving environmental outcomes, especially when global environmental degradation continues at a rapid pace.

The purpose of this volume is to probe how accountability is being used within GEG and to establish if accountability is a useful tool for improving governance, with the aim of addressing global environmental deterioration. Conceptually, accountability in GEG remains underanalyzed

(Biermann 2014; Gupta and Biermann 2011), although the contributors in this volume are at the forefront in examining how specific accountability processes operate. We make three claims: first, that GEG institutions exhibit a normative bias; second, that these biased logics determine the framing of problems and accountability procedures; and third, that functionalist or compliance-based accountability processes alone cannot enable the organizational learning that is necessary for effective environmental governance and therefore outcomes. This argument seeks to unpack the *meta-governance* or governance of global environmental governance, which includes how the norms underpinning international institutions shape how governors design and execute environmental interventions (Jessop 2002; Kooiman and Jentoft 2009).

In the international realm, institutions for governing the global environment are not homogenous (Biermann 2014).[1] We propose that scholars of accountability must investigate the goals of the multiple actors engaged in public, private, voluntary, and hybrid global environmental institutions. These actors have different goals for governing the environment. An understanding of how these goals differ is vital for understanding the accountability trap. We contend that various actors' goals shape attendant accountability processes. Authority holders, or those governing the environment, are guided by distinct goals that determine to whom and for what to account. This influences the framing of environmental priorities and how accountability is measured.

Given the multiplicity of actors in GEG, we provide a theoretical framework that traces how public, private, voluntary, and hybrid governance institutions prioritize different goals, and how these priorities shape interventions in environmental problems. Designing governance institutions in certain ways, and not others, shapes the accountability procedures that are established to hold governors to account for environmental interventions. Thus, public actors prioritize being responsive to constituencies; private actors prioritize economic benefit and profit; and voluntary actors focus on moral value as determined by shared agreement among concerned stakeholders. These distinct goals influence the design and execution of GEG and their attendant accountability mechanisms.

The theoretical framework for analyzing accountability in global environmental governance is informed by a constructivist understanding of the world, where social actors are engaged in intersubjective interactions that constitute and give meaning to material facts. Through daily interactions, public, private, and voluntary actors constitute systems of governance. This engenders distinct logics of action for these institutions. These three logics of action (public, private, and voluntary), determine how problems are framed and how those in authority subsequently devise attendant accountability procedures. Individuals within these institutions may act against those goals (for example, for personal enrichment) but are constrained by what is socially acceptable (Schillermans and Busuioc 2015, 194).

A constructivist approach does not preclude examining individually rational actions. Indeed, actors may seek to behave in an optimal way to achieve their interests. However, actors take on the interests and preferences that are rational within the broader social structure within which they exist (Johnston 2001; Schimmelfennig 2005). These social structures prioritize specific normative aims. In other words, the social structures within which governors of the environment act help shape what counts as rational behavior. Chapters 4 and 6 of the book use the Principal-Agent model in their analysis of actors establishing accountability processes. These chapters fit within the volume because they emphasize how actors view their social environments as having set logics with concomitant interests.

In sum, divergent public, private, and voluntary goals shape how global environmental institutions are designed and how they conceive interventions to mitigate negative environmental impacts. These goals influence actors' understanding of the purpose of accountability. We maintain that the environment is subservient to the prior goals of each of these institutions.

In order to demonstrate the accountability trap, the theoretical framework proposes examining two tiers of environmental governance: first, the design of three types of institutions; and second, the execution of their accountability processes for evaluating environmental interventions. Examining two tiers of governance is imperative because authority holders may be held accountable for their actions without necessarily mitigating negative environmental impacts. Herein lies the accountability trap: authority holders are held accountable through existing governance institutions which bias goals such as short-term economic gains over environmental goals. Accountability holders may not be accountable despite accountability procedures because those establishing GEG are not held to account for the first tier of governance, where problems are framed, priorities identified,

and solutions devised. While scholars are aware of competing and conflicting interests in bringing authority holders to account, such as Koppell's
(2005) multiple accountability disorder (MAD), they have not linked the
goals of actors to the design of environmental institutions, focusing instead
on the execution of discreet interventions. The practice of accountability in
GEG therefore privileges applying accountability to established governing
processes, rather than investigating whether, for what, and to whom those
in authority were answerable when designing governance institutions in
the first place.

This volume seeks to understand how the goals of GEG institutions
shape accountability processes as well as investigating whether accountability procedures work to ensure that authority holders are accountable. We
therefore address an important gap in the literature by critically examining
how accountability processes were established and what their relationship
is to improving environmental governance and outcomes. Throughout the
chapters, we analyze whether there is a feedback loop from the design of
institutions to the creation of accountability mechanisms, whose operation
in turn affects the goals of GEG institutions. We take the idea of a feedback
loop up in our conclusion as a necessary factor for accountability to be a
meaningful tool for effective GEG.

The value of this framework is to locate failure in GEG in terms of agents
and structures. This provides an opportunity to examine how the design
and execution of GEG is built on the normative bias of actors. Doing so provides an opportunity for reflection and learning. Our agreement is much
deeper than suggesting that GEG merely set the wrong goals. Indeed, this
critical analysis details how certain ways of doing environmental governance became possible. This, then, provides insight into how actors can
seek alternative means to redesign and re-execute environmental governance through learning from the results of accountability practices. We
explicitly lay out how accountability processes were either not evident
in the original design of governance institutions or were later devised to
improve preexisting GEG structures.

Our introduction is structured in three parts. First, we examine the nature
of accountability mechanisms that have grown alongside the continued
deterioration of the environment. Second, we map accountability processes
and develop a theoretical framework for analyzing the following: how the
goals of those governing the environment shape the design of institutions;

how this in turn directs the execution of specific interventions in the environment; and finally, how these interventions lead to subsequent accountability processes for holding governors to account. The introduction then provides an overview of the contributions to the collection.

The Trap: More Accountability without More Environmental Benefits

As with governance more broadly (Bostrom and Garsten 2008; Held and Koenig-Archibugi 2005), there has been a proliferation of institutionalized accountability processes in global environmental governance (Cashore et al. 2004; Park 2010). Some see this as the rise of an "audit society," where the spread of technical practices can be understood as deriving from an attitudinal commitment to problem solving (Power 1997). A variety of accountability procedures within GEG have been established to increase transparency, provide actors' justification and reasoning for their governance decisions, and monitor and evaluate governance efforts (Ebrahim and Weisband 2007, 3–5). Authority holders thus aim to establish that they are responsible and answerable for how they govern the environment, and increasingly, how this impacts resource-dependent communities.

The types of accountability processes highlighted by Ebrahim and Weisband are detailed here in relation to GEG. First is the rise of transparency by all actors in GEG to enable scrutiny (Gupta 2010; Gupta and Mason 2014). This is increasingly evident before, during, and after multilateral environmental agreement (MEA) negotiations. It is also apparent in the willingness of corporate and voluntary actors to provide public reporting on their activities (on nonstate holders of authority, see Cashore 2002). Voluntary actors such as environmental nongovernment organizations (ENGOs) have been asked to explain their "financial practices, partnerships and methods" (Balboa 2015a, 159). It is also manifested in various transparency initiatives such as the Global Reporting Initiative and the Carbon Disclosure Project.

Second, across different media and platforms, environmental governors are increasingly providing justification and reasoning for their decisions. Most tangibly, some governance institutions such as the Forest Stewardship Council and the Marine Stewardship Council (FSC and MSC, on the latter, see chapter 6, in this volume) have even formalized deliberative decision-making procedures. Providing justification and reasoning has been internalized by some authority holders regarding how they govern. Third, there has been a proliferation of efforts to assess compliance through monitoring and evaluation. This is particularly evident in intergovernmental organizations (IGOs).

For example, the World Bank, which has a large environmental impact, has its Independent Evaluation Group and internal units such as the Quality Assurance Group to evaluate its environmental impact. Corporate actors have also been challenged to provide evidence of their compliance with voluntary standards such as the UN Global Compact and the various voluntary initiatives to which they have agreed to (see chapter 5, this volume). The ISO 14000 series now dominates such efforts, including environmental auditing. However, internal procedures remain nontransparent and difficult to assess. Meanwhile, ENGOs are required to be financially accountable to the state while holding each other to account for voluntary professional standards (Balboa 2015, 162).

As this short overview demonstrates, the problem is not the absence of accountability initiatives, but the continued deterioration of the environment despite their growth. Prescribing more accountability mechanisms is not necessarily better, because the mechanisms may not have an impact in terms of reducing environmental degradation. Scholars therefore question the utility of accountability in GEG. For example, Lohmann (2009) claims that interventions such as carbon accounting and cost-benefit analysis create black boxes of measurement, which are ill-conceived for attending to the complexity of global environmental problems. Hence,

carbon accounting's indifference to where or how emissions cuts are made discourages attention to path dependence, positive feedbacks and innovation; its conflation of reductions and offsets leads to a running together of probability with uncertainty, ignorance and indeterminacy; and its focus on means of achieving short-term efficiency obstructs social thinking about long-term directions and the drawbacks of having to monitor geographically distant effects (Lohmann 2009, 530).

In this example, accountability procedures have been tacked onto environmental interventions, which produce incommensurable categories that create perverse incentives for credit seekers and provide political clout to blend fundamental differences in localities, actors, and issues. Lohmann argues that this is part of a Weberian drive "to make an uncertain, complex, nonlinear, largely unpredictable world amenable to management and governance" (2009, 514). Attempts to manage the environment also speak to a process of "governing by indicators," or creating measurable and comparable statistics for assessing accountability, which may be inappropriate for addressing the problem (Shore and Wright 2015). Although this identifies the gap between governance instruments and desired environmental outcomes, it does not explain variance in the impact of accountability instruments, or even whether they can positively impact environmental outcomes.

Demands for accountability persist because accountability procedures do not respond to the expectations of environmental stakeholders (i.e., those affected by the environmental problem and those that claim to speak for the environment). This failure is twofold. First, despite the proliferation of GEG and attendant accountability procedures, the environment continues to deteriorate across 88 of the 90 indicators outlined in the *Global Environmental Outlook-Five* assessment (IPCC 2015; UNEP 2012). This is a widely recognized failure of outputs, leading many to question whether those in authority are being held to account for governing the environment or whether we need more or better accountability. The second reason why there has been an increase in the desire by policymakers, individuals, and institutions for greater accountability is based on input accountability, the continuing demand by different actors to shape decisions for governing the global environment (Biermann 2014; Chan and Pattberg 2008; Chesterman 2008). Both are addressed next.

First, widespread calls for accountability are based on output accountability, the demand that those governing be answerable and responsible for not delivering on their aim to mitigate the human impact on the biosphere. The conflation of environmental outputs, such as meeting emissions targets, and the resultant outcome for the environment is discussed below. Output accountability is the "oversight of operations, or accounting for results or impacts" (Davenport and Low 2013, 88–89). ENGOs push states to be held responsible for their environmental impact and advocate for binding agreements to limit environmentally damaging behavior through international negotiations. Once such agreements have been concluded ENGOs (and corporations) seek to hold states accountable for meeting agreed standards.

Of course, private actors are also recognized as legitimate actors (Hall and Biersteker 2002), with authority for governing the global environment (Green 2013).[2] While corporations are held to account through national regulations, ENGOs have also demanded corporations recognize their environmental footprint and that they are answerable for it. ENGOs then monitor whether private actors comply with (usually industry-set) standards. Assessing the compliance of those governing the environment is one component of accountability. GEG remains weak in the use of enforcement or sanctions to punish a lack of transparency, answerability, or compliance. Output accountability remains a challenge because, as we outline below, accountability procedures prioritize other normative goals such that environmental outcomes are subsumed. The solution is not to expand the concept of accountability to address all GEG limitations but to illuminate how accountability can be applied to the design of the standards to which governors are held and the execution of GEG against which compliance is measured.

The ongoing demand for accountability in GEG is based on the assumption that holding those governing to account will improve governance outcomes. In examining the normative logics of GEG institutions we go beyond constructivist research that identifies the emergence of "good norms" that advance a liberal progressive position (Risse et al. 1999; Park 2010). Instead, this volume seeks to uncover the existing normative bias in GEG institutions that gives rise to accountability mechanisms that seek to verify, measure, and monitor compliance for some things but not others. These accountability processes were designed to improve the governance of the global environment, with predictions by those governing the environment that they would lead to improved environmental outcomes.

An assessment of academic publication patterns in four leading interdisciplinary accounting journals upholds the argument that accountability processes are assumed to lead to better environmental outcomes. Research publication patterns show a dramatic increase in scholarship on social and environmental accounting since the late 1980s (Parker 2005). The practice of using accountability frameworks as management tools for governments and corporations is widespread (Lober et al. 1997; Caraiani 2015). In some international organizations, accountability is seen as a necessary condition for improving performance. For example, during decades of reorganization in the World Bank, the absence of accountability for mainstreaming environmental issues was identified as a clear obstacle to achieving better environmental results (Liebenthal 2002). Activists and the press also identify the lack of accountability as the main culprit behind acute and chronic environmental disasters (Mathews 2015, Greenpeace 2018).

Scholars, policymakers, corporations, and civil society actors associate—implicitly or explicitly—with imbue accountability processes as leading to specific environmental benefits.

Evidence is still required to support the argument that any kind of accountability measure has a positive effect on GEG. To date, evidence on environmental accountability shows mixed results at best (Larrinaga-Gonzalez and Bebbington 2001). There is a tendency to equate accountability mechanisms, understood as mostly public renderings on transparency, answerability, compliance, and sanction, with effective environmental action. Yet, in the modern, bureaucratized state system upon which the international system is built, we are surrounded by examples of accountability arrangements that do not achieve environmental benefits.

For example, there is a proliferation of state-regulated protected-area systems that provide for legal accountability mechanisms, but which do not necessarily translate into the conservation of the species that the systems were designed to protect (Kramarz 2013). There is a risk in the overwhelming preference within accountability scholarship for applying accountability solely to functional, end-of-pipe concerns like verification, measurement, and compliance. The accountability mechanism can identify whether actors are being held to account for meeting their stated aims. But to understand how and why particular accountability mechanisms were devised, we need to go beyond functionalist accounts and analyze the goals of particular governance institutions.[3] While the counter-factual may also be true—that the environment might be worse without accountability processes—it still needs to be proved.

The second reason why there has been an increase in the demand by policymakers, individuals, institutions, and ENGOs for greater accountability in GEG is based on input accountability (Chan and Pattberg 2008). This is in line with broader demands for global governance to be more responsive and answerable for *how* decisions are made, including determining who can demand that authority holders be held accountable. For much of the last decade, global governance has been described as having a "democratic deficit" where decisions are made absent connections back to the "public" (Held and Archibugi 2005). Demands for greater input accountability challenged IGOs that were only accountable to their member states, absent transparent decision-making processes. With a shift toward globalization, international decisions were increasingly felt locally, particularly as a result of transnational private governance (Dingwerth 2008). Pushback from groups in global civil society led to greater IGO transparency and hotly contested debates over the power of private interests in international regulation. In reaction to ENGOs' highly visible role, the voluntary sector also came under fire for being unaccountable (Balboa 2015).

Increasing participation in governing the environment may lead to better environmental outcomes (Dingwerth 2008). However, accountability is a tool that can only hold those governing the environment responsible and answerable for their actions within the context of preexisting institutions. As with democratic processes, accountability procedures are not inherently pro-environmental. Input accountability is structured differently in public, private, and voluntary (and hybrid) governance institutions with different values placed on open and participatory decision-making. We argue that a common feature across these governance institutions is the subordinate value placed on the environment. This is so even for hybrid governance institutions, such as public-private or public-voluntary arrangements, designed to address environmental problems.

In the absence of a broader input accountability, competing goals and agendas are not publicized, debated, and agreed upon when institutions are created. The dual hope of environmental accountability is that it will improve problem solving and responsiveness to stakeholders affected by environmental problems, although there may be tensions in addressing both. For example, resource dependent communities may be displaced in the name of conservation without any accountability to these populations for that decision (Chapin 2004). This volume suggests that those negatively affecting the environment have not, thus far, been able to address that impact through accountability processes. The lack of input accountability is evident when communities have been unable to contribute to the design or execution of environmental interventions that affect them.

There is ample evidence that those governing the global environment are increasingly holding themselves to account to primary or principal stakeholders and committing themselves to incorporating the voices of these stakeholders in global environmental decision-making. Two broad sources of evidence demonstrate this standard of accountability. The first is derived from international law, and the principle of Free Prior and Informed Consent (FPIC), which many IGOs such as the Food and Agriculture Organization hold as the gold standard of participation in sustainable development projects (FAO 2016, Tamang 2005). Although many critics see FPIC as soft law and aspirational, it is nonetheless a standard to which actors are holding themselves accountable.

The second source for a standard of accountability to primary stakeholders are statements from authority holders themselves. In these statements, they repeatedly commit to the inclusion of, and responsiveness to, vulnerable communities. Those communities respond to the accountability standard set by these authority holders and demand a response. For example, in 2007, Pygmy communities in the Democratic Republic of Congo (DRC) filed a request with the World Bank's Inspection Panel because Bank forestry projects were being designed and executed without the consultation or participation of forest dependent communities. The requesters stated that "the design and implementation of a new commercial forest concession system may cause irreversible harm to the forests where they live and on which they depend for their subsistence. They contend that these developments are taking place without giving them information, consulting with them, or providing them with an opportunity to participate" (World Bank Inspection Panel 2007, x). In response, the Bank acknowledged the need to "do better" for communities and increased communications on its involvement of local communities in forest sector reforms in the DRC. It justified its actions with frequent references to civil society participation (Anton and Shelton 2011). Whether community participation is rhetoric or a priority goal for IGOs like the World Bank, the salient fact is that they hold themselves accountable to this standard of environmental governance.

We therefore question whether there is a failure of accountability processes within GEG (Najam and Halle 2010). Instead, we suggest that the accountability trap is best understood by investigating two tiers of governance: the original design of GEG and the execution of GEG to which accountability procedures have been applied. As we argue below, tracing accountability from the design tier to the execution tier is essential for accountability to improve the governance of the global environment. Najam and Halle (2010) identify this in relation to MEAs but we need to interrogate the design of new institutions (and the retrofitting of old ones) by state and nonstate actors alike. Institutions are continually being created to mitigate environmental problems with accountability procedures to assess their effectiveness. Environmental accountability must go beyond evaluating whether authority holders are responsible and answerable for their actions within these institutions to ensure that they are responsive and answerable for their actions not just to the institution but to nature and the primary stakeholders of the environment. For example, recent studies such as that discussed in chapter 6 (this volume) demonstrate that having formalized justification and reasoning processes in GEG is no indication that those designing the process were held to account when they did it. Indeed, Gulbrandsen and Auld demonstrate that not being accountable in designing nonstate certification schemes (even those with transparent justification and reasoning processes and monitoring and evaluation procedures) can still lead to problems of accountability when operationalizing certification.

A Framework for Accountability in Global Environmental Governance

The theoretical framework provided here presents accountability as a useful tool in understanding how environmental governance institutions can be improved in terms of their institutional capacity for mitigating environmental damage. Establishing accountability procedures includes identifying what the object is for holding people to account, such as mitigating environmental damage, as well as how they should be held to account through transparent standards of assessment. Yet identifying such procedures does not explain why accountability mechanisms may fail to make an impact. Accountability is a limited tool for improving the environment through better governance because authority holders may point to accountability procedures (transparency, justification and reasoning, monitoring and evaluation) as leading to outputs (labeling standards, treaties, conventions, protocols) but not necessarily to outcomes (preventing or mitigating harm, decelerating desertification, reversing carbon dioxide trends). While there is difficulty in identifying how environmental outputs lead to better environmental outcomes, the failure of existing accountability procedures can be traced to the goals of GEG.

Central to this argument is the recognition that actors have different goals, which delimit the options considered when designing environmental institutions and the types of interventions deemed appropriate. To theorize the distinction between goals and means of accountability, we rely on a constructivist interpretation of constitutive versus regulative norms in international relations. Constitutive norms and rules "create new actors, interests, or categories of action," while regulative norms and rules "order and constrain behavior" (Finnemore and Sinkkink 1998, 891). The goals are the main purpose of the institution, with corresponding responsibilities to target audiences. In this case, goals have a constitutive effect on actors' understanding of the purpose of accountability (Searle 1995). Goals generate accountability procedures that regulate processes, standards, and sanctions, which are the regulative rules or the means of accountability. Every governance choice involves bias. Revealing those biases, including whether those designing public, private, voluntary, and hybrid institutions are accountable, brings us closer to understanding how accountability processes can be used to improve environmental governance outcomes.

Goals influence how different actors are held responsible in environmental institutions, which determines how their actions are rendered to a relevant community at two tiers. The first tier is the original design of governance institutions, where problems are framed, priorities identified, and solutions devised. This opens up a set of interrelated questions: Who gets to choose the approach for addressing an environmental problem? What biases animate these choices? To whom are actors accountable in prioritizing certain goals? For example: to whom were the proponents of the UN Global Compact accountable when they assumed that norms could trump self-interest (Chesterman 2008, 47–8)? To whom is Conservation International accountable for promoting a hotspot approach to conservation? Who is the World Wide Fund for Nature (WWF) responsible to for supporting a Forest Stewardship Council standard of certification over alternatives (Cashore 2002, 507)? What are the intrinsic goals of these institutions and where is the accountability for choosing these goals?

The second tier of GEG is the execution of environmental interventions. The accountability literature concentrates on whether authority holders are transparent, provide justification and reasoning, include monitoring and evaluation procedures, and are compliant with their aims in relation to the execution of specific interventions (i.e. whether actors do what they are supposed to do). We liken our distinction between the first and second tiers of GEG to "process integrated" versus "end-of-pipe" types of environmental approaches. The former relies on *ex ante*—in the design stage of environmental governance, such as processes of clean production; while the latter relies on *ex post*, in the execution stage of environmental governance

Table 1.1
Applying Accountability to the First and Second Tiers of GEG

		First-tier accountability "process-integrated" ↓		Second-tier accountability "end-of-pipe" ↓
Goals of Public/ Private/ Voluntary Governors	→	Design of environmental Institutions	→	Execution of environmental interventions

(table 1.1). In order for accountability to be a meaningful tool for action it must be applied to both tiers. This is because they are intrinsically linked[4].

We map how the first and second tiers of GEG interact across three ideal governance institutions: public, private, and voluntary (Mashaw 2006; Chan and Pattberg 2008, 105)[5]. This is important because the proliferation of institutions "based on private authority, private regimes, or some mix of public and private actors" (Risse 2005, 166) has led some to argue that other types of accountabilities exist beyond public accountability, where "market" and "voluntary" accountability have different standards, procedures, and sanctions (Mashaw 2006). We adapt a map of accountability first described by Dubnick and Justice (2004) to highlight how these institutions have distinct logics of action (figure 1.1). In public systems, what counts as accountability is being answerable to an electorate or political community for protecting the public good; in private systems, what counts is providing economic benefits to consumers and shareholders; in voluntary systems, what counts is upholding or diffusing agreed upon moral standards of conduct among self-selected, like-minded individuals.

These are the goals of the global environmental institutions. Consequently, actors internalize a need to act and render an account of their actions based on bureaucratic, utilitarian, or moral standards. Understanding the motivations for accountability that animate different authority holders, and where, if at all, the environment appears in those motivations to account (subsumed by political, economic, and moral preferences), can reveal important governance dysfunctions, and ultimately failures to curb environmental degradation of the earth's systems.

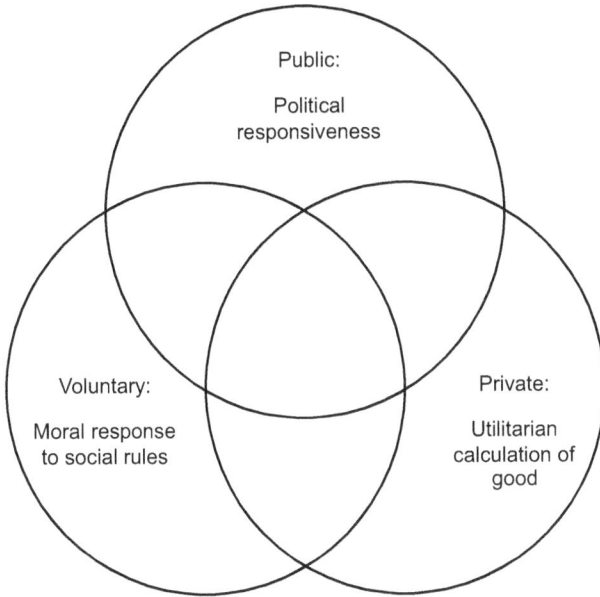

Figure 1.1
Public, private, and voluntary environmental governance goals

These categories, like all ideal types, do not describe the complexity of GEG. A decreasing number of institutions fit neatly into a single category. As the Venn diagram here suggests, GEG initiatives involve hybrid institutions that create more complexity for understanding accountability relationships and responsibilities for effective environmental action (we do not see governance progressing from one type to another, contra Chan and Pattberg 2008, 108). Chapter 5 of this volume, on the accountability of corporations to the United Nations Framework Convention on Climate Change (UNFCCC), straddles traditional public and private governance. Chapter 6 in this volume, on certification schemes in the MSC, examines governance institutions that crosses private and voluntary types. Other research investigating how ENGOs enforce the Convention on International Trade of Endangered Species (CITES) multilateral agreement for states spans public and voluntary governance (see chapter 7, this volume). Public, private, and voluntary governance categories are useful for distilling principles of accountability for types of institutions. It is also useful for mapping which types of accountability hybrid arrangements adhere. Although hybrid institutions straddle more than one type of governance, they tend to prefer particular goals, which shape not only what they are accountable for but also how they are accountable.

Different accountability procedures meet the goals of the three institutional types. To parse out the relationship between the goals, which shape the design of institutions, and the execution of environmental interventions, we examine six standard accountability questions. These questions are as follows: who is being held to account; to whom is accountability owed; for what are they accountable; what process demonstrates accountability; what standards does an agent use to demonstrate accountability; and what happens when the agent fails to meet these standards (Mashaw 2006, 118).

Public Accountability

As states remain the primary holders of authority, public accountability is the default setting for discussions of responsibility and answerability for environmental degradation. A states' goal is to represent the *demos* within sovereign states. Public accountability is "to express a belief in that persons with public responsibilities should be answerable to 'the people' for the performance of their duties" (Dowdle 2006, 3). Public officials are held to account through democratic elections and bureaucratic procedures, although these processes are problematic (Rubin 2006, 76–77). Elected officials and bureaucrats respond to public demands for curbing environmental degradation and for establishing and upholding legislation and international agreements.

The six accountability questions should be applied to both the first and second tiers of governance. Discussions of accountability tend to concentrate on the execution of public accountability through holding signatory states responsible to agreements and targets. Internationally, public governance is articulated through a patchwork of treaties, protocols, and agreements between states that have emerged over the last seventy years. There are now over 1,200 MEAs and 1,500 bilateral agreements between states covering the global environment (Mitchell 2002, 2015). States have also created and repurposed IGOs to enforce and operationalize these agreements.

In many MEAs and attendant governance institutions an accountability analysis would provide a forensic account for explaining who got to choose the "right" approach for addressing environmental problems,

Table 1.2
Mapping Accountability for Goals and Means in GEG

Governance Institutions	First-Tier Accountability: Constitutive Goals				Second-Tier Accountability: Regulative Means		
	What is the primary *purpose*?	*Who* is held to account?	*To whom* is accountability owed?	Normative priority: For *what* are they accountable?	Inputs: What *process* demonstrates accountability?	Outputs: What *standards* demonstrate accountability?	What *sanctions* when there is failure to meet standards?
Public	To represent	Elected officials and civil servants	Electorate and political communities	Responding to regulatory demands, upholding and obeying the law, not abusing powers, serving the public interest	Transparency of deliberative process, disclosure of information, open access to information, public consultations, report cards, participatory audits, budget reviews	Legislation, treaties, conventions, protocols, enforcement, monitoring	Removal from office, legal action through the courts, fines, loss of trust
Private	To profitably generate goods and services	Producers	Consumers, shareholders, and employees	Maximizing social welfare through employing people to supply products and services at the quantity, quality, and price consumers demand.	Disclosure of financial position, accurate forecasts of risk and exposure, adherence to standards of business practice	Price, availability, ease of access to desired goods and services. Social and environmental benchmarks.	Firm collapse, legal action through the courts, reputational loss, profit loss, fines
Voluntary	To promote moral conduct	Norm champions	Social networks	Constructing ethical frames and socializing a standard of accepted conduct	Information campaigns, lobbying, transparency of deliberative processes, accurate reporting on norm spread	Agent-based uptake of desired conduct	Reputational loss, naming, shaming, fines, loss of influence

while revealing the biases that animated those choices and determining whether they were accountable (and to whom) in prioritizing certain goals. The traditional focus on states has privileged demonstrating accountability through increasing transparency in international decision-making, disclosing information, establishing public consultations, report cards, participatory audits, and budget reviews (Warner 2005). Compliance and audit processes for evaluating accountability have accelerated with global patterns of interaction (Davenport and Low 2013). Public accountability outputs include the establishment of standards that environmental actors agree to adhere to: legislation, treaties, conventions, protocols, monitoring, and evaluation targets. Thus, the institutional focus that contributes to an accountability discussion has been limited to enhancing information flows between states and tracing commitments and compliance.

This suggests that accountability is narrowly conceived as compliance but not identified as promoting certain agendas. Thus, the biases of authority holders designing GEG remain unexamined. Those governing the environment remain unaccountable because the point of departure for accountability is based on the predetermined goals and installed capacities of public governance institutions. What is neglected is the meaning and value that state discourses attach to the environment. States are crucial for sustaining major environmental discourses that shape how problems are framed and the policies created to tackle them.

An accountability analysis at the design tier would investigate the design of the goals of public governance, including how problems are framed. Three modern environmental discourses have been identified: the construct of globalized systems of knowledge production; the emphasis of economic efficiency over ethical frames; and favoring imperatives of modernization and development (Warner 2005, 287). Most MEAs have an economic framing of the world's resources. Although two equity norms have emerged from international conventions—that the environment is the "common heritage of humankind" and that states have "common but differentiated responsibilities"—the success of these norms is attributable to how well they fit into the existing global neoliberal economic order because they do not require a restructuring of trade, states, and sovereignty (Okereke 2008, 25–26).

The shift from state-based regulation from the 1990s has allowed the private sector to gain authority to prescribe and proscribe self-regulated environmental interventions (Green, 2014). This antiregulatory discourse and shift in authority threatens democratic deliberation that can render environmental governance goals accountable. It prioritizes governance institutions that bias other purposes and objects of accountability over environmental problems. Yet firms also demand from states regulated and predictable landscapes to be able to project profitable business models (and advance their regulatory preferences internationally, see Buthe and Mattli, 2011). The merging interests of private industry and accountability-supplying regulatory states have shaped the goals of states, including a focus on scientific consensus for environmental decision-making domestically (Dowdle, 2006).

In GEG, bureaucratic forms of accountability are particularly emphasized (Rubin 2006, 54). For example, the United Nations Environment Programme (UNEP) is held to account for their activities by their member states. Member states' authority and accountability in turn rests on state sovereignty (and increasingly on popular sovereignty). This constitutes a delegation chain from member states to management to staff. Scholars of the World Bank have examined the various means through which bureaucracies are held to account through oversight procedures and management plans (Nielson, Tierney, and Weaver, 2006). Failure to meet standards set by elected officials or bureaucrats should lead to a removal from office or a loss of trust, although evidence of the former remains scarce (Schillermans and Busuoic, 2015).

Beyond traditional forms of accountability, current scholarship focuses on how to make IGOs more accountable to stakeholders (Ebrahim and Weisband, 2007; Held and Koenig-Archibugi, 2005). As identified earlier, being environmentally accountable means not only being held responsible and answerable for one's actions, but being responsible and answerable for protecting the environment and principal stakeholders rather than being held to account for meeting the goals of political, private, or voluntary institutions that are authoritative in a given context. Who counts as a stakeholder? If the World Bank lends donor funds to borrower countries for environmentally damaging projects (such as coal-fired power plants), and both donors and borrowers are satisfied, then the World Bank is perfectly accountable to both. This contractual relationship omits being held to account by those outside the contract who are nonetheless affected by the World Bank. This draws attention to the limits of traditional accountability delegation chains. We have to go beyond a framework that privileges bureaucratic accountability. Typically, in projects, stakeholders are assessed according to how they are affecting the problem and who is affected by the problem along a power-versus-interest continuum. In the case of the World Bank and the coal power plants example, the stakeholders are not only those immediately affected but also people who may not live in the country requesting the plant but are nevertheless subject to the environmental effects of that state's decision (see also Mason 2005).

Benner, Reinecke, and Witte (2004, 193) argue that asymmetries in global governance lead to operational and participatory gaps in accountability that require a pluralist approach to accountability. Public accountability is hierarchical, reproducing assumptions about whom should be held to account in a sovereign state system with unequal power resources, while obscuring gaps in accountability for the powerless (Ebrahim and Weisband 2007, 3–5). There is profound inequality between those producing environmental degradation and those affected, as well as inequality in those that have the power and the means to rectify environmental damage (Benner et al. 2004; Mason 2005; Chesterman 2008, 44). Power asymmetries, the differentials between those who incur the greatest cost of environmental deterioration, as well as intergenerational responsibilities to those future generations who cannot make governance demands on current elected officials and bureaucrats, all reinforce our argument for scrutinizing the biased choices behind the design of GEG. Doing so promises greater utility for accountability to improve the environmental outcomes of GEG.

In short, much of the public accountability focus has been on ensuring that specific interventions are carried out. Public accountability has processes, standards, and sanctions for evaluating the execution of public GEG. This includes certifications schemes, green accounting, and carbon markets. Where there is no discussion of the goals of GEG, then being held accountable to mechanisms decided by others absent transparency, consultation, deliberation, and buy-in from those likely to be affected is of limited utility.

Private Accountability

Private (and hybrid) governance institutions are particularly important considering the rise in power and authority of market actors (Cashore 2002; Buthe and Mattli 2011). States have delegated authority to the private sector, or enabled private entrepreneurship (Green 2013) over governance institutions, leading to very different accountability goals. The primary goal of private governance is to maintain industry profitability while maximizing social welfare. Consumers and shareholders hold producers accountable for meeting market demands in a way that generates profit while abiding by, and promoting their own, regulatory and social standards of appropriate business practice. Environmental issues are incorporated into market transactions as a constraining factor on profit-making rather than a compelling goal on their own right. Accountability processes, standards, and sanctions in private governance reflect the authority of supply and demand and the secondary priority given to environmental issues. Thus, processes of accountability are built into the business model through internal business practices, supply chains, logistics, annual financial reports, and certification schemes. Standards that demonstrate accountability include the price, availability, and ease of access to desired goods and services. Added onto to these are social and environmental benchmarks. Failure to meet these standards could result in the firm's collapse, litigation, and reputational and profit loss.

As the framings on debates on corporate environmentalism demonstrate, the focus is on maximizing firms' profits as a first-order concern while still leaving behind a living planet for future generations (Freeman et al. 2000). Traditional neoclassical economic paradigms treat environmental degradation as an externality whose cost is not assumed by producers. Corporate environmentalism attempts to reverse that practice by internalizing environmental costs into market transactions, yet unlimited growth and profit remains a dominant paradigm over an ecocentric approach informed by the earth's carrying capacity (Banerjee 2002).

First-tier governance applications of accountability would examine to whom the private sector is accountable to when establishing new environmental institutions. Private transnational regulation has become an accountability concern as market actors devise new standards absent engagement and participation from those affected (Dingwerth 2008). As Chesterman (2008, 40) notes in relation to transnational regulation, "[P]articipation in these disparate decision making processes varies widely, but there is rarely a general right for affected parties to challenge a decision; frequently it is not possible even to seek reasons as to why a particular decision was made."

Even the creation of hybrid governance institutions such as the MSC should be interrogated according to the six standard accountability questions. To whom were Unilever and the WWF accountable to when creating the MSC? To their shareholders and members? To the environment and affected stakeholders? Were they accountable for determining that the MSC would not have direct membership or local affiliations as per the structure of the FSC (Auld and Gulbrandsen 2010, 98)? Private and private-voluntary governance institutions like both the FSC and MSC establish environmental initiatives that downplay the need for rapid and deep environmental action requiring industry-wide changes, reflecting instead the dominance of market-oriented policy instruments (Chan and Pattberg 2008, 113).

The dominance of the market has led scholars to suggest that private actors cannot be held to account in the way that public actors can. Private accountability systems revolve around the tenets of supply and demand. Product, capital, and labor markets are built on the buying and selling of goods and services determined by market signals and consumer preferences. Private or market accountability is "often mutual" and more fluid than the hierarchy of public accountability (Chan and Pattberg 2008, 105). Rubin (2006, 66) argues that devolving responsibilities to private actors to make their own rules is not accountability because it "misleads us into thinking that the firm is being supervised or controlled, while in actuality it can violate public norms with impunity." Market actors operate within both public and private law where "constraints are designed largely to make the competitive process work more effectively" (Mashaw 2006, 123).

Others suggest that the purpose of the accountability that characterizes public governance institutions can be integrated into the private sphere through "publicization," where private actors commit to public goals as the price of accessing opportunities to supply goods and services, for example (Freeman 2006, 83–6). Given the dramatic shift toward private GEG, publicization signals the possibility of ensuring environmental action commensurate with environmental demands. Yet efforts to establish accountability in private governance tend to focus on functional requirements, leading scholars and policymakers to view accountability as an end in itself. When examining second-tier environmental interventions in nonstate certification schemes, for example, the extent to which they are decreasing deforestation or improving fish stocks is unclear. Despite their popularity in the West, there are structural barriers to the global uptake of these schemes which stem from the design of these governance institutions. Among other barriers, this includes the uneven geographic representation stemming from the dominance of industrialized companies in creating rules compared with the lack of infrastructure, economic capacity, and expertise for developing-country companies to meet certification requirements (Pattberg 2005, 366; Dingwerth 2008).

A burgeoning scholarship on private and hybrid governance institutions examines how they have taken up "public" accountability mechanisms to denote their commitment to accountability, leading to not dissimilar processes and standards from public accountability in some cases (Auld and Gulbrandsen 2010). Thus, both the FSC and the MSC have processes for greater transparency and more deliberative and participatory decision-making, in addition to disclosing information, ensuring public consultations, and establishing reports assessing their conduct (Auld and Gulbrandsen 2010; Cashore 2002; chapter 6, this volume; Gulbrandsen 2008; Chan and Pattberg 2008). Some, such as the MSC, have also established formal recourse mechanisms to challenge decisions (chapter 6, this volume).

Yet as Chesterman (2008, 42) points out, regimes (including transnational private ones) are more commonly "designed with an accountability deficit in place." In other words, despite allowing for greater "public" accountability in the structure of private-voluntary governance institutions, the design of such "open" institutions may meet other primary goals which need to be further interrogated. In the case of the MSC, accountability processes may be used "instrumentally" to advance the goals of the governance institution, such as ensuring its legitimacy in maintaining profitability rather than sustainability (Auld and Gulbrandsen 2010, 98; Gulbrandsen 2008). This reinforces the argument that accountability can only be a meaningful tool for environmental action if it is used to interrogate the choices made by authority holders in determining the design of GEG and the environmental interventions and accountability processes that follow.

Voluntary Accountability

Transnational activists have been powerful drivers of change in GEG, aiming to promote moral conduct (Finnemore and Sikkink 1998). Voluntary accountability is focused on meeting standards of appropriate conduct promoted by norm champions within social networks (Mashaw 2006, 124).

This involves being held morally accountable to other individuals, as well as to formal and informal social networks outside the state and marketplace (including family, friends, and associations). Indeed, the "creation of most environmental groups can be traced back to core values within civil society" (Cashore 2002, 522). Voluntary accountability systems are much more fluid and flexible than the "rigidly defined and jurisdictionally cabined" administrative and legal "subcategories" of public governance (Mashaw 2006, 126–127). Obligations may be formal or informal and are "informed by judgments of appropriateness" (Chan and Pattberg 2008, 105).

Voluntary actors such as ENGOs are accountable for constructing ethical frames and socializing a standard of acceptable conduct and for holdings themselves to it. The processes voluntary actors use to demonstrate their accountability is to provide information of their practices, and to engage in campaigns, lobbying, and marketing to spread their ideas. The standards of accountability to which they are held is determined by their social networks (Balboa 2015, 172). Failure to be responsible and answerable for spreading new ideas and ethical frameworks could lead to reputational loss, or being "named and shamed," leading to a loss of influence and materially undermining the operation of the organization or association.

Carbon Action Rationing Groups (CRAGs) provide an excellent illustration of voluntary accountability. These community-based groups voluntarily cap their carbon emissions and self-impose fines if they surpass their annual targets. CRAGs primary goal is to promote personal, responsible conduct *vis-à-vis* climate change. CRAGs, as a localized response to climate action, originated in the United Kingdom and spread to the United States, Canada, and China (Hoffmann 2011). CRAG members form a social network of shared values and hold themselves and each other accountable to an annual target of carbon reductions. Members self-report on their carbon emissions, and the group fines those who exceed agreed targets. Previously, accountability relationships in the voluntary sector were based on the kind of trust that CRAGs exemplify but have since shifted to bureaucratic compliance and auditing processes as the connections between actors multiply via globalization (Davenport and Low 2013, 88–89) and as ENGOs are pushed to meet public accountability processes by donors (Balboa 2015).

Beyond self-imposed social standards, the voluntary sector is important because of the role that activists play in demanding that environmental degradation be subject to public regulation and that private actors be held to account (Mason 2005). Being able to hold actors in positions of authority responsible and answerable for their actions is to determine what broader social goals matter and what are the legitimate grounds for making authority holders accountable. Social networks are therefore a site of "meaning-making" regarding what constitutes acceptable behavior (Mashaw 2006, 126). Voluntary accountability can bring actors together into a hierarchical authority relationship where none existed before (Gulbrandsen 2004, 578).

In a first-tier governance examination of voluntary accountability, the six standard questions should be applied: for what, who, to whom, and what processes, what standards, and what sanctions are voluntary governance institutions accountable? While the CRAG example presented here is a case of a pure voluntary governance institution, first-tier interrogations should also be applied to hybrid governance institutions. Voluntary actors with the biggest influence are those that "shout the loudest" (Chesterman 2008, 49) and are not representative of all affected stakeholders (Dingwerth 2008). Even those promoting environmental concerns bias other priorities, such as offering moderate reforms over radical ones, in order to influence public and private governance institutions (Maniates 2001). This is particularly pronounced in using "market-oriented policy instruments ... to address matters of concern to global civil society" (Cashore 2002, 503, 514). This has meant that environmentalism has successfully created a "new societal occupation" but it has not stopped serious environmental degradation (Engels 2010, 128). The influence of transnational activists has not necessarily been matched by new accountability mechanisms (Chan and Pattberg 2008, 106). If there is no accountability for the goals the voluntary sector promotes, it is unsurprising that environmental problems persist, continuing stakeholder demand for responsiveness from governing institutions.

Voluntary actors advocate for greater accountability of second-tier governance "end-of-pipe" environmental interventions such as processes of certification because they are complicit in choosing the goals for governing the environment, designing corresponding institutions, and supporting others, even if they "do not address environmental groups fundamental critiques and concerns" (Cashore 2002, 518). To illustrate, there has been an accountability shift in global forest governance from private to "collaborative civil society based regimes" (Chan and Pattberg 2008, 104). Despite the move toward stakeholder governance, accountability deficits remain. Authority holders in these environmental institutions choose to adopt specific accountability processes not based on what might be effective in holding actors to account for their actions but because they were considered appropriate by voluntary actors (Gulbrandsen 2008).

To explain, "[P]opular organizational accountability recipes may or may not enhance control [over the organization through monitoring] and responsiveness [to stakeholders demanding accountability], but as long as the organization adopts those recipes it is deemed successful by external audiences" (Gulbrandsen 2008, 569). The upshot, as Gulbrandsen (2004, 577) argues, is that the "spread of particular accountability arrangements appears to be driven more by expectations and demands in organizations' institutional environments [ENGOs] than the instrumental function of these arrangements," leading to more formal accountability processes but less responsiveness to critics and stakeholders. Thus, "accountability understood in this way could become a meaningless ritual of justifying conduct by answering only those questions that the answerable party has decided upon" (Gulbrandsen 2008, 578) The appearance of accountability here demonstrates how "accountability mechanisms have frequently been responsive to the realities of power not merely in implementation but in design" (Chesterman 2008: 47). This volume identifies how accountability mechanisms are tied to the inherently biased goals of GEG institutions.

Overview of Contributions

In summary, the book recognizes three aspects of global environmental governance: (1) that there are distinct governance logics exhibiting different normative biases; (2) these biased logics determine the framing of problems and accountability procedures; and (3) examines if the current scholarly emphasis on functionalist (compliance-based) accountability practices prevent organizational learning necessary for effective environmental outcomes.

This volume interrogates the use and utility of accountability in GEG across the institutional types of public, private, and voluntary, as well as recognizing the complexity of GEG through an examination of hybrid arrangements: public-private, public-voluntary, and private-voluntary. The introduction provides the theoretical framework for the volume. Each subsequent chapter then analyzes one of these governance types. They document how the normative bias of the governance arrangement influences the structure and goals of the accountability processes that are ostensibly devised to improve environmental outcomes. While problematizing the institutional arrangement, the collection addresses key environmental issue areas: climate change, biodiversity, and fisheries, as well as trade and global value chains, although the theoretical framework could be easily applied across all environmental problems. The aim here is to reveal how institutional goals for addressing environmental problems shape accountability procedures in order to discern whether accountability can play a role in improving environmental outcomes. In each chapter, the authors work through the standard questions of accountability: to whom, by whom, for what, and what constitutes accountability processes, standards, and sanctions.

Section two of the volume examines accountability from the perspective of our framework's first tier of environmental governance. These chapters consider how goals of public, private, and voluntary governance institutions shape the substantive content of accountability mechanisms that were established to track performance for meeting environmental goals. In particular, this section of the volume highlights the normative underpinning of the governance arrangement: specifically who is being held to account, to whom is accountability owed, and for what are they accountable (i.e., what is the normative priority?). Here, the design of public (chapter 2), private (chapter 3), and voluntary (chapter 4) GEG institutions are interrogated.

In each of the first three chapters, the authors examine how the constitutive rules for governing institutions across these three ideal types were created. The chapters identify how the goals of the governance arrangement shape accountability practices, including processes, standards, and sanctions, and whether feedback loops exist to challenge the normative bias of environmental governors. In chapter 2, Gupta and van Asselt analyze how public governance is exemplified through states' commitments to the United Nations Framework Convention on Climate Change (UNFCCC). They probe how accountability for climate reductions is dependent on states agreeing to "pledge and review" their actions under the 2015 Paris Agreement. As with other international treaties, state sovereignty (based on representing the interests of the national polity) for the provision of competing public goods at the national level is a normative priority beyond any environmental aim.

In chapter 3, Hamish van der Ven identifies how accountability procedures within global value chains represent a form of private governance. He traces how pressure on corporations, especially lead firms, from nongovernmental organisations (NGOs) amongst others has led to efforts to address environmental impacts across entire global value chains. To this end, corporations have entrusted the establishment of sustainability standards and the verification of compliance with those standards to independent third-party organizations. In this respect, corporations are attempting to become more accountable for their impact on the environment, not directly to consumers or NGOs, but indirectly by being held to account to a third party. Deciding to follow a sustainability standard is entirely voluntary but choosing to do so is part of a larger market transaction. Van der Ven unpacks the design of this private governance arrangement and its consequences for achieving environmental outcomes.

In chapter 4, Cristina Balboa documents how ENGOs enact accountability in voluntary governance. While there is a wealth of literature on how ENGOs pressure either public or private actors in order to hold them to account for their environmental impacts, Balboa unpacks what accountability for ENGOs looks like. Delving into the realm of conservation governance, she shows us that the normative commitment to biodiversity at the highest level exists among conservation NGOs, yet there remains disagreement as to how this should be met. Conservation, preservation, and new conservation approaches remain in conflict. This normative contestation, combined with increasing pressure from donors and stakeholders, means that the tier one design-level questions over how to govern the environment remain fundamental for voluntary governance.

The third section of the book gathers contributions that examine accountability from the perspective of our framework's second tier of environmental governance. Here, we focus on how accountability processes work: we assess whether they address environmental problems and whether feedback mechanisms can tackle impediments for environmental gains. We also question whether this can be brought back into the redesign of governance arrangements. The contributors seek to evaluate the extent to which regulative accountability rules and mechanisms are enacted across public-private (chapter 5), private-voluntary (chapter 6), and public-voluntary (chapter 7), arrangements.

This section of the volume examines a rising phenomena: hybrid governance arrangements. Here, we extend concerns about the impact of public–private and private-voluntary governance to include a chapter on less analyzed but equally important institutions: public-voluntary governance. This is a critical and relatively under-explored area for environmental governance relying on both governmental and nongovernmental actors to enforce environmental regulations.

Chapter 5, by Oscar Widerberg, Philipp Pattberg, and Lieke Brouwer, sketches how public-private governance arrangements have proliferated under the UNFCCC umbrella. As part of the broader phenomenon of polycentric governance, hundreds of private initiatives have emerged to reduce corporate and public carbon emissions. In this chapter, the authors examine four cases of public-private governance arrangements to reduce carbon emissions: Lean and Green, the Compact of States and Regions, the Portfolio Decarbonization Coalition, and the Roundtable on Sustainable Biofuels. They detail how there is a wide variety of processes, standards, and sanctions for demonstrating accountability with no clear sense of which if any are the most optimal for meeting UNFCCC targets. It is vital to assess how the various standards, processes, and sanctions feed back into the design of interventions, or what we call tier one of global climate governance.

In chapter 6, Gulbrandsen and Auld investigate the private-voluntary initiative that is the MSC. Here, they identity how the MSC is structured and how the various private and voluntary actors work together and in tension with each other to certify sustainable fisheries. They examine attempts to review and reform the MSC in order to better address concerns that its normative commitment to sustainable fisheries lags behind its efforts to ensure the MSC certification standard will be taken up by fisheries seeking to brand themselves as sustainable. This criticism is similar to criticisms leveled by NGOs that the MSC does not go far enough to ensure sustainable standards. The role of sustainability experts within the certification process has changed, and there are now improved accountability procedures in place that enable challenges to the assessment of the fisheries certifiers. While becoming much more transparent and accountable, there remain heated debates over whether the changes help improve the MSC's efforts to certify sustainable fisheries.

In chapter 7, Lorraine Elliott and William Schaedla examine how public-voluntary governance operates in efforts to combat the illegal wildlife trade. They detail how public actors have looked to NGOs for support in various aspects of treaty-based compliance and enforcement, including law enforcement of trade in illegal wildlife, and how those hybrid arrangements can recalibrate understandings of the logics of action and accountability. ENGOs are at the forefront of combating the illegal trade of endangered species. Frequently, voluntary actors operate at the local level to collect evidence and to be present when perpetrators are apprehended. This gives voluntary actors a high degree of technical knowledge and expertise. It also informs their guidelines, which have been taken up by states and international organizations for creating the processes and standards of accountability. However, it does raise questions as to how these standards, processes, and sanctions feed back into the design tier of wildlife trade governance and whether the NGOs are themselves accountable for their chosen approach to accountability.

All of the chapters in this section consider the operational success of regulative accountability mechanisms, or how accountability mechanisms function to hold actors governing the global environment to account. Hence, the contributors focus on identifying how accountability is enacted in GEG. Specifically, they examine what constitutes the processes and standards of accountability and what sanctions are devised to address failures to meet those standards. The section examines accountability mechanisms for what they seek to achieve and assesses whether they contribute to meaningful environmental action. We evaluate hybrid institutions because they are reflective of contemporary GEG. However, we argue that despite their hybridity, they tend to be underpinned by understandings of accountability that align with public, private, or voluntary ideal types and can begin to be interrogated from this perspective. For example, private-voluntary governing institutions, such as the MSC, tend to hew to market mechanisms for evaluating environmental performance, including accountability mechanisms.

The volume demonstrates that accountability procedures are important for determining whether actors are being held to account for their actions in governing the environment, but that analysis of the first tier of governance that constitutes the foundational design decisions of environmental interventions remains unaccountable to the environment and its stakeholders. Accountability at this stage can reveal why and how some purposes and audiences are chosen over others. Comparing logics of action exposes how normative biases shape accountability processes in public, private, voluntary, and hybrid arrangements. The conclusion more fully explores how feedback mechanisms between regulative rules of accountability in tier two of governance could be used to reshape and reconstitute the first tier of environmental governance so that accountability enables learning and improves global environmental outcomes.

Notes

1. *Governance* refers to the means through which individuals and institutions direct or steer (international) society.

2. We distinguish between corporate and voluntary "private" actors here, as we argue that they have different normative logics. *Legitimacy* refers to the normative belief that a rule, ruler, or institution is valid and ought to be obeyed. Ian Hurd, "Legitimacy and Authority in International Politics," *International Organization* 53, no. 2 (1999): 379–408.

3. Moreover, those in authority may not be interested in whether accountability mechanisms work as per the "forum model." Thomas Schillermans and Madalina Busuioc, "Predicting Public Sector Accountability: From Agency Drift to Forum Drift," *Journal of Public Administration Research and Theory* 25, no. 1 (2015): 191–215.

4. The "promise of accountability" refers to the "idea that governance can be enhanced by facilitating or requiring account giving behavior" through accountability mechanisms, including "promoting behavior driven by the expectations of relevant and significant others." Melvin J. Dubnick and H. George Frederickson, "Introduction," in *Accountable Governance: Problems and Promises*, ed. Melvin J. Dubnick, and H. George Frederickson (Armonk, NY: M. E. Sharpe, 2011), 17. We argue that this should run through both the design of GEG as well as its execution rather than be limited to verification, measurement, and compliance.

5. In keeping with the GEG literature we differentiate between public and private governance compared with the "state" and "market," as used elsewhere. We also use the "voluntary sector" rather than "social" or "society" because we identify the role of collective actors that are not beholden to the state or private actors acting voluntarily within society, and see that all sectors have socially accepted standards of behavior.

II Analyzing the Goals of Accountability in Global Environmental Governance

2 Transparency and Accountability in Multilateral Climate Politics

Aarti Gupta and Harro van Asselt

Introduction

This chapter analyzes the shifting dynamics of state-to-state accountability in the multilateral climate regime established under the United Nations Framework Convention on Climate Change (UNFCCC).[1] Our central concern is with exploring whether evolving accountability mechanisms, centered on reporting and review, can both make visible and enhance climate action in this contested multilateral context. In a widely acclaimed development, countries adopted a new agreement in Paris in December 2015 for the post-2020 phase of collective action to address climate change. The Paris Agreement institutionalizes a pledge-and-review approach to climate change action. Under this approach, transparency of action and (financial, technological, and capacity-building) support is becoming an ever more central component of multilateral climate governance, with an "enhanced transparency framework," consisting of reporting and review arrangements, designed to be one of the key pillars of the Paris Agreement.

It is now widely assumed that these transparency arrangements will be vital to making visible who is doing what, in order to assess progress toward fulfilling individual country climate pledges, thereby helping to hold countries accountable for their action or inaction. Going further, transparency in this context is also assumed—at least by some—to help with enhancing individual and collective ambition in combating climate change. Yet, are UNFCCC transparency arrangements realizing such far-reaching hopes? And in aiming for such enhanced environmental outcomes, who is being held to account by whom, and for what standards of performance? If transparency is gradually becoming the main vessel for promoting state-to-state accountability in the climate regime, how are these arrangements working and to what end? We address these timely and urgent questions associated with first-tier accountability (discussed in chapter 1, in this volume) in this chapter.

Our interest, furthermore, is with *state-led* governance, and thereby with public accountability, broadly stated (see also chapter 1, in this volume). This is aligned with our view that it is imperative to bring attention (back) to *state-to-state accountability* in global environmental governance, given an evolving research context that increasingly prioritizes examining the accountability challenges facing private and hybrid governance (e.g., Chan and Pattberg 2008; Bäckstrand 2008; and Karlsson-Vinkhuyzen and McGee 2013), even as the elephant in the room—state-to-state accountability—remains either underexamined or is assumed to be relatively more straightforward.

We follow the understanding of accountability advanced by Park and Kramarz (chapter 1, in this volume); i.e., as a relational concept whereby "some actors have the right to hold others to a set of standards, to judge whether they have filled their responsibilities in light of those standards, and to impose sanctions if they determine that those responsibilities have not been met" (Grant and Keohane 2005, 29). Our analysis is organized according to the key questions related to first-tier accountability identified by Park and Kramarz: Who is accountable? To whom? For what? And what normative priorities can be identified in the design and practices of this accountability system?

We proceed as follows: we first briefly consider the challenges of securing greater state-to-state accountability in anticipatory governance challenges such as climate change, and then examine transparency as a key mechanism to further such accountability. The following sections then address, in turn, the "who" and "to whom" of accountability, as it is operationalized within the UNFCCC, as well as "accountability for what" (i.e., the negotiated standards of performance that those accountable have to meet). We conclude with drawing out implications of our analysis, with a key lesson being the need for critical scrutiny of the overarching aims or, as Park and Kramarz put it, the normative priorities that underpin the design and practices of accountability mechanisms in this context.

Our overarching focus is on assessing the relationship, if any, between the scope and practices of accountability mechanisms (consisting primarily of the UNFCCC system of reporting and review) and the pursuit of stringent environmental outcomes. Given that the details of the Paris Agreement's transparency arrangements are still subject to further negotiations, and since the Paris outcome specifically calls upon countries to build upon existing arrangements, we focus here on the reporting and review arrangements within existing UNFCCC processes in the pre-Paris (pre-2020) phase of collective climate action, including agreements reached at the 2010 UNFCCC Cancún meeting. Given that their implementation history is still very recent, the functioning and effects of such reporting and review processes have to date been little analyzed. Because the Paris arrangements will build on these existing processes, it is both timely and instructive to analyze their workings here, including assessing the extent to which they are designed—and able—to further state-to-state accountability for effective climate action.

Our analysis draws on participant observation of UNFCCC negotiations intermittently since 2013, and analyses of primary and secondary literature, including UNFCCC decisions on the scope and design of transparency systems.

Furthering State-to-State Accountability: Ex Post and Ex Ante Transparency Arrangements

Our point of departure is the continuing importance of analyzing multilateral, state-to-state accountability, yet in a manner that goes beyond notions of principal-agent and/or delegated accountability assumed to prevail in public accountability settings (whether domestic or international). In the multilateral state-to-state accountability context of the UNFCCC, the same actor is both principal and agent (given that each demands accountability from the other, and is accountable to the other). Thus, the dynamics of state-to-state accountability are shaped not so much by standard principal-agent relationships (Biermann and Gupta 2011; Karlsson-Vinkhuyzen and van Asselt 2015), but rather by the contested politics of answerability and enforcement in these multilateral contexts (such as, for example, geopolitical conflicts over responsibility and burden sharing for climate action in the UNFCCC). There is a pressing need, therefore, to analyze how the scope and practices of state-to-state accountability are being negotiated and operationalized in this highly contested, multilateral governance setting.

In our view, renewed attention to state-to-state accountability is also required in light of an ever-growing need for ex ante accountability, i.e., accountability in the context of *anticipatory* governance challenges such as climate change. By *anticipatory governance,* we mean governance in the face of fundamental normative and political uncertainties and conflicts over the very nature of harm and its distribution; that is, about the need to antici-pate future environmental harm and its distributive effects in designing governance arrangements in the present (Gupta 2004). If so, the design of ex ante, state-to-state accountability arrangements are likely to raise dis-tinct challenges in this contested multilateral context.

As such, we also seek to unpack the ex ante and ex post dimensions of accountability. Ex post accountability has long been associated with multilateral environmental treaty negotiations, in the form of reporting and review with regard to implementation of obligations and compliance (Raustiala 2001), as well as in seeking to hold to account for harm done (Mason 2008; Pellizoni and Ylönen 2008). There is nonetheless a growing need for, and specific set of challenges associated with, ex ante accountabil-ity in contested areas of anticipatory governance such as climate change. Ex ante accountability comes into play, for example, in assessing (and holding to account for) not only whether countries are (and will in the future) real-ize their existing obligations, but also whether such obligations are fair and ambitious enough to mitigate, adapt to, and/or redress future harm (see also Newell 2008).

Ex ante accountability then encapsulates some of the most critical accountability conflicts in governing climate change, given temporal interdependencies complicating the search for accountability in this and other anticipatory governance challenges (see Biermann and Gupta 2011 for a discussion of the spatial, functional, and temporal interdependencies underpinning accountability challenges in an era of earth system gover-nance). Yet this element has received relatively little sustained scholarly attention to date. Our analysis sheds light on the different nature and chal-lenges of securing both ex ante and ex post accountability (or combina-tions thereof), and the role for reporting and review systems in realizing accountability.

We turn next to our analysis of how the design, scope, and practices of transparency are shaped by and linked to contestations around account-ability relations (who, to whom) and/or standards of performance (for what), which in turn reflect (contested) underlying normative priorities that might underpin accountability arrangements.

Transparency Arrangements in the Climate Regime

The UNFCCC was adopted at the Earth Summit in Rio de Janeiro in 1992. It put in place an overarching objective of "avoiding dangerous anthropogenic interference with the climate system" (article 2), as well as several principles guiding its parties in the further development of the regime . Notably, this included the principle of common but differentiated responsibilities and respective capabilities, which suggest that developed countries are to take the lead in addressing the problem of climate change. Though the UNFCCC enjoys near-universal participation, it did not establish any concrete emission reduction targets, but merely required participating nations to adopt policies and measures to mitigate climate change. This changed with the adoption of the Kyoto Protocol in 1997, under which developed countries took on economy-wide greenhouse gas emissions targets. The protocol further introduced market-based flexibility mechanisms (i.e., the Clean Development Mechanism, Joint Implementation, and international emissions trading) to allow those countries to pursue their targets cost-effectively, and it also established a new mechanism to promote compliance with the treaty obligations.

With the Kyoto targets only covering the period up to 2012, discussions on the future of the climate regime continued in the 2000s. These discussions signaled a shift from the "targets-and-timetables" model of the Kyoto Protocol toward a system of non-legally binding pledges, combined with a system of reporting and review. This direction was already indicated in the 2009 Copenhagen Accord (and the Cancún Agreements adopted one year later) and fully confirmed in the 2015 Paris Agreement.

Based on provisions in both the UNFCCC and Kyoto Protocol, an elaborate reporting and review system has been developed under the auspices of the climate regime over the past two decades, as a way to hold countries to account for meeting obligations. As regimes are rarely constructed on a blank slate and continuously evolve, the enhanced transparency framework of the Paris Agreement will build on these arrangements.

To set the stage for the analysis of the central accountability questions in the following sections, we will first provide a descriptive overview of the climate regime's existing transparency arrangements. We organize this background overview in four subsections covering transparency arrangements under (1) the UNFCCC; (2) its Kyoto Protocol; (4) the UNFCCC Cancún Agreements; and (4) the Paris Agreement.

Transparency Arrangements under the UNFCCC

The UNFCCC contains various obligations for developed countries (Annex I parties) to report on their progress with regard to the implementation of their obligations. Much of this information is contained in countries' national communications. The national communications by developed countries are subject to regular in-depth reviews by expert review teams (ERTs), which comprise experts nominated by parties to the UNFCCC and, at times, from intergovernmental organizations (UNFCCC 2014). The ERTs review the data and information provided by countries and assess progress made. The process is intended to be nonpolitical, facilitative, and transparent. The reviews usually include in-country visits in addition to desk-based studies, although centralized reviews are possible for economies in transition with low emission levels. The process allows for parties to respond to the review reports before their release. The reports are forwarded to the UNFCCC's Subsidiary Body for Implementation (SBI) and are made publicly available. National communications are also required from developing countries (non-Annex I parties), but these are not subject to review.

In addition to national communications, all parties need to communicate national greenhouse gas inventories. Developed country parties need to prepare inventory reports, which follow a common format and guidelines, and need to be transparent, accurate, consistent, comparable, and complete (UNFCCC 2013). Since 2003, inventory reports have been subject to a technical review process (UNFCCC 2014). In this process, the UNFCCC secretariat carries out initial checks of individual reports, and synthesizes the information from all reports, followed by detailed reviews by ERTs. Such reviews include desk-based reviews, centralized reviews, and in-country visits. Non–Annex I parties (i.e., developing countries), are not required to submit separate inventory reports, but they are required to include the results of their greenhouse gas inventories in their national communications.

Transparency Arrangements under the Kyoto Protocol

Building on the reporting and review system put in place by the UNFCCC, the Kyoto Protocol provided for further transparency arrangements for Annex I parties, requiring them to report annually on (and demonstrate compliance with) their emission reduction obligations. Given the crucial role of emissions accounting for the environmental integrity of the treaty, the information in these reports is more detailed than what is required under the UNFCCC (UNFCCC 2005a). The reports include information supplementing the information contained in the national communications under the UNFCCC, such as the use of the Kyoto Protocol's flexibility mechanisms, policies, and measures, and the provision of finance and the transfer of technology. In addition to these regular reports, the Kyoto Protocol requires several one-off reports: (a) an initial report clarifying parties' assigned amounts (i.e., allowed level of emissions) under the protocol; (b) a report on the "demonstrable progress" made with the implementation of commitments by 2005, as required by the protocol; and (c) a "true-up period" report, through which parties' compliance with their Kyoto emission reduction obligations can be assessed.

With the exception of demonstrable progress reports, all reports are reviewed by ERTs. Thus, ERTs are responsible for a number of specific reviews (UNFCCC 2005b):

• *Annual review of inventory reports*: This review, which encompasses the review under the Convention for developed country Kyoto parties, starts with an initial check for completeness, timeliness and consistency, accuracy, transparency, and comparability, followed by an in-depth review, which may involve an in-country visit. ERTs can identify problems and, if necessary, apply adjustments to the emissions data.

• *Periodic review of national communications:* This review, which also covers the review under the convention for developed country Kyoto parties, includes an in-country visit, along with centralized or desk-based reviews. National communications are checked for completeness, and ERTs carry out a detailed examination of the various sections of the national communications. The report needs to include a technical review and discuss potential problems identified in the national communication, linked to the criteria of transparency, completeness, and timeliness.

• *Review of initial reports:* This review, which was carried out in 2007–2009, focused on the inventory, the calculation of assigned amounts, the national system,[2] and the national registry, and provided a timely assessment of whether the national system and registry were in place at the start of the protocol's first commitment period in 2008.

• *Review of true-up period reports:* This review (carried out in 2015) was to determine whether parties have complied with their targets. ERTs were to check if the information was provided according to guidelines, whether it was consistent with other information sources, and whether a country met its target.

ERTs are mandated to carry out technical assessments and are also permitted, in this process, to raise "questions of implementation," though they are to refrain from political judgments. If these questions cannot be resolved, the ERT can refer the matter to the Kyoto Protocol's Compliance Committee, which may adopt a variety of measures to promote compliance.

In this context, it is useful to briefly note the compliance mechanism established by the Kyoto Protocol, given specific emission reduction obligations for Annex I parties contained therein. This mechanism consists of a Compliance Committee, with a Facilitative Branch and an Enforcement Branch. The compliance procedure of the Kyoto Protocol can be triggered in three ways (UNFCCC 2005c): (1) ERTs may, as noted earlier, raise questions of implementation with regard to the reports submitted; (2) a party may refer itself to the Compliance Committee; and (3) another party may refer a party.

In practice, however, only the first trigger has been used. The mandate of the Enforcement Branch is quite broad and includes compliance with the emissions-related commitments of Annex I parties, as well as some key reporting requirements. If a party is found to be in noncompliance, it may need to draft a compliance action plan, it may be barred from participation in the protocol's flexibility mechanisms, or it may be required to reduce more in the second commitment period of the protocol (2013–2020).

The Facilitative Branch is mandated to address any questions of compliance not addressed by the Enforcement Branch and is intended to provide an early warning function for noncompliance with the emission targets. Its available means are softer than those of the Enforcement Branch, and it is mainly aimed at providing advice and facilitating assistance. Since it started operating in 2006, the Compliance Committee has successfully dealt with several cases of noncompliance, yet these have mainly been related to methodological issues and reporting, rather than the Kyoto targets themselves (Doelle 2012; Oberthür 2014).

The Cancún Agreements: Toward a New Transparency System

The Copenhagen Accord not only introduced voluntary pledges (for both developed and developing countries) for the period leading up to 2020, but also signaled a new direction for transparency arrangements under the UNFCCC. These arrangements were fleshed out in the Cancún Agreements (UNFCCC 2010). The new transparency arrangements build on the existing system under the UNFCCC, with more elaborate rules for developed countries. However, they also introduced new reporting and review obligations and processes for developing countries.

As per the Cancún Agreements, in addition to already required national communications and annual inventory reports, developed country parties are expected to submit biennial reports on progress in achieving emission reductions and providing finance, technology, and capacity-building support to developing countries. The reports follow a specific format and guidelines (UNFCCC 2011a). Biennial reports are subject to a process of "international assessment and review" (IAR) every two years.

IAR includes two separate steps: a technical review and a multilateral assessment. Common guidelines for the technical review of national communications, biennial reports, and inventories were agreed in 2014 (UNFCCC 2014). When submitted simultaneously, biennial reports and national communications are subject to a joint in-country review; otherwise, a centralized review will be carried out. Technical reviews examine in-depth issues not covered in the inventory review, including information related to emission reduction pledges and the provision of support. The review focuses on transparency, completeness, timeliness, and adherence to reporting guidelines. ERTs can ask questions and request information from the party, as well as offering suggestions and advice.

The multilateral assessment, the second step in the IAR process, considers in a state-to-state multilateral setting the outcomes of the technical review, the party's reports, and supplementary information on the achievement of the party's emission reduction target. Other parties can submit written questions or raise questions in a session of the SBI devoted to this process. The first round of multilateral assessments took place at sessions in 2014 and 2015, resulting in a review of forty-three developed country parties. The second round took place in 2016 and 2017, during which forty-two parties were reviewed.

As part of the Cancún Agreements on transparency, parties also agreed that developing countries—except for least-developed countries (LDCs) and small island developing states (SIDS)—should submit new biennial update reports every two years from 2014 onward, either in conjunction with already required national communications or separately (UNFCCC 2010). Biennial update reports should include information on, among others, national circumstances and institutional arrangements, mitigation actions, and financial, technical, and capacity needs (UNFCCC 2011a).

These reports are to be subject to a process of "international consultation and analysis" (ICA), under the SBI, a process designed to "increase transparency of [developing-country] mitigation actions and their effects" (UNFCCC 2010, paragraph 63). The ICA process is expressly intended to be nonpunitive, nonintrusive, and to respect national sovereignty. For the purposes of ICA, LDCs and SIDS can be analyzed in groups, rather than individually. The two-step process in an ICA somewhat mirrors the two-step IAR process for Annex I countries. It starts with an analysis by a team of technical experts in consultation with a party (UNFCCC 2011a). Based on the experts' report, a "facilitative sharing of views" is to take place, which can include questions and answers between parties. The first facilitative sharing of views sessions took place during four workshops in 2016 and 2017, covering a total of thirty-five developing-country parties.

The Paris Agreement's Enhanced Transparency Framework
With the success of the Paris Agreement hinging upon the effective implementation of the non-legally binding nationally determined contributions (NDCs), transparency plays a central role in the new agreement. The Paris Agreement establishes an enhanced transparency framework applicable to all parties. However, the framework provides for "built-in flexibility," taking into account parties' different capacities (article 13).

Although the details of the transparency framework are subject to negotiation at the time of writing (e.g., UNFCCC 2016a), the Paris Agreement and its accompanying Decision (UNFCCC 2015) offer some initial insights into how the framework will function. First, the new transparency arrangements are to build on the existing ones under the UNFCCC, meaning that elements of the existing reporting and review process will be drawn upon. Moreover, the new system will ultimately supersede existing transparency arrangements (UNFCCC 2015, paragraph 99). Second, the framework applies to both "action" (i.e., measures to mitigate or adapt to climate change) and "support" (i.e., financial, technological, and capacity-building assistance), making the latter a clearer and more prominent focus of the transparency arrangements. Specifically, the Agreement requires developed countries to report biennially on the support provided, and encourages other parties providing support to do so on a voluntary basis. Third, in terms of reporting, the Paris Agreement specifies that each party needs to submit annual inventory reports, as well as "[i]nformation necessary to track progress made in implementing and achieving its [NDC]" (Article 13.7) on a biennial basis (except for LDCs and SIDS; see UNFCCC 2015). Fourth, like the arrangements established by the Cancún Agreements, the review process will include two main elements: a technical expert review and a process of "multilateral consideration." The technical expert review is to identify "areas of improvement" for the party under review and examine the consistency of the reported information with multilateral guidelines. The multilateral consideration focuses on the implementation and achievement of NDCs, as well as the obligations related to providing climate finance.

In addition to the enhanced transparency framework, the Paris Agreement also establishes a "mechanism to facilitate implementation of and promote compliance" (Article 15). However, it is unclear whether the mechanism, which is to be served by a committee that is to be "facilitative in nature and function in a manner that is transparent, non-adversarial and non-punitive" (Article 15), would be related to the enhanced transparency framework and, if so, how.

Moreover, the Paris Agreement launches a five-yearly "global stocktake" from 2023 onward (Article 14), which offers parties an opportunity to assess the extent to which they made progress toward the agreement's long-term goal to keep the global average temperature increase to well below 2°C. The transparency framework is also intended to feed into this process, but the specific modalities are still a work in progress.

Following this background on how transparency arrangements within the climate regime have evolved, we turn next to assessing the scope and practices of state-to-state accountability that these systems reflect, and institutionalize, within this multilateral context.

Furthering Accountability in Multilateral Climate Politics through Transparency: An Assessment

This section draws on the description of the evolving reporting and review processes given previously to analyze who is being held to account to whom, and for what, in the UNFCCC context, and with what implications for collective climate action.

Who Is Accountable to Whom?

This crucial element of the accountability *problématique* (who is held to account?) goes to the heart of whether and how transparency is able to further accountability in multilateral climate governance. In the UNFCCC context of state-to-state accountability, the key point of contention has always been who—that is, which states should be accountable (and for what; see later in this chapter). The central issue of which states should be accountable lies at the heart of the notion of differentiation in the UNFCCC context.

Differential treatment of developed and developing countries has consistently been the make-or-break issue in multilateral climate politics, shaping the fate and effectiveness of the UNFCCC regime (examples include the primary reason for US president George W. Bush's withdrawal from participation in the Kyoto Protocol in 2001 or the breakdown of the Copenhagen Conference in 2009) (Rajamani 2013). Differentiation is a lightning rod for conflict because it underpins fundamental disagreements about historical and continuing responsibility and burden sharing for actions on climate change. These conflicts are also represented in differentiating who has to do what, and therefore, who has to be transparent about what.

Transparency arrangements under both the UNFCCC and the Kyoto Protocol have been consistently differentiated. For instance, while national communications have to be submitted by all countries, the reporting requirements and timing are more flexible for LDCs and SIDS. Moreover, the in-depth review process only applies to Annex I parties. Similarly, while inventories have to be submitted by all parties, the requirements and timing are different and more flexible for non-Annex I parties, and the technical review process only applies to Annex I parties. Differentiation is clearest in the transparency arrangements of the Kyoto Protocol, with elaborate reporting and review requirements applying only to Annex I parties.

Differentiation between developed and developing countries continued with the establishment of two separate transparency systems in the Cancún Agreements, following extensive and contested negotiations over these systems both prior to and in the immediate aftermath of Copenhagen (van Asselt et al. 2010; Rajamani 2011). Yet the establishment of the IAR/ICA systems also signaled a move toward greater convergence in the transparency arrangements, as it introduced some form of international scrutiny for the domestic measures taken by developing countries (Dagnet et al. 2014). Before Copenhagen, this shift had been advocated by developed countries, whereas countries like China and India had opposed such a move, insisting that domestic verification would be sufficient (Dubash 2010; van Asselt et al. 2010). However, as part of a trade-off to strengthen the transparency of support provided by developed countries, developing countries agreed to the system (Morgan et al. 2010).

In the negotiations leading up to the Paris Agreement, the fault line shifted slightly, with the group of like-minded developing countries (LMDC)—a negotiation coalition including China and India—insisting that the Cancún transparency arrangements should be the default for developing countries in the new agreement (LMDC 2013), whereas the United States called for "a single system with built in flexibility" (United States 2013, 5).

Ultimately, the Paris Agreement confirmed the trend toward convergence through the introduction of a common, "enhanced" transparency framework applicable to all countries in the Paris Agreement. However, reflecting the contentious nature of differentiation, the relevant provision includes references to "flexibility," with specific reference to countries' capacities.

A crucial site of further negotiation is precisely what such flexibility entails (van Asselt et al. 2016; see also Rajamani 2016). For instance, is it related only to technical capacities, hence suggesting that at some moment, flexibility ends when capacities have been sufficiently increased? As the United States submission on transparency to the UNFCCC prior to the Marrakesh climate meeting in November 2016 unequivocally stated: "flexibility is for those developing countries that need it *in light of their capacities* …," going on to state that "flexibility can be applied in a number of different ways across the transparency guidelines but provisions that are not linked to capacity will not need flexibility" (UNFCCC 2016b, 69–70, italics added). For many developing countries, however, flexibility is related not only to technical and human resource capacities but also to burden sharing in the context of differing national circumstances and fairness. For instance, the LMDC group suggests that *all* developing countries require flexibility (UNFCCC 2016b, 37, italics added).

Flexibility is thus emerging as a key site wherein the geopolitics of differentiation will be contested, negotiated, and revealed. It is also linked to a discernible shift in framings of differentiation in the UNFCCC in recent years, sought in particular by Annex I parties. This is a shift away from an emphasis on the responsibility component of the UNFCCC principle of common but differentiated responsibilities and respective capacities to differentiation almost solely on the basis of capacities. While this focus on capacities does speak in pragmatic terms to developing country needs, and hence is welcomed by many developing countries, including LDCs and SIDS (Rajamani 2016, 23), such a shift in framing away from responsibility to capacity has as yet understudied implications for the geopolitics of multilateral climate action.

Contestations over who should be transparent, and whether the transparency burden should be harmonized across countries or remain differentiated, relates to concerns voiced by developing countries that a common transparency framework may build pressure for greater uniformity of mitigation commitments. Even if the types of mitigation actions (e.g., economywide emission reduction targets, energy efficiency targets, or emissions intensity targets) that developed and developing countries take on vary, developing countries are encouraged by the Paris Agreement to "move over time towards economywide emission reduction or limitation targets" (Article 4.4), and a convergence in transparency arrangements may be a precursor for more harmonized mitigation action. Indeed, it is often stated that monitoring emissions is an important first step and prerequisite for a country to take further mitigation action (see also Ellis and Moarif 2015, 17). The concern that transparency might become a means to pressure developing countries to take on more ambitious targets is voiced in particular by the LMDC group. As India made clear in its submission prior to the Marrakesh climate meeting in November 2016, "the transparency framework should not result in the creation of a top-down regime for the establishment of subsequent NDCs or of creating de facto limitations on the extent to which Parties, particularly developing countries, may exercise national determination in shaping and communicating their NDCs" (UNFCCC 2016b, 33).

These divergent views on the meaning and operationalization of the enhanced transparency framework in the context of differentiation imply that countries see a potentially transformative role for transparency, not only revealing but also shaping actions. Thus, the transparency system is not only deeply interlinked with the general debate on burden sharing and its accountability dimensions, but it also might push this debate in specific directions.

This brief discussion highlights how transparency relationships under the UNFCCC reflect broader conflicts and negotiations about who should be accountable to whom. We turn next to assessing the "accountability for what" dimension, or the standards of performance against which countries are to be held accountable, i.e., the aspects of individual climate-related performance that the transparency framework is intended to make visible.

Accountability for What?

In the context of the climate regime, the standards to which transparency arrangements apply refer to the commitments entered into by countries under the UNFCCC, including the Kyoto Protocol and the Paris Agreement. These commitments are related to climate mitigation, adaptation, and (financial, technological, and capacity-building) support, among others. Thus, they extend beyond specific emission reduction targets to include a wide spectrum of climate actions and support.

As these commitments vary, it follows that the UNFCCC's transparency arrangements apply to a range of standards of performance. These include generating and reporting on mitigation-related data on greenhouse gas emissions and removals (through inventories). Others include generating information on the measures taken to implement climate-related obligations, not necessarily limited to mitigation but also including adaptation (through national communications and biennial update reports). And some standards of performance relate to both legally binding and non-legally binding quantified emissions targets. The reporting and review processes under the Kyoto Protocol generate information that allows for determination of whether a country has met its Kyoto target. The IAR process allows for an assessment of the progress made toward achieving the quantified economy-wide emission reduction targets put forward by developed-country parties following the Copenhagen Accord.

In addition, transparency arrangements have increasingly started to require the reporting and review of information related to various types of support provided to developing countries. Here too, the development of transparency arrangements follows broader contestations in multilateral climate politics. The UNFCCC requires developed countries to provide new and additional financial resources to developing countries and makes the effective implementation of commitments by non-Annex I parties dependent on the effective implementation of commitments on financial and technological support by Annex I parties (Article 4.6). Throughout the last decades, multilateral climate talks have been marked by calls from developing countries for developed countries to provide adequate, predictable, and sustainable finance.

Against this backdrop, developing countries have in recent years also consistently demanded improved transparency of (mainly financial) support provided by developed countries (e.g., UNFCCC 2011b, 3; 2011c, 5–6; LMDC 2014, 10; South Africa 2014, 7), particularly following announcement of the goal that developed countries would jointly mobilize $100 billion at the Copenhagen climate summit (see also Clapp et al. 2012). Further measures to strengthen the transparency of (financial) support have been agreed to as a consequence. Under the UNFCCC's Standing Committee on Finance, a biennial process has been created to specifically review flows of climate finance (UNFCCC 2011a). Moreover, as part of their biennial reports, developed countries need to provide information on the provision of financial, technological, and capacity-building support (UNFCCC 2011a). The Paris Agreement continues this trend by establishing a transparency framework for support as well as action. However, the emphasis of the framework to date is mainly on transparency of action, in particular mitigation-related transparency (e.g., there is as yet no agreed system for reporting on climate finance; see Roberts and Weikmans 2017).

Broader political contestations are also reflected in what climate transparency arrangements do not seek to make visible. First, they do not seek to provide information on parties' individual ambition levels. Although the decision accompanying the Paris Agreement offers basic guidance on the information that needs to accompany parties' ambitions (i.e., their NDCs), this guidance is couched in hortatory language (see UNFCCC 2015, paragraph 27), and is not linked to the enhanced transparency framework. Likewise, the transparency arrangements say little about (making visible and assessing) even collective (let alone individual) ambition. Although the new five-yearly global stocktake included in the Paris Agreement will "assess the collective progress towards achieving the purpose of this Agreement and its long-term goals" (Article 14.1), it remains unclear how the enhanced transparency framework of the Agreement will actually feed into this process (van Asselt et al. 2016).

Second, the transparency arrangements do not seek to uncover information about the fairness or equity of parties' efforts. Neither the Kyoto Protocol's nor the Cancún Agreement's transparency arrangements focus on whether the targets (or pledges) that parties have taken on can be considered to be fair. While the Paris Agreement does not change this status quo, it is interesting to note that parties are invited to specify why they think their respective NDCs are fair. While this shows that discussions on the (perceived) fairness of parties' efforts is not beyond the realm of the feasible in the international climate regime, the transparency arrangements themselves eschew shedding light on these issues. This is perhaps not surprising, as information on whether a party's effort is "fair" or "equitable" requires agreement on the benchmarks for such an assessment. Although proposals for such benchmarks have been made in the negotiations—such as burden-sharing on the basis of historical responsibility, as proposed by Brazil (UNFCCC 1997)—such proposals were and remain contested.

In essence, then, the aspects of substantive climate performance that the transparency framework makes visible relate primarily to national monitoring of current emissions, and implementation of self-selected contributions/commitments, but not to how these are related to the ambition or fairness of efforts. Thus, there is transparency of emissions and implementation in this multilateral climate context, but not transparency of ambition or fairness. The reason is that these latter, arguably more stringent, substantive standards of performance (ambition or fairness) *are not standards that parties are willing to be held to account for*; hence, the transparency arrangements are also not called upon to assist in such a holding to account.

In addition to emission levels and implementation of commitments as the substantive standards of performance that transparency arrangements currently illuminate, there are also a number of procedural standards of performance against which countries are judged in the context of UNFCCC transparency arrangements. These procedural standards of performance relate to the nature and quality of the reporting about agreed aspects of climate actions (such as emissions trends and implementation) that the transparency framework seeks to make visible. These are also the procedural standards used to guide the ERTs in their review of reports. These standards or procedural performance criteria include the following: transparency (i.e., information is presented in a way that is clear and understandable, for instance, by explaining the underlying methodologies and assumptions); consistency (i.e., information is in line with the format or other requirements for its submission, and in line with information reported earlier and elsewhere); comparability (i.e., information can be compared with that of other parties, for instance, because the same indicators are used); completeness (i.e., information provided is complete); accuracy (i.e., emission estimates are relatively exact); and timeliness (i.e., information is submitted on time). As we discuss briefly in the next section, assessing performance against even such procedural criteria faces various challenges, with implications for the extent to which transparency can further answerability in this context.

We turn next to a brief discussion of how the contours of the UNFCCC transparency and accountability relationships discussed in this section (who, to whom, and for what) are functioning to date, with an eye to further delineating the normative priorities underpinning the scope and practices of reporting and review processes in this multilateral context.

UNFCCC Accountability in Practice: the Workings of Reporting and Review

Surprisingly little research has been carried out on how the reporting and review systems of the UNFCCC have worked in practice. Perhaps more important, to the extent that such studies exist, they focus on the patterns or quality of reporting and the impacts of review on the quality of national reports (e.g., Herold 2012; Ellis and Moarif 2015; Zahar 2015; Briner and Moarif 2016; Pulles 2017), rather than investigating the extent to which reporting and review helps countries to better implement (more ambitious) climate policies (i.e., the extent to which they improve environmental outcomes). This finding is not too surprising given that, as we will explain below, the review processes are explicitly instructed to eschew normative judgments on how well a country is doing, and how ambitious it is.

To give but one example of a study on country reports, Ellis and Moarif (2015) examine the reporting record of countries under the UNFCCC. They find that the record of mitigation-related reporting by developed-country parties is generally seen as adequate, albeit with some variation. For developing countries, the challenge of ever more regular and comprehensive reporting mandated by evolving UNFCCC transparency arrangements can be discerned from the fact that, by the end of 2016, only thirty-five developing countries had submitted their first biennial update report (which were due by the end of 2014).[3] Although reporting requirements for developing countries are less stringent than those for developed countries, particularly in the pre-Paris era, this record suggests that developing countries are experiencing difficulties with aspects of reporting. This may be related, among other factors, to a lack of financial resources, data, or established domestic reporting infrastructures (Ellis and Moarif 2015, 24). In other words, reporting challenges are associated, in many instances, with capacity constraints. This framing is underlined by the Paris Agreement, which has put in place a new Capacity Building Initiative for Transparency.

In line with the earlier differentiation discussion, a key question that arises here is what this focus on overcoming capacity constraints to developing-country reporting implies for enhancing the accountability of collective climate action through transparency. In particular, one question to consider is whether this focus shifts the lens away from a more far-reaching scope for state-to-state accountability (including developed country accountability) within the UNFCCC and Paris Agreement transparency arrangements.

Given that the capacity of Annex I countries to report on emissions trends and implementation (the main categories of performance that countries are currently called upon to report) are sufficiently advanced, the focus of transparency-related activities and debates within the UNFCCC is increasingly shifting to developing country transparency and on the means to enhance this transparency, including through capacity building. This may divert attention from the fact that the transparency arrangements have a limited scope, insofar as they do not call for making visible how (comparatively) ambitious and fair individual countries' efforts are.

Be that as it may, reporting shortfalls, including in developing countries, may also be related to factors other than capacity, such as the unwillingness of a party to subject itself to international reporting at predetermined intervals, given national sovereignty concerns. China, for example, has not yet submitted its biennial update report, although it remains unclear why this is the case. The experiences to date within non–Annex I parties in generating biennial update reports, and their political willingness to do so, remain very little analyzed, suggesting a key gap in the knowledge required to assess the transformative potential of transparency in the context of climate action.

A key reason for the fact that we know little about the transformative potential of reporting and review under the UNFCCC is that the relevant processes tend to eschew making judgments about whether (substantive or even procedural) standards are being met, regardless of whether they are carried out by technical experts or involve a state-to-state multilateral assessment process. The in-depth expert reviews of national communications mandated under the UNFCCC (for both developed and developing countries) are not intended to include political assessments of the measures adopted (Yamin and Depledge 2004, 340); thus, what is being assessed is confined to technical matters (see also chapter 1, in this volume). Yet their political consideration within the UNFCCC context is also minimal. The outcomes of the technical reviews are merely forwarded to the SBI for consideration, with no follow-up required from the party in question, and little debate about their content in this negotiating context.

Under the Kyoto Protocol's transparency arrangements, the stakes were higher, as the outcome of an ERT review could lead to "questions of implementation," which could subsequently lead to a state being brought before the protocol's Compliance Committee. However, the technical expert reviews became a site for political negotiation. While the ERTs are ostensibly independent and should avoid conflicts of interest, they are often the same government officials involved in their own country's reporting. Even as the ERTs involved in the reviews of Kyoto Protocol reports have increasingly become part of a political dialogue with parties amounting to compliance facilitation (Huggins 2015), they also "have an interest not to come down too hard on [other countries] or expose them during the review of the national communication or inventory, for this could lead to similar treatment of their own country's reports" (Zahar 2015, 75). In other words, political judgments tended to be avoided, thus limiting enhanced state-to-state accountability in deference to state sovereignty as the overarching normative priority.

The avoidance of political judgments notwithstanding, country reports and reviews can provide valuable information to other parties and observers (Yamin and Depledge 2004), which can facilitate the holding to account of states (Karlsson-Vinkhuyzen and van Asselt, 2015). Moreover, in some cases, ERTs also carry out a substantive assessment of a party's progress. For instance, in its review of Canada's fifth national communication in 2012, the ERT "noted with strong concern that on the basis of the information provided ... and during the review, Canada could potentially become noncompliant with its commitments under Article 3, paragraph 1, of the Kyoto Protocol [i.e., its Kyoto target]" (UNFCCC 2011d, paragraph 83). While the ERT thus flagged potential noncompliance, the actual engagement with the party had to be left to the protocol's Compliance Committee—which ultimately failed to take it up (Zahar 2015, 79).

The final step in the judgment phase of UNFCCC transparency arrangements, particularly those established by the Cancún Agreements, is the international party-to-party review, consisting of the multilateral assessment for Annex 1 parties under IAR, and the facilitative sharing of views for non–Annex 1 parties under the ICA. By their very design, these are political processes, in which countries can give an account of their performance and be subject to questioning from their peers. They involve, by and large, the same government officials who are part of country delegations simultaneously negotiating in the climate talks.

The multilateral assessments that have taken place to date have involved a great number of questions posed by parties to each other, for instance related to individual parties' use of market-based mechanisms and the progress made (or lack thereof) in achieving climate pledges (Kong 2015). Although, given the recent nature of the multilateral assessment process, empirical analyses are few and far between, this process has been said to, among other things, create greater clout at the domestic level for ministries involved in implementation; contribute to policy exchange and learning; clarify technical issues in reporting; and offer space for asking political questions (Deprez et al. 2015, 12; Briner and Moarif 2016, 31). The facilitative sharing of views offers a similar forum for information exchange. However, both processes are hampered by limited participation by states. This reflects resource limitations: for smaller countries, it is not always possible to engage in detail with the lengthy reports and their reviews (Briner and Moarif 2016, 31). Moreover, and importantly for our purposes, it remains to be seen whether and how these state-to-state processes produce outcomes that change state behavior.

Avoiding political judgments is likely to be a characteristic also of the enhanced transparency framework under the Paris Agreement. Like the ICA, the framework is to "be implemented in a facilitative, non-intrusive, non-punitive manner, respectful of national sovereignty" (Article 13.3). This means that the transparency arrangements, as designed and currently organized, eschew a key element for furthering accountability: a judgment. The same can be said for the implementation and compliance mechanism, whose committee is to be "facilitative in nature and function in a manner that is transparent, non-adversarial and non-punitive" (Article 15.2). Nevertheless, the transparency framework and implementation and compliance mechanism may help strengthen accountability to the extent that they provide other states insights into the performance of the state under review.

The review process that could arguably most likely lead to increased ambition is the global stocktake, which should in theory provide parties with an indication of how well they have been doing in achieving their overall goals, as well as an idea of how much more they need to do in the future. However, not only is the design of this mechanism still under negotiation, it also very much remains to be seen whether the global stocktake can meet these high expectations in reality.

Conclusion

We began our analysis by noting that transparency is widely assumed to be an essential prerequisite or at least one key mechanism for securing greater accountability. Our analysis has revealed the validity of exploring two other prospects: that transparency is a site mirroring the same accountability conflicts, or even a distraction from these accountability conflicts. As explored in this chapter, the scope and practices of existing transparency arrangements reflect ongoing disputes around responsibility, differentiation, and burden-sharing for climate action, and hence reflect key conflicts around the first-tier accountability questions of who (which states) are to be held accountable, and for what. Instead of transparency mediating conflicts (as is the dominant assumption) and thereby facilitating accountability, our analysis suggests that existing UNFCCC systems of transparency mirror these disputes in their scope and design.

This is evident in the manner in which contested accountability relations, standards of performance, and judgments are reflected in existing transparency arrangements. With regard to relations (who is accountable to whom?), we find that the negotiations over differentiation between developed and developing countries that have been a *leitmotif* throughout the development of the climate regime also reemerge in the question of who should be transparent. In terms of standards (accountable for what?), our analysis shows that the scope of current transparency arrangements is limited to holding to account countries for monitoring emissions and for making progress toward implementing existing commitments/contributions. Achievement of these contributions falls outside the scope of existing UNFCCC accountability arrangements (with the notable exception of the Kyoto Protocol's compliance mechanism), even though the transparency arrangements can generate essential information to make independent assessments of whether countries are achieving their individual pledges or targets. This will also be the case for the Paris Agreement, which does not include a legally binding obligation for any country to implement, let alone achieve, its NDC. Furthermore, substantive performance criteria such as ambition or fairness are not standards against which countries' climate actions are being judged in this multilateral context.

Our analysis further shows that existing transparency arrangements review progress in implementation in a manner that is predominantly facilitative (again, with a limited exception in the case of the Kyoto Protocol's compliance mechanism). Again, this is the case not only for developing countries, but also for developed countries.

In light of these observations, an important empirical question remains whether transparency is transformative, in spurring additional actions (rather than only reporting on existing ones), thereby serving as a feedback loop between enhancing the visibility of existing efforts and ratcheting up such efforts. The enhanced transparency framework under the Paris Agreement may well provide new opportunities for collaboration and support, particularly for those developing countries establishing such processes of information generation and reporting for the first time. Yet this remains contested as well, insofar as countries might be wary of more comprehensive reporting obligations leading to pressures to enhance mitigation actions. In other words, it remains to be seen whether transparency as an accountability mechanism in multilateral climate politics can actually improve environmental outcomes (see also chapter 1, in this volume).

Finally, it is worth noting that the global stocktake might well serve as a potential feedback loop between scrutinizing collective existing actions and stimulating more ambitious efforts. This is to be held at five-yearly intervals from 2023 onwards and is touted to play a key role in enhancing (collective) ex ante accountability for actions to be taken in the future, to meet the Paris Agreement's aspirational goal to keep average global temperature increases to below 2°C. Yet, its details are still to be decided, and it remains unclear how the outcomes of the transparency framework will feed into this evaluative moment. Thus, the transparency dimensions of the global stocktake, and whether transparency itself will stimulate additional climate action by all, remain important issues for further empirical assessment.

Meanwhile, in highly contested political contexts like climate change, current trends imply that transparency may well become an end in itself, as suggested by the shift in focus within the UNFCCC on building capacity to establish ever more comprehensive transparency reporting infrastructures, including in developing countries. As such, our analysis implies that widely assumed relationships between transparency, accountability, ambition, and trust do not always materialize, and hence require further explication.

Strikingly, the word *accountability* does not appear in the Paris Agreement. This signals the challenges of seeking far-reaching, state-to-state accountability in this contested multilateral context, with long-standing national sovereignty constraints militating against a broader scope for "accountability of what" (extending beyond reporting on emission trends and progress on existing actions, to also include ambition and fairness of such actions).

We conclude that the link between transparency and accountability is far from straightforward. It depends fundamentally upon how the first-order question "Who is being held to account by whom, and for what?" is being operationalized in any given context. Our analysis of the UNFCCC suggests that transparency and accountability are sites wherein long-standing, contested aspects of collective action on climate change are being (and will continue to be) negotiated, reinterpreted, and operationalized.

Notes

1. This chapter is an adapted version of Gupta and van Asselt (2017). It has been adapted to engage with the analytical framework advanced in Park and Kramarz, in this edited volume, thus addressing a somewhat distinct set of questions.

2. National systems are needed for the accurate estimation of emissions and thereby for the functioning of the Kyoto Protocol's flexibility mechanisms. They further provide information necessary to assess compliance with the Kyoto targets.

3. United Nations Framework Convention on Climate Change (UNFCCC), "Submitted Biennial Update Reports (BURs) from Non Annex I Parties," last updated on April 3, 2018, https://unfccc.int/national_reports/non-annex_i_natcom/reporting_on_climate_change/items/8722.php.

3 Private Accountability in Global Value Chains

Hamish van der Ven

Introduction

Corporations are increasingly being held accountable for their impact on the environment. The fragmented nature of global production has pushed accountability across borders to encompass the members of a corporation's global value chain. Apple Computers, for example, is held accountable to some extent for the actions of the companies that manufacture its products in China and elsewhere. In an effort to reconcile the environmental values of consumers with the practices of distant producers, a range of private accountability mechanisms have arisen across commercial sectors and environmental issue-areas. This chapter analyzes the complex accountability relationships that exist among actors within, and adjacent to, global value chains. Complementing the broad definition in this volume of *accountability* as when "some actors have the right to hold other actors to a set of standards, to judge whether they have filled their responsibilities in light of those standards, and to impose sanctions if they determine that those responsibilities have not been met" (Grant and Keohane 2005, 29), this chapter conceptualizes private accountability as a complex causal sequence through which downstream consumer demand for environmental accountability filters upstream to change practices at the site of production.

At each stage of this sequence, this chapter identifies a logic of action that guides behavior and explains how this dominant logic affects the goals and outcomes of private accountability. The chapter's central argument is that existing accountability mechanisms offer tremendous potential for advancing Tier 2 concerns related to effective execution and enforcement of environmental goals, but they also may have adverse effects on Tier 1 concerns about the appropriate design of private environmental governance institutions (see chapter 1, in this volume).

As observed in the first chapter to this volume, environmental goals are often subsumed by a narrower logic of action underlying accountability mechanisms. In this case, the economic consequences that provide a strong imperative for accountability also distort the original goal of accountability as it moves up a value chain. In this way, accountability in global value chains often resembles a game of "broken telephone," wherein an original message becomes more distorted with each new transmission. A key implication is that while accountability exists at each level of a global value chain, it normally falls short of achieving the type of on-the-ground environmental improvements that it is intended to produce.

The chapter proceeds as follows. It begins by explaining the rise of private accountability in global value chains and introduces the concept of "lead firms" as central actors in creating the demand for accountability mechanisms. Next, it diagrams and traces the complex causal sequence through which demands for accountability filter up from environmentally conscious consumers to suppliers around the world. It then identifies the predominant logic of action and normative priorities that inform accountability at each stage of the accountability causal sequence. Following this, it examines the substantive consequences of these logics of action for the efficacy of accountability mechanisms at each stage of the causal chain. The chapter concludes by offering some thoughts on whether value chain accountability can achieve meaningful environmental gains or whether, as the editors argue, it subsumes broader environmental goals by restricting the design of global environmental governance (GEG) to institutions that align with the extant global economic order.

The Role of Lead Firms in Global Value Chains

Corporations are accountable to more parties than just their customers, shareholders, and employees. Over the past thirty years, scholars of strategic management have come to recognize the influence of a broader community of stakeholders in corporate accountability (Freeman 1984). These stakeholders can include nongovernmental organizations (NGOs), trade unions, political groups, social movements, communities, and any other group or person with an interest in the corporation. The broadening of the community of stakeholders capable of influencing corporate behavior reflects an expanding global public domain and rising social expectations about the role of corporations in society (Porter and Kramer 2006; Ruggie 2004).

As described in chapter 4 in this volume, expectations of "publicness" have spread to the NGO sector; these same expectations have spread to the private sector as well. The influence of norms of corporate environmentalism have been particularly pronounced for large, heavily branded multinational corporations (MNCs) (Dauvergne and Lister 2012). Across regions and demographic categories, consumers want to know that the brands that they encounter every day share their environmental values (Nielsen 2015). They are also increasingly willing to move away from brands that fail to uphold these values (Llopis 2014).

This, in and of itself, is nothing new. The roots of corporate environmentalism can be traced back to the nineteenth century or earlier (Carroll et al. 2012). However, the scope of business operations being held to account is fundamentally novel. Globalization and the deterritorialization of production has created a need for private governance and accountability mechanisms that transcend national borders. Accountability to the environment increasingly extends not just to businesses directly owned or managed by big brand MNCs, but also to their arms-length suppliers around the world. A company's environmental reputation is only as strong as the weakest link in its global value chain. Take, for example, the Virginia-based company Lumber Liquidators. At one point, Lumber Liquidators was the largest retailer of hardwood flooring in North America. Yet its share price fell by 75 percent after a *60 Minutes* newscast documented dangerously high levels of formaldehyde in laminate flooring imported from its Chinese suppliers (Steele 2016). The company came under further fire when activists and journalists revealed that its suppliers had sourced wood from forests in Russia that provide habitats for endangered animals like Siberian tigers and Amur leopards (Harbert 2016). Neither environmental faux pas was perpetrated by units directly under the company's management, but the actions severely tarnished the company's brand nonetheless. Two years later, its stock remains at roughly a fifth of its 2014 value (Steele 2016).

Lumber Liquidators helps illustrate an important characteristic of accountability in global value chains. Accountability for environmental problems largely falls on *lead firms,* which are those corporations in a global value chain that wield the most economic clout. They can be found in both buyer- and producer-driven chains (Gereffi and Korzeniewicz 1994). In buyer-driven chains, the purchasing power of lead firms like Walmart or Costco offers them tremendous power over suppliers, power that can be used to specify what, how, when, where, and by whom goods are produced. By contrast, producer-driven chains are dominated by large manufacturing lead firms such as General Motors and IBM, who outsource components of manufacturing to selected suppliers (Gereffi and Korzeniewicz 1994).

In both variants, lead firms occupy a unique role, insofar as they are both accountable to a broad community of stakeholders and responsible for holding other entities to account. The environmental indiscretions of suppliers can impose material and reputational costs on lead firms. Yet lead firms can also impose material losses on their suppliers by dumping the ones that expose them to reputational risk. In this way, both lead firms and their suppliers fit within the private model of accountability conceptualized in chapter 1 of this book. The sanction for failing to meet accountability standards is reputational damage, profit loss, and potentially, firm collapse.

Accountability as a Complex Causal Sequence

Public outcry over environmental degradation does not immediately create change at the site of production. Rather, accountability in global value chains is best conceived as a complex causal sequence. Environmentally conscious consumers send a signal at one end of a value chain. This signal gradually filters up to producers and suppliers at the other end. Thus, to explain how accountability works (or fails to work), it is first necessary to map the actors and accountability mechanisms that exist at each stage of this causal sequence. This exercise is equally helpful for exploring who is being held accountable and what they are being held accountable for. The accountability sequence in global value chains is diagrammed in figure 3.1. For each actor, an arrow points toward the party that they hold accountable. The primary accountability mechanism is summarized in italics.

At the root of calls for accountability in global value chains, we find so-called green consumers and environmentalists. *Green consumers* exist across regions, income levels, and commercial categories and constitute a growing and affluent market that is coveted by big brand MNCs worldwide (Nielsen 2015). Recent survey data suggests that two in three consumers would be

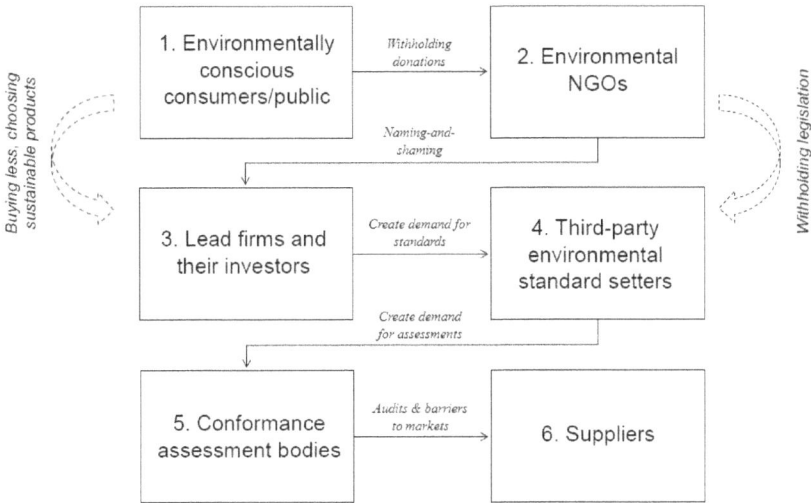

Figure 3.1
The accountability sequence in global value chains

willing to pay a premium for environmentally responsible goods (Nielsen 2015).

Paradoxically, however, heightened attention paid to the environmental impact of products coincides with an increased demand for discount products (Laird 2009; Shell 2009). Corporations like Walmart and Target have seen their global sales grow by billions of dollars annually on the strength of demand for cheap consumer goods. Consumers have a number of options to satisfy their twin desires for cheap but environmentally friendly goods. As individuals, they can modify their consumption patterns by buying fewer things or choosing sustainable products. Both actions would have the effect of holding lead firms accountable for their environmental impacts.

Yet, existing evidence suggests that most consumers do not pursue either of these options. Global consumption levels show few signs of abating, especially with an emerging middle class in the BRICS countries (namely, Brazil, Russia, India, China, and South Africa) (Princen, Maniates, and Conca 2002). Moreover, pervasive confusion about which products are genuinely sustainable has limited the ability of consumers to vote with their wallets (Eden, Bear, and Walker 2008). Taken together, these factors suggest that individual consumers face barriers in holding value chain members accountable through direct actions.

More commonly, consumers donate to environmental nongovernmental organizations (ENGOs) as a means of expressing their environmental values. In the United States alone, citizens donated roughly $10.5 billion to environmental charities in 2015 (Charity Navigator 2015). Groups like Greenpeace, World Wildlife Fund (WWF), and the Natural Resource Defense Council act as a sort of collective conscience for donors. ENGOs perform a key aggregation function by translating broad public support for environmental causes into specific actions. These actions advance the values and interests of their donors but also provide the basis for ongoing monetary support. Many ENGOs rely heavily on donations from individuals to fund core operations. Their survival often depends on their ability to reaffirm their relevance and impact.[1] Thus, at the second stage of the accountability sequence, ENGOs are accountable to their donors: environmentally conscious consumers and the public (see chapter 4, in this volume).

One immediate consequence of this accountability relationship is that ENGO campaigns are frequently designed to be eye-catching. Conservation campaigns focused on charismatic megafauna, like polar bears or harp seals, tend to garner more public support than those focused on less cute and cuddly creatures (Martín-López, Montes, and Benayas 2007). A similar dynamic exists in campaigns focused on corporations. Broad attention and donor support is best achieved by targeting lead firms with recognizable brand-names. Household names like Disney, Walmart, Home Depot, and others have all been the targets of ENGO campaigns over the last ten years (Dauvergne and Lister 2013). Targeting big-brand lead firms has the twin advantages of allowing ENGOs to raise their profile with donors while simultaneously achieving the most impact with the least amount of resources, a strategy that has been elsewhere termed "leverage politics" (Keck and Sikkink 1998, 2).

ENGO efforts to hold corporations accountable come in a number of forms and with varying levels of coercion. Mainstream ENGOs like WWF and Conservation International favor collaborative partnerships. By contrast, more radical groups like Friends of the Earth or People for the Ethical Treatment of Animals (PETA) often use coercive naming-and-shaming campaigns. While the mechanisms of steering differ, both carry an implicit or explicit threat of sanctions through reputational damage and profit loss to the target firm if they fail to respond to NGO concerns (see chapter 1, in this volume).

This threat manifests in several ways. It can come from reduced revenues through boycotting campaigns, but more proximately, it often comes through a negative impact on share price. Past research has established a discernible negative effect of naming-and-shaming campaigns on both sales and stock prices (Bartley and Child 2011, 426). The risk is even more pronounced for firms with recognizable brand names (Bartley and Child 2011, 439). Thus, at the third stage of the accountability causal sequence, we find that lead firms and their investors are accountable to ENGOs. Admittedly, the level of accountability varies considerably, based on a range of factors, including where the firm operates, which sector it occupies, and how directly it relates to consumers. Nonetheless, accountability exists in some form, largely as a function of an ENGO's ability to affect a corporation's bottom line.

Senior executives in lead firms have a fiduciary duty to protect their owners/investors from risks to corporate value from naming-and-shaming campaigns.[2] Faced with angry environmental activists outside their headquarters, there are any number of strategies that executives may choose to manage risks to their shareholders. Lead firms may use corporate social responsibility (CSR) programs or in-house production standards to manage their environmental impacts. However, a drawback of these options is that they lack the appearance of impartiality, and therefore risk being perceived as inadequate and illegitimate in the eyes of ENGO critics and the public.

Both consumers and ENGOs remain understandably wary of the ability of corporations to self-regulate. Hence "going it alone" is a risky strategy for lead firms. Past experience has shown that superficial corporate environmentalism, either as pure "greenwash" or as poorly conceived and executed programs, can expose lead firms to long-lasting reputational damage (Chen and Chang 2013). A fraudulent ecolabel or environmental claim pours gasoline onto the fire of a naming-and-shaming campaign by adding deliberate deception to the list of corporate misdeeds.

As a less risky option, lead firms can engage the services of a third-party environmental standard-setter. Third-party environmental standards and certifications emerged decades ago as a response to consumer skepticism about environmental claims made directly by lead firms (chapter 6, in this volume; Harrison 1999). They function by offering an ostensibly impartial set of rules designed to mitigate environmental impacts along a global value chain. Much has been written about the rise of third-party standard-setters as a form of transnational and private-voluntary environmental governance (Auld 2014; Bartley 2007; Büthe and Mattli 2011; Cashore, Newsom, and Auld 2004; van der Ven 2015). In essence, these organizations serve two functions for lead firms. First, they offer an additional layer of impartiality and legitimacy to corporate environmentalism that can help minimize the risk of ENGO naming-and-shaming campaigns. Second, they offer lead firms the prospect of garnering "club goods" or exclusive benefits that provide an advantage over competing firms (Potoski and Prakash 2005; Potoski and Prakash 2010). In competitive sectors, having an environmental label or certification can be an important source of differentiation from competitors.

Thus, at the fourth stage of the accountability causal sequence we find third-party environmental standard-setters. These standard-setters have dual accountabilities. On one hand, they are accountable to ENGOs for generating credible and impactful environmental standards. Many ecolabels grew directly out of the efforts of ENGOs to hold corporations accountable. The WWF, for example, cofounded the Marine Stewardship Council (MSC) to advance its work in global fisheries. However, even those ecolabels that do not have formal ties to ENGOs are still accountable to them in many ways. A third-party standard-setter essentially serves as a trust-broker between producers and consumers within a complex global value chain.

The value proposition of an environmental standard, certification, or label lies in its ability to affirm that a product or service has been produced in a way that is not detrimental to the environment, even if the buyer of the product has no way of ascertaining this information. Hence, a third-party standard-setter's core business is trust. Its value proposition lies in its perceived ability to create neutral and impartial rules that govern different value chain participants. In the realm of corporate environmentalism, ENGOs are often the arbiters of which types of environmental practices are trustworthy or not. Thus, their support is critical to the success of third-party standard-setters (Cashore 2002). As Gulbrandsen and Auld (2016) document in the case of the MSC, ENGOs can withdraw their support and challenge the legitimacy of a standard if they feel its criteria is slipping, thereby throwing its trustworthiness into question and potentially affecting its core business. This creates an accountability relationship between ENGOs and third-party standard-setters.

On the other hand, third-party standard-setters are also accountable to lead firms for making sure that their standards and certifications are used. After all, an environmental standard with no corporate uptake has a net environmental impact of zero. It can modify neither production nor consumption in a way that benefits the environment, nor can it provide a source of revenue from certification and logo licensing, both of which are vital to standard-setters. For example, the MSC derived 72 percent of its total income in the 2013–2014 fiscal year from royalties accrued through logo licensing (MSC 2014).

Thus, to have an environmental impact and gain the resources necessary to operate, third-party standard-setters have to ensure that their standards are used by as many firms as possible. One of the easiest ways to achieve this market uptake is by targeting lead firms. The rationale behind this strategy lies in the commanding position that lead firms hold in global value chains. As Mayer and Gereffi (2010, 8) note: "[F]irms with large market shares, whether marketers, retailers, or producers, usually have the option to source from many smaller suppliers, each of which may have few options other than doing business with the lead firm." Lead firms act as gatekeepers to their broader networks of suppliers, thereby affording them a certain degree of power over nominally independent standard-setters (van der Ven forthcoming). Third-party standard-setters recognize the commanding position of lead firms in the global marketplace and often target these firms in the hopes that they will push demand for their standards up global value chains.

This strategy for market transformation is explicitly diagrammed in the WWF's communication materials around its certification and labeling efforts (WWF 2012). Lead firms are conceptualized as the stem of a champagne glass, providing a crucial bridge between producers (the base of the glass) and consumers (the bowl of the glass). In targeting a small number of lead firms (principally retailers), third-party standard-setters can change the production patterns of millions of producers and the consumption habits of billions of consumers. Bonsucro, a third-party standard-setter for sustainable sugarcane, provides an example of this strategy. In lieu of convincing millions of individual sugarcane farmers to use its standard, or billions of consumers to purchase products containing certified sugarcane, Bonsucro targets lead firms like Coca-Cola to use its standard. A decision by Coke to source exclusively through the Bonsucro standard would fundamentally transform the sugarcane value chain overnight and secure Bonsucro's long-term survival.[3]

The importance of both lead firm and ENGO assent to third-party standard-setters creates a complicated accountability dynamic. The standard-setter must set the bar for certification at a level that is achievable to lead firms because they are the single most important actors for ensuring that an environmental standard is broadly used. At the same time, the standard-setter is also accountable to ENGOs, which are vital for the credibility and legitimacy of the standard. Third-party standard-setters, therefore, maintain a difficult balancing act between setting the bar for certification high enough to maintain credibility but low enough to ensure broad market uptake. The dual nature of the accountability relationship at this stage in the causal sequence has implications for the broader goals of accountability mechanisms that will be discussed in the section entitled "Implications for Accountability," later in this chapter.

Once a lead firm has identified a reputable third-party environmental standard and decided to procure exclusively to that standard, it falls on the standard-setter to design an appropriate assurance process for verifying compliance with its standard. A standard-setter that conducts auditing and assurance itself would present a conflict of interest,[4] hence this responsibility is often delegated to an independent conformance assessment body (CAB). CABs have no influence on the content of environmental standards, but they are tasked with objectively verifying a supplier's conformance with a standard's criteria. The CAB is therefore accountable to the standard-setter for maintaining the integrity and efficiency of the certification program. Should it fail to perform its duties on either count, it risks losing the ability to certify to that particular standard, and potentially, its principal source of revenue.[5]

At the last link in the causal sequence are suppliers, the actual producers of consumer goods. Suppliers are most directly accountable to CABs. Their ability to sell goods to a lead firm or one of its subsidiaries depends on their ability to pass a CAB audit and correct any nonconformities with a third-party environmental standard. Failure to pass an audit in today's fragmented system of global production can cause a lead firm to drop a supplier and source in favor of another supplier capable of meeting its standards (Dauvergne and Lister 2012). This is particularly true for value chains where levels of asset specificity are low, like agricultural products. For example, when Unilever recently decided to source tea exclusively from Rainforest Alliance–certified suppliers, tea farmers had little recourse but to conform to the Rainforest Alliance standard and submit to a CAB audit (Rainforest Alliance 2014). Failure to do so would mean losing a contract with a major buyer. CABs, therefore, have the most direct accountability relationship with the producers and suppliers of goods.

Private accountability in global value chains is thus a complex causal sequence. A signal at one end is transmitted through various intermediaries before emerging at the other end. Admittedly, the causal sequence diagrammed and outlined in this chapter is imperfect. One can see how certain stages in the causal sequence might be bypassed entirely. For example, a lead firm may choose to take action directly with its suppliers, bypassing third-party standard-setters and CABs.

In addition, there is far more complexity in the relationships between actors in a global value chain than can be captured in a simple diagram. In certain cases, suppliers may feel directly accountable to end-use consumers, depending on the nature of the product.[6] Moreover, there are any number of intermediaries, distributors, and other parties not captured in the diagram who may play a role in accountability. Thus, the complex causal sequence depicted in figure 3.1 offers a common representation of how accountability works in a global value chain, but by no means is it the only possible image. It is primarily intended as a heuristic exercise designed to open a broader conversation about who the most important actors in a global value chain are and what accountability relationship exists between them.

The Logic of Action Underlying Accountability in Global Value Chains

At each stage in the accountability causal sequence depicted in figure 3.1, an important distinction can be made concerning which logic of action is most readily identifiable in holding actors to account. March and Olsen (2006) distinguish between two ideal logics of action in political life: a logic of consequence and a logic of appropriateness. Under a *logic of appropriateness*, action is driven by rules of appropriate or exemplary behavior. Perceptions of appropriateness include dynamic cognitive and normative components, but generally, the authors suggest that "rules are followed because they are seen as natural, rightful, expected, and legitimate" (March and Olsen 2006,

689). In this context, consumers may purchase environmentally friendly goods or support ENGOs because they feel like it is the "right thing to do" in their particular cultural and temporal context. By contrast, under a *logic of consequence*, action is usually predicated on a rational calculation of consequences and expected utility (March and Olsen 2006). Behavior tends to follow a relatively static set of unitary interests. In this context, executives in lead firms attempt to protect their share price because they fear repercussions from investors if they fail to do so.

Of course, these are ideal types, and it is important to recognize that action can often be explained through a combination of both logics. Nonetheless, closer scrutiny of which logic of action is most readily identifiable at each level of a global value chain is useful for thinking about how accountability works. Beyond who is involved, a focus on logics of action can help illuminate the normative underpinnings of private accountability, and accordingly, why the ultimate goal of accountability to the environment is sometimes lost in translation (see chapter 1, in this volume).

Perhaps tellingly, consequentialist concern for economic self-interest is readily observable across most dimensions of a global value chain. While a logic of appropriateness is indispensable for explaining the broader movement to embed environmentalism in value chains in the first place, it does not adequately account for the specific actions of NGOs, lead firms, standard-setters, CABs, and suppliers at each stage. These actions are often more consistent with a logic of consequence and a concern for material sanctions. Consequentialist imperatives become more pronounced the further one moves along the causal sequence, culminating in extremely strong consequences for suppliers, who may be dropped if they fail to measure up to the environmental standards demanded by lead firms (Dauvergne and Lister 2010). For this reason, the results of accountability mechanisms in global value chains often skew wide of the environmental targets considered appropriate by broad segments of society.

Beginning in the first stage, a logic of appropriateness is instrumental for explaining decisions by environmentally minded citizens to push for greater accountability in global value chains. As noted earlier in this chapter, citizen support for environmental causes often manifests as donations to ENGOs. A logic of appropriateness is at work here because support for embedding environmentalism in markets reflects an evolving and dynamic belief that economic growth and environmental protection are not irreconcilable goals (Bernstein 2001). In addition, there are very few identifiable consequences for not donating to environmental causes, leaving aside the social sanctions that may play a role in certain communities. Citizens and consumers contribute to ENGO campaigns because they feel they should, not because they must.

The logic of action at work becomes somewhat more complicated at Stage 2. ENGOs attempt to steer the behavior of lead firms, both because their identities and interests are formed by the same environmental norms that lead donors contribute to their campaigns and also because there are material consequences for doing so. In the first instance, one can safely assume that people who work at ENGOs share common values and beliefs, such as a duty to care for the environment. Viewed through this lens, efforts to hold corporations accountable can be interpreted as an appropriate response, given the impact of corporations on the environment. On the other hand, ENGOs also know that high-profile campaigns help burnish their reputation (Bartley and Child 2014; Jasper 2004). Campaigns that target large, easily recognizable lead firms tend to garner more attention, and consequently more donations. These donations enable ENGOs to expand their operations, hire more staff, and launch new campaigns. So there is an element of economic self-interest at work as well (see chapter 4, in this volume). ENGOs hold corporations accountable both because it is appropriate to do so and because doing so advances their material self-interest (see chapter 1, in this volume).

Consequentialist imperatives become more pronounced at Stage 3, in explaining why lead firms choose to take action on environmental issues. Most existing explanations of corporate environmentalism assume that firms are rational, profit-maximizing actors, and that corporate environmentalism is simply another means of maximizing profit (Brown, Vetterlein, and Roemer-Mahler 2010).[7] Decisions to push environmentalism up the value chain and into nonowned business units can be viewed as an extension of the desire to grow or protect share price.

There are several ways in which value chain environmentalism supports a healthy bottom line. It can help realize hitherto unexplored production efficiencies, for example, by reducing energy consumption (van der Ven, Bernstein, and Hoffmann 2017). It can help mitigate information asymmetries and improve lines of communication with suppliers (Thauer 2014). However, one of the most commonly noted values of value chain environmentalism is protecting brands against the risk of ENGO naming-and-shaming campaigns (Bartley 2007, 299). Notwithstanding the emergence of concepts like "shared value" (Porter and Kramer 2006) and "triple bottom-line" (Elkington 1998), the only legal duty that executives in lead firms hold is to their shareholders. Since naming-and-shaming campaigns constitute a material threat to share price, it makes sense to interpret value chain environmentalism as a move to protect and increase share price. Hence, lead firms often engage third-party environmental standard-setters to neutralize the threat of naming-and-shaming and guard against material consequences.

Multiple logics of action may be at work at the fourth stage of the accountability causal sequence. Much like ENGOs, it is easy to see how the individuals who create and manage third-party environmental standards could be driven by a concern for demonstrating appropriate behavior within the current social structure. Many third-party standard-setters use multistakeholder processes to create, revise, and shape the content of their standards. Any number of identities and interests may be represented in standard-setting processes and it is important to recognize the role of individual values, socialization, and a logic of appropriateness in explaining where the bar for certification is set (van der Ven 2016).

However, as noted earlier, environmental standards must balance effectiveness carefully against a need for broad uptake in the market. Above all else, certifications must be widely used to have an impact and be self-sustaining; hence, there is a strong consequentialist imperative toward constructing environmental standards in a way that does not preclude broad market presence. Indeed, WWF quite openly touts its goal of constructing certifications that allow the top 20 percent of producers in a given sector to attain certification immediately (WWF 2012). This reflects both a deliberate strategy for market transformation and a means of building certifications that will be able to survive without ongoing grant funding. Hence, both logics of action are at work in Stage 4 and may pull a third-party standard-setter in opposing directions.

At the fifth stage, concerns for appropriate behavior are largely absent in CABs. Unlike lead firms or third-party standard-setters, they are not accountable to broader communities of external stakeholders for upholding environmental values. Their role is to impartially assess against a standard, regardless of what the standard specifies. CABs, therefore, are directly accountable to standard-setters because the latter create the demand for CAB services. Failing to perform their duties both efficiently (i.e., in a timely fashion) and effectively (i.e., without making mistakes) can lead a standard-setter to switch to a new CAB.

Thus, CABs face dual, and sometimes conflicting, consequentialist imperatives. They must ensure that they audit suppliers thoroughly and consistently to preserve the integrity of an environmental standard. However, at the same time, they must perform their duties quickly enough that they do not prolong assessments and provoke anger in a standard-setter's clientele—that is, producers and suppliers (Gulbrandsen and Auld 2016). This creates a tension between "doing it fast" and "doing it right."

At the final stage, there are any number of consequentialist imperatives for suppliers to adjust their production practices in a way that allows them to pass a CAB audit. The fragmented and competitive nature of global production often means that suppliers must do whatever is necessary to maintain relationships with lead firms and their intermediaries. For suppliers in sectors with low levels of asset specificity (particularly agriculture and goods manufactured by unskilled labor), this means meeting whatever standards are imposed or risking replacement by competitors (Dauvergne and Lister 2010). A logic of appropriateness may hold some influence over supplier behavior, but it is largely subsumed by the need to survive in a competitive globalized marketplace. Here again, we find evidence of Kramarz and Park's assertion that the dominant logic of action underlying accountability mechanisms often subsumes broader environmental goals (see chapter 1, in this volume).

Implications for Accountability

Multiple logics of action can be observed at each stage of the accountability causal sequence. Attributing behavior exclusively to norms or self-interest at any given stage would belie the complexity of forces that shape identities and interests across a global value chain. It would also ignore the considerable gray area that exists between these two ideal types. Nonetheless, it is worth noting that a preponderance of consequentialist imperatives motivates accountability at each level in a global value chain. Lead firms face consequences for not listening to ENGOs, suppliers face consequences for not adopting third-party environmental standards, and so on. The presence of a logic of consequence at each stage holds two implications for accountability in global value chains. On one hand, it offers tremendous potential for Tier 2 concerns related to the effective execution of accountability mechanisms (see chapter 1, in this volume). If accountability is ultimately about ensuring that authority holders are answerable for their actions, then it could be argued that a logic of consequence is better suited to steer behavior because it invokes material consequences for noncompliance instead of appealing to softer concerns for demonstrating appropriate behavior. On the other hand, the presence of consequences may have adverse effects on Tier 1 concerns about the appropriate design of GEG institutions. If actors along a value chain are more concerned about their own economic self-interest than about their ultimate impact on the environment, then they may fall well short of achieving broader environmental objectives.

Beginning with the former implication, the distribution of power in a global value chain creates an ideal environment for enforcing accountability. The concentration of purchasing power in the hands of fewer and fewer MNCs provides a rich target for ENGOs. They can maximize their profile and impact by directing resources at a handful of huge multinational lead firms. Lead firms, in turn, wield considerable economic leverage over their suppliers. This leverage transcends borders and is capable of penetrating states where domestic environmental standards are either weak or nonexistent (Börzel, Hönke, and Thauer 2012).

A decision by a lead firm to push sustainability up through its value chain creates a ripple effect of consequences. Viewed in this light, there is tremendous potential for environmental accountability in global value chains. If lead firms were to agree to source goods exclusively through robust third-party environmental standards, the collective environmental impacts could outweigh those produced through decades of multilateral environmental agreements. As Gerald Butts, the former president and chief executive officer (CEO) of WWF Canada, notes:

We could spend 50 years lobbying 75 national governments to change the regulatory frameworks for the way [that aluminum, citrus, sugarcane, glass, and coffee] are grown and produced. Or these folks at Coke could make a decision that they're not going to purchase anything that isn't grown or produced in a certain way—and the whole global value chain changes overnight ... Coke is literally more important than the United States. (Dauverge and Lister 2013, 19–20, citing Houpt 2011)

Yet, the same logic of action that makes accountability more enforceable at various stages of a value chain also has an impact on the nature and design of accountability goals. These Tier 1 impacts can be observed at each stage of the causal sequence. At Stage 1, ENGOs are under concerted pressure to "do something" by environmentally minded citizens. Yet the precise substance of what to do remains beyond the grasp of most ENGO donors. Steering a lead firm toward sustainable sourcing through a third-party environmental standard is a major victory for an ENGO, and one likely to help the ENGO secure ongoing support from donors.

However, existing research suggests that consumers have a limited understanding of what ecolabels actually represent outside of well-established labels like *organic* and *dolphin-safe* (Gutierrez and Thornton 2014). Consumer confusion is rampant amid a proliferation of competing standards that make similar claims (van der Ven 2015). Hence, while there are strong incentives for ENGOs to get lead firms to meet third-party environmental standards, incentives ensuring that those standards and certifications are designed in a way that actually achieve environmental outcomes are much weaker.

A similar dynamic exists at Stage 3. Lead firms face material consequences from ENGO naming-and-shaming campaigns. However, the nature of this threat engenders a conservative approach to the design of value chain accountability. Firms are clearly threatened by the environmental irresponsibility of their value chains, but the evidence is far less clear that they benefit from exemplary environmental performance among suppliers. Assuming that firms are rational profit-maximizing actors for the most part, the imperative to avoid naming-and-shaming campaigns would push lead firms to manage their value chains in a way that avoids being "worst-in-class." Put differently, they will incur costs and exert control over their value chains to avoid being singled out as environmental pariahs, but it is not clear that they will incur these same costs to emerge as environmental leaders.

As David Vogel (2007) astutely notes, the market for virtue is limited. Lead firms generally will not commit themselves to environmental accountability beyond a baseline level. Once the threat of environmental shaming is removed and the low-hanging fruits of efficiency have been obtained, there is little incentive to push for more ambitious environmental goals in the absence of concerted internal or external pressure (van der Ven 2014).

Tier 1 implications can also be observed at Stage 4. For third-party standard-setters, the two answers to the question "To whom are they accountable?" create implications for how environmental standards are designed. Standard-setters face material consequences for failing to be answerable to both ENGOs and lead firms. Setting the bar for certification too low can lead to accusations of greenwash or a failure to obtain legitimating ENGO endorsements, both of which affect a standard-setter's core business. Setting the bar for certification too high risks alienating lead firms. Absent the power of lead firms to demand certification from suppliers, third-party environmental standards risk being confined to niche markets, where they will be unable to obtain sufficient revenue from certification and logo licensing.

The dual nature of accountability for these groups creates a *Goldilocks approach* to standard-setting: environmental standards must be not too high and not too low, but just right. Hence, a broader accountability to the environment is subsumed by a more proximate need for economic viability in third-party standard-setters. This can result in an incrementalist approach to value chain accountability. A third-party environmental standard might be better than nothing but still fall far short of mitigating environmental impacts on a level necessary to deal with persistent global threats.

At Stage 5, CABs have few incentives to ensure that the criteria in environmental standards are actually having an impact at the site of production. Their accountability is limited to standard-setters and the suppliers that pay their auditing fees. Unlike ENGOs or lead firms, they are not accountable to broader constituencies of environmentally minded stakeholders. CABs face material consequences from standard-setters for failing to perform audits quickly and effectively.

This conflicting imperative means that audits often rely heavily on the examination of paperwork, which provides the dual advantage of being quicker to evaluate and less prone to errors of interpretation as on-the-ground practices. The speed with which audits are performed can mean that they lack the requisite depth to truly evaluate a standard's implementation (Boiral and Gendron 2011). Moreover, the reliance on paperwork assumes, perhaps naively, that written policies constitute an accurate representation of a supplier's actions (Jiang and Bansal 2003). Both factors make it difficult for CABs to accurately capture whether accountability mechanisms are actually having the desired effect at the site of production.

Finally, for suppliers, the threat of being replaced by lead firms should they fail to measure up to third-party environmental standards has discernible consequences for environmental outcomes at the site of production. For most suppliers, conforming to an environmental standard is a commercial requirement more than a genuine attempt to embed environmentalism in their operations. Given that much supplier behavior in a fragmented marketplace is consistent with a logic of consequence, it is unclear whether third-party environmental standards actually lead suppliers to internalize environmental values and practices or simply teach them how to meet conformance assessment requirements superficially.

Past research has shown that the daily practices of workers remain largely decoupled from the prescriptions of environmental standards because employees often have little understanding of the rationale behind the standards (Boiral 2007). Absent this deeper internalization, environmental practices at the site of production rest on an unstable foundation that is prone to changing with the requirements of the market. If a lead firm drops an environmental standard or switches to a less demanding standard, so too will its suppliers.

A second consequence of environmental accountability for suppliers is that it further subsumes their power in the global economy. Specifically, the extant that accountability system may disadvantage smallholders (McDermott, Irland, and Pacheco 2015). Conformance with third-party environmental standards tends to place a heavy administrative and financial burden on suppliers. They must keep records of their production practices, conduct routine inspections, and pay for routine audits. In many cases, suppliers are ill equipped to afford these costs. A consequence is that large industrial production facilities are often better positioned to comply with third-party environmental standards than smaller producers (Mutersbaugh 2005). One can therefore envision a scenario in which small, well-managed, and sustainable operations are replaced by large industrial ones that demonstrate a better commitment to the environment on paper, but not in practice. Similarly, one could easily envision agricultural producers switching to less regulated and more environmentally harmful crops in order to avoid incurring expenses associated with third-party environmental standards.

In sum, the nature of accountability relationships and the logic of behavior that underpins accountability at each level in a global value chain creates a powerful instrument for holding private actors to account.

Yet, this same causal sequence is also capable of distorting environmental goals. Much like a game of broken telephone, a message transmitted from one party to another loses some of its clarity and original meaning with each subsequent transmission. This condition of *lost in translation* partially explains the trap laid out in chapter 1 of this volume: an increase in accountability mechanisms does not necessarily produce commensurate environmental gains. The introduction of environmental accountability to global value chains has yet to stem the tide of environmental impacts at the sites of production.

Conclusion

Large corporations are increasingly held accountable for their environmental impacts. This accountability extends to their value chains. Yet, value chain accountability is far from a direct or straightforward process. Each actor in a global value chain is directly answerable to at least one other party, but no actors are directly accountable to the environment.[8] Instead, accountability is produced through a complex causal sequence triggered largely by concern for material sanctions at each level of a global value chain. The upshot of this system is that it holds tremendous potential for enforcing accountability, or what Kramarz and Park refer to as the "second tier of GEG" (see chapter 1, in this volume).

Commitments made by lead firms to source exclusively from third-party certified producers have led to a considerable upswing in environmentally certified production worldwide. For example, UTZ, a third-party certifier of sustainable cocoa, increased its sales of certified cocoa by 814 percent between 2011 and 2014, in part because of a commitment by Mars to source 100 percent sustainable cocoa by 2020 (UTZ 2016). Therefore, the power of lead firms to drive sustainability up through their value chains offers tremendous potential for achieving environmental objectives, particularly in areas where domestic environmental regulations are lacking and international regimes are weakly enforced.

However, a downside to this system of accountability is that the strength of the original signal sent by consumers is greatly weakened by the time it reaches the site of production. Like a game of broken telephone, the final message often bears little resemblance to the original because it has been reinterpreted to convey goals that diverge markedly from the message's original intention. Thus, the sheer length and complexity of the account-ability chain in global value chain governance invites opportunities for failure. If just one part does not function as it should—if NGOs fail to scru-tinize corporate activity properly, or if CABs do not perform their duties consistently and effectively—then the whole enterprise breaks down.

In many ways, the simplest way to achieve accountability in the private production of goods is to reduce the distance between buyers and sellers. Doing so would greatly reduce information asymmetries between the two parties and allow environmental preferences to filter upstream with fewer disruptions. There are signs that this is already happening through "Buy local" movements around the world. However, there are few indications that this localized mode of production and consumption is scalable or will reverse the tide of economic globalization that has elongated global value chains over the past few decades.

Viewed in the broader context of GEG, private accountability in global value chains holds both promise and peril. On one hand, governing through accountable value chains offers a pragmatic alternative to the gridlock that has too often characterized multilateral environmental negotiations (Hale, Held, and Young 2013). Lead firms have a capacity to steer environmental behaviors swiftly and broadly in a way that states and international orga-nizations often do not. On the other hand, accountable value chains do little to curb one of the root causes of global environmental degradation: consumption.

While notable progress has been made in reducing the environmen-tal impacts of particular products, and there is evidence that this success could be replicated in other sectors, environmentalists, academics, and practitioners would do well to heed Dauvergne and Lister's (2012) caution that rising levels of global consumption could displace any advances made in production efficiency. The same lead firms that are pushing environ-mental accountability up their value chains are also furthering the demand for cheap, disposable, and environmentally harmful goods. Thus, while improving accountability in global value chains can form a partial and immediate solution, preventing irreversible environmental degradation ultimately will also require concerted efforts to curb rising levels of global consumption.

Scholars of environmental governance, therefore, should direct fur-ther attention toward whether there is a feedback loop between extant accountability mechanisms and the broader design of private accountability institutions in GEG, or what Kramarz and Park label the first tier of GEG (see chapter 1, in this volume). The very existence of value chain accountability takes the existence of global value chains as a given, potentially inhibiting a wholesale rethinking of the way that goods are produced and distributed in the global economy. In this sense, Hoffmann (2016) is correct in acknowledging that a focus on accountability may actually be counterproductive to shaping the overarching goals of GEG. A narrow focus on accountability in global value chains risks legitimizing an unsustainable economic model, while constraining the design of GEG institutions to those that allow limitless economic growth.

Notes

1. Greenpeace is a prime example of such an organization. It accepts donations from neither governments nor corporations.

2. The motivations for corporate environmentalism are more diverse than simply fear of reputational risk; nonetheless, evidence suggests that this remains one of the key motivators. Hamish van der Ven, "Socializing the C-Suite: Why Some Big-Box Retailers Are 'Greener' than Others," *Business and Politics* 16, no. 1 (2014): 31–63.

3. Coca-Cola has committed to sourcing 100 percent sustainable sugarcane by 2020, although its progress toward this goal remains unclear. Tim Smedley, "Sustainable Sugar: Coca-Cola and BP Signed up but Will It Go Mainstream?" *The Guardian*, September 15, 2014, https://www.theguardian.com/sustainable-business/2014/sep/15/sustainable-sugar-can-coca-cola-bp-shell-bonsucro.

4. Standard-setters derive revenues from certification and logo licensing. Thus, there is an economic incentive to overcertify if auditing and assurance is handled by the standard-setter.

5. Many CABs are also accountable to an accreditation body that independently certifies their capacity to operate as a neutral body that acts with integrity when certifying or inspecting for conformity assessment. Hence, there is an additional layer of accountability, but not one that alters the accountability dynamic between CABs and third-party standard-setters.

6. Previous research has documented the strong accountability relationship between suppliers of kosher food products and end-use consumers. Shana Starobin and Erika Weinthal. "The Search for Credible Information in Social and Environmental Global Governance: The Kosher Label," *Business and Politics* 12, no. 3 (2010): 1–35.

7. However, it is worth acknowledging that there are diverse motivations for corporate environmentalism. Hamish van der Ven, "Socializing the C-Suite."

8. One can envision a future scenario where lead firms, fearing the collapse of an entire commodity, feel a direct accountability to the natural environment. For example, McDonalds has expressed concern about the long-term availability of the Alaskan pollock that it uses in its Filet-O-Fish sandwiches. Greenpeace, "Where Do McDonalds Filet-O-Fish Sandwiches Come From?" August 1, 2014, http://www.greenpeace.org/usa/mcdonalds-murkowski.

4 Participation versus Performance: The Crisis of Accountability for Environmental Nongovernmental Organizations[1]

Cristina M. Balboa

Introduction

"... we were the original conservationists" [but now] "we are enemies of conservation"

These two quotes were recorded at the 2005 World Conservation Congress in Bangkok, Thailand. They were spoken by the Maasai leader Martin Saning'o (Dowie 2005). Saning'o's people had practiced nomadic grazing of their cattle, reducing their impact on any one piece of land and distributing seeds throughout the biological corridor to increase biodiversity. However, much of their grazing range had been deemed off limits to them in the effort to conserve the ecosystem. The conservation practiced by the Maasai of Kenya and Tanzania—the pastoral and nomadic cattle grazing upon which their life and livelihood depended—was constricted by a different approach to resource governance, one championed by environmental nongovernmental organizations (ENGOs) (Dowie 2005). The traditional Maasai cattle farmers and the ENGOs both wanted to conserve the resources of Eastern Africa, but their approaches to the issue—their experiences with the resources, problem-definition, communication and management strategies, and interests—were different and even conflicting (Dhume 2002; Keck and Sikkink 1998). This is not a unique dilemma: ENGO-community interactions in the Amazon Basin, Guatemala, Papua New Guinea, and a myriad of other places mirror this dynamic where communities legalize their own land tenure in order to protect their resources from outsiders, while conservationists aim to establish protected areas that are off-limits to all people, including local communities (Chapin 2004; Grandia 2004; Balboa 2014).

The mission statements of ENGOs state that these organizations were created to "protect nature"[2] or save "wildlife and wildplaces,"[3] while others discuss responsibility to future generations. This focus on nonhuman or not-yet-human stakeholders creates unique accountability problems for ENGOs. In the absence of a clear consensus on how best to govern natural resources or serve the planet, the environmental field has evolved and incorporated a multitude of disparate views regarding resource conservation. For each organization working to govern resources, there is a different idea of how that is to be done and different demands on how to hold environmental actors accountable.

The conservation field in particular includes conflicting approaches and philosophies: a preservationist approach, which promotes peopleless tracts of land and sea; a conservationist approach, which incorporates people as part of the environment; and a "new conservation" approach, which focuses on "greening" extractive and consumptive industries. The conflict between *preservation*, which seeks to stop what it sees as despoliation of natural resources, and *conservation*, which incorporates the planned use of natural resources based on scientific principles and evidence began in the late 19th and early 20th century (Vandermeer 1994) and remains today (Wilshusen, Brechin, and Fortwangler 2002). In reaction to the criticisms that conservationists did not take into account the wants and needs of resource-dependent communities, ideas of "participatory conservation" have become prevalent in the past four decades, pushing the intellectual territory of conservation out of the exclusive domain of governments and scientists to involve local communities and other parts of civil society (Kothari 2000). Whether conservation projects should be considered integrated conservation and development projects (ICDPs) that address participation and livelihood issues of resource-dependent communities remains a controversial topic (Terborgh 1999). The latest iteration of environmental approaches—"new conservation"—argues that the underlying cause of environmental degradation is consumption and thus, conservation must focus on transforming extractive industries to reduce their impact on the earth (Dauvergne 2016; Hance 2016). As part of this approach, focus has shifted from resource-dependent communities toward working with big industries in agriculture, logging, fisheries, and mining. All of these shifts have inspired environmentalists to point fingers at one another—each accusing the others of not serving environmental ends.

Initially presented as a means to ensure the incorporation of multiple actors' voices into environmental work (Ribot 2002; Newell and Wheeler 2006), the term "accountability" has become a staple in the conservation literature. If ENGOs are more accountable to resource-dependent communities, it is reasoned, their conservation projects will be more participatory, more culturally-appropriate, and, therefore, more sustainable and successful in the long term (Chapin 2004; Dowie 2005; Balboa 2018). If ENGOs are more accountable to traditional conservation organizations, their research and interventions will stand up to scientific rigor (Hance 2016). Funders call ENGOs to account for their outcomes and efficiency (Jepson 2005). The field of nongovernmental organizations (NGOs)—environmental and otherwise—call for professional standards of practice for NGO management, reporting, accounting, and internal governance. While many ENGOs have heard the call for more accountability in conservation—indeed, many of the ENGOs have joined in the call themselves (Steiner 2007)—ENGOs, funders, and resource-dependent communities remain unsatisfied by both these accountability relationships and conservation gains (Jepson 2005). Kramarz and Park (chapter 1, in this volume) call this an accountability trap: environmental governance increasingly relies on accountability processes to demonstrate good governance but without any real assurance that these processes result in increased environmental gains.

Kramarz and Park challenge us to analyze the accountability trap by examining the two tiers of governance: how the design of institutions drives accountability goals; and the execution of accountability interventions. This chapter does this work for ENGOs, arguing that they face a unique dilemma in their accountability states because of conflicting elements of their design. First, as voluntary institutions in governance, ENGOs are required to uphold a set of "agreed upon moral standards" (chapter 1, in this volume) to serve the planet. ENGOs hold each other to account to ensure that their actions all point to these standards. This design stage is also "where problems are framed, priorities identified, and solutions devised" (chapter 1, in this volume). However, as the introductory section of this chapter indicates, there is a lack of consensus on *how* best to serve the planet, resulting in voluntary institutions with very different approaches to environmental governance. Moreover, ENGO reliance on funding through grants pushes these organizations to distinguish themselves from each other through their missions and approaches to environmental governance. Thus, while they hold each other accountable, they have diverging and often conflicting ideas on how to best serve the planet. These opposing pressures—to uphold a common moral standard to serve the planet and to promote unique missions and interventions to serve the planet—create a scenario where more accountability might not result in achieving mission.

As the following pages argue, voluntary institutions face a crisis of accountability. Either they can try to answer all the calls for accountability from the growing number of agents, endeavoring to balance between the current and future generations of human and nonhuman stakeholders, but leaving no resources to actually achieve their mission; or they can shirk the demands of various agents of accountability in order to achieve environmental gains in the way they think best serves the planet. In the first scenario, the organization suffers from multiple accountabilities disorder (MAD) and falls into a crisis of participation (Koppell 2005a) . In the second scenario, the organization must assume that its mission and approach are the most representative of what future generations and nonhuman stakeholders would demand (as opposed to what other agents of accountability are demanding), falling into a single accountability disorder (SAD) and a crisis of performance. In either case, the lack of consensus on how to govern natural resources, combined with the motivation of voluntary governance to be accountable to a moral standard (disputed as it may be), makes balancing accountability demands and achieving mission elusive. Indeed, to which moral standard should ENGOs be accountable? To the standard that allows indigenous peoples to graze their animals nomadically or the standard that makes these lands off-limits to everyone? To the standard that condemns extractive industries or works with them to make incremental changes? While diverse approaches to environmental governance might be acceptable, the environmental field has evolved to a point of having mutually exclusive or directly conflicting approaches, making balanced accountability elusive.

To make this argument, this chapter will focus on conservation NGOs as an illustrative example. First, it will explain how ENGOs have augmented both their roles and their numbers as what Kramarz and Park call "voluntary governors" (see chapter 1, in this volume), thus making them the focus of more calls for accountability. In increasing their numbers, ENGOs also increase the competition for finite funding, requiring them to distinguish their missions in ways that make accountability to each other elusive.

Next, looking theoretically, empirically, and normatively, this chapter will explore to whom conservation NGOs owe accountability. Here, this chapter will illustrate how the design of voluntary governance creates the disconnect between the growing number of agents of accountability and the agents these NGOs prioritize based on their missions. Since there is no one ideal form that voluntary governance takes, and no one umbrella institution enforcing their operational practices, each NGO individually negotiates with funders, governments, other NGOs, and a plethora of other stakeholders to be seen as legitimate governors. In the next section, the chapter will suggest how this disconnect between perceived and actual agents of accountability creates an accountability crisis for NGOs. To explain this crisis, I offer a three-part typology of accountability states for ENGOs: MAD, SAD, and balanced. The case study of the International Marinelife Alliance (IMA), a conservation NGO focused on combating destructive fishing in the live reef fish trade in the Philippines and Southeast Asia, was purposively selected to demonstrate this argument. Using internal organizational documents, publications, and 32 interviews conducted in 2006, I trace how this particular ENGO moved between accountability states: from SAD and a crisis of performance to MAD and a crisis of participation, despite its efforts to balance accountability demands.

ENGOs: Why Are They Being Held to Account?

This chapter argues that a convergence of trends brought the environmental field to the point where there is an accountability trap for ENGOs. To build the first part of this argument—the increased reliance on accountability—this chapter demonstrates the convergence of 1) increased environmental mandates globally; 2) decreased state capacity to address those mandates; and 3) increased voluntary governance as the ENGO field expanded to fill this governance gap. These three trends in global environmental governance (GEG) explain the increased participation, power, and publicness of NGOs on the GEG landscape, resulting in increased calls for ENGO accountability.

MEAs over time

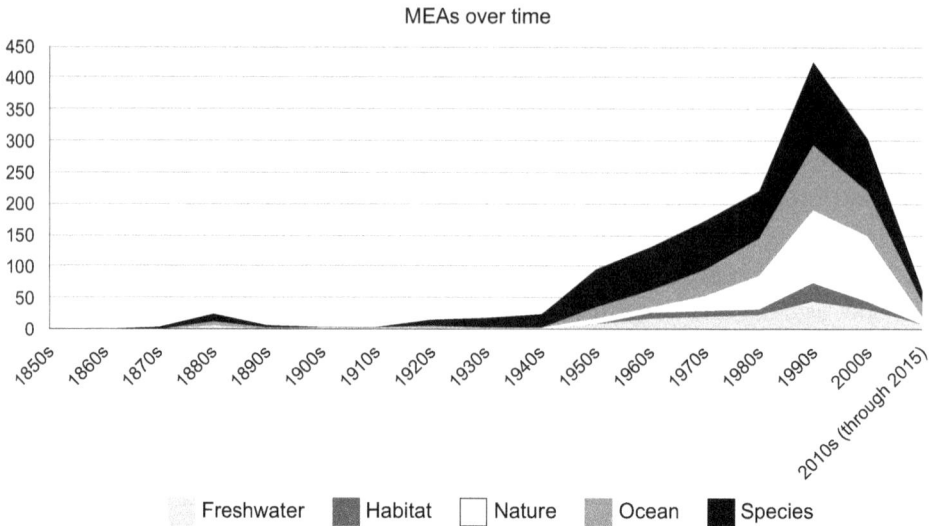

Figure 4.1
Conservation oriented MEAs over time. Source: data from Ronald B. Mitchell. 2002–2015. International Environmental Agreements Database Project (Version 2014.3).

Increased Environmental Mandates Means There Is More Environmental Governance

One manifestation of the growing nature of environmental governance is the dramatic increase of multilateral environmental agreements (MEAs) demonstrated by data from the International Environmental Agreement Database (Mitchell 2015). Figure 4.1 plots the number of conservation-focused MEAs (divided into four categories) over time by signatory date and shows a dramatic spike in the number of agreements in the 1990s. This proliferation of MEAs in the past few decades has intensified environmental governance.

Decreased State Capacity to Address Environmental Mandates Creates A Governance Gap

At the same time that globalization has increased the number and complexity of environmental governance agreements, the capacity and will of many states to address policy issues deeply and accurately appears to be decreasing. Embracing a suite of management reforms characterized by the rule of the free-market and a greater role for private citizens and organizations

(Minogue 2001; Behn 2001), many developing and industrialized states, either by choice or by necessity, have reduced the size of central government by decentralizing or delegating authority over many issues to non-state actors (Ribot 2002; Green 2013).

For the environment in particular, recent studies demonstrate that regulatory expansion for environmental issues (in both Western and non-Western state agencies) is not accompanied by growth in state funding or staffing (Sommerer and Lim 2016). Indeed, one study examined twenty-one national ministries of the environment or environmental protection agencies of Organisation for Economic Co-operation and Development (OECD) countries from the 1990s to the early 2010s, and found that five countries (the United Kingdom, the Netherlands, Denmark, Canada, and Australia) experienced sharp declines in the number of staff in environmental agencies, and five other countries (the USA, Japan, Finland, Sweden, and Norway) show stagnation in their staff numbers. This same study indicates that between 1995 and 2012, public environmental expenditures in the EU have been stagnating or decreasing for most European OECD countries while the United States Environmental Protection Agency's (USEPA) budget has stabilized (Mol 2016, 53). Thus, while the number of MEAs has increased, and while states follow parallel adoption rates on core environmental policy, the state itself is not expanding to address these issues, creating a governance gap on environmental issues.

Increased Voluntary Governance as the NGO Sector Grows to Fill This Governance Gap

As policy issues grow beyond domestic boundaries and public demand for leaner, result-based governance grows, NGOs—whose arenas of influence are not constrained by national boundaries—have taken a much larger role in the policy process. In response to these new roles, the ENGO sector has experienced dramatic growth, which can be demonstrated in two ways. First, there has been a drastic increase in the number of ENGOs in the past forty years in both industrialized and nonindustrialized countries (see figures 4.2 and 4.3). As Longhofer and Schofer (2010) demonstrate, industrialized countries have experienced almost a 300 percent rise in domestic environmental organizations since the 1970s. Industrialized countries' membership in international NGOs (INGOs) has also increased, although to a much lesser extent. Figure 4.3 demonstrates that nonindustrialized

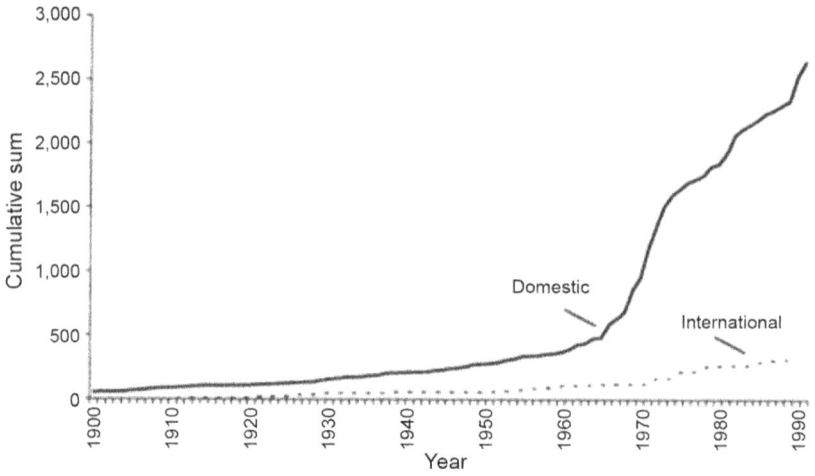

Figure 4.2
Growth of domestic environmental organizations and INGO memberships in industrialized countries, 1900s to 1990s. Source: Longhofer and Schofer 2010. Reprinted with permission.

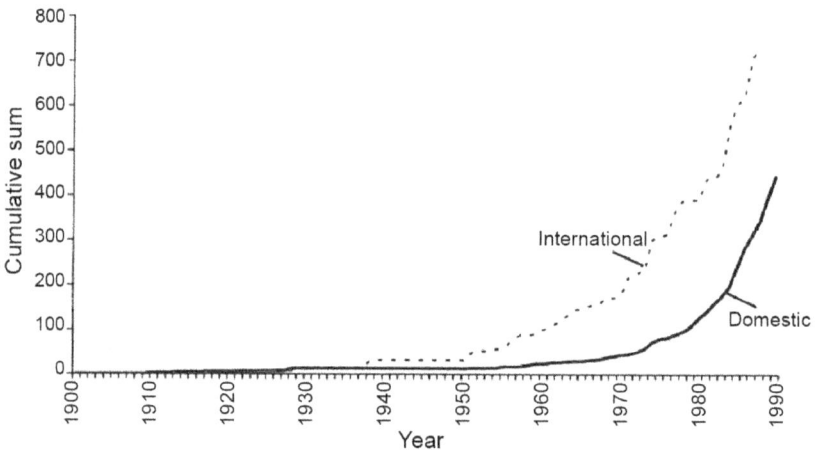

Figure 4.3
Growth of domestic environmental organizations and INGO membership in nonindustrialized countries: 1900–1990. Source: Longhofer and Schofer 2010. Reprinted with permission.

countries have also experienced considerable expansion of both domestic NGOs and INGOs. In these countries, membership in INGOs has grown to almost four times its size since the 1970s, with the growth in domestic ENGOs demonstrating a drastic increase since the 1980s. This growth points to an increase in the prevalence of NGOs on the governance landscape. As Jessica Green succinctly states, "[T]here is more governance, and as a consequence more governors are responsible for doing it" (2013, 164). Moreover, with no clear mandate from their nonhuman or not-yet-human constituencies, each organization promotes their own process of problem identification, root causes, and remedies for environmental ills. This proliferation of the sector marks a parallel diversification of approaches to solve environmental problems. The growth of NGOs raises an important question for accountability at the first tier of governance: if organizations are designed based on competing visions of appropriate action (see chapter 1, in this volume), then to what common standard do they hold each other accountable?

Substantial and growing funding is the second indicator of ENGO growth. Data aggregated from each decade of foundation funding to ENGOs demonstrates a steady increase in the funding of private US-based actors working on environmental issues (see figure 4.4).

In 2012, more than $1.3 billion was granted to environment-serving organizations (excluding animal protection and rescue organizations like The Humane Society), with the majority of these grants given to organizations

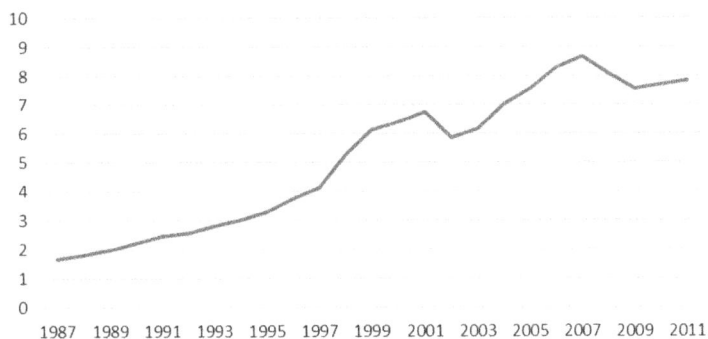

Figure 4.4
Total giving to environmental and animal protection causes in the US (in billions of dollars). Source: data from Giving USA 2012.

in California, Washington DC, and New York. While this data does not name the individual organizations, these three states are the location of the headquarters of several NGOs whose programs are focused outside of the United States. Indeed, one might question how Washington DC could be the second-largest recipient group of foundation funding (after California), if one was not aware that Washington DC is home to the second-largest number of internationally-focused NGOs in the US (after New York City) (Balboa, Berman, and Welton 2015). This $1.3 billion does not include the $125 million in 2012 that was granted directly to ENGOs outside of the US (Foundation Center 2014).

The annual revenues of the big three ENGOs are another indicator of their increased prominence in environmental governance. In the decade between 2004 and 2014, Conservation International increased their revenues from $92.2 million to $164.8 million (Conservation International 2005, 2015); the Nature Conservancy (TNC) increased theirs from $865.8 million to $1.11 billion (The Nature Conservancy 2004, 2015); and the World Wildlife Fund (WWF) more than doubled their revenue from $126.3 million to $266.3 million (WWF 2005, 2015). Clearly, these actors' prominence as voluntary governors of the environment is on the rise.

While funding from US philanthropy is one indicator, the Global Environment Facility (GEF)—the largest public funder of projects to improve the global environment—also demonstrates a growth in funding to ENGOs. Since its inception in 1992, the GEF funding to NGOs has more than quadrupled (from $20.94 million to $89.8 million, see figure 4.5), and the number of projects given to NGOs has increased almost fivefold (from 720 to over 2,500) (figure 4.6).

Thus, the increased demand for environmental governance is met by increased voluntary governance by ENGOs. The approach these ENGOs take to governing natural resources—preserving resources by restricting human use, conserving resources through planned use, or working with extractive industries to make them more sustainable—remains vehemently contested (Hance 2016). Without clear direction on the best way to serve the planet's nonhuman and not-yet-human constituents, the voluntary governance by ENGOs is diffuse in the goals it sets and the institutions it creates to achieve these goals.

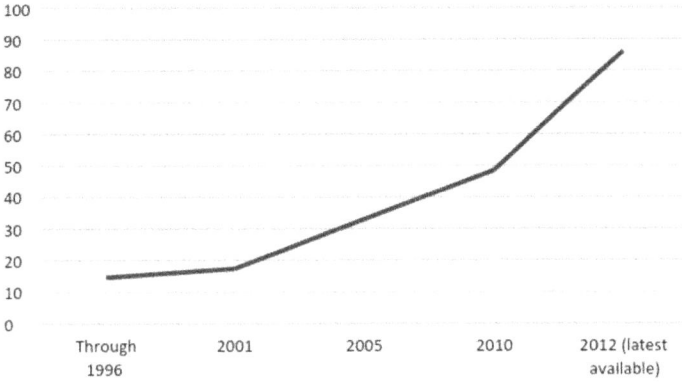

Figure 4.5
GEF funding to NGOs (in millions of real US dollars). Source: data from GEF reports 1996, 2005, 2010, 2012, 2014, 2015a, 2015b.

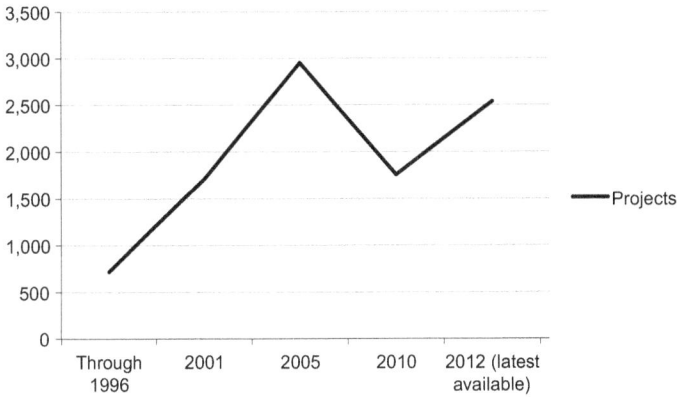

Figure 4.6
GEF projects directly implemented by NGOs. Source: data from GEF reports 1996, 2005, 2010, 2012, 2014, 2015a, 2015b.

How Does Accountability Manifest for Conservation NGOs?

Kramarz and Park assert that there is an accountability trap in environmental governance: a visible increase in accountability mechanisms which does not necessarily ensure an increase in environmental gains. As others have claimed for global governance organizations, the growing power and publicness of ENGOs (documented in the trends described previously) coupled with the lack of traditional democratic relationships result in increased calls for accountability of NGOs (Koppell 2005b). This section will explain the second part of this trap for ENGOs.

Accountability is a relational term where actors (agents of accountability) determine whether or not other actors (objects of accountability) have fulfilled their responsibility to uphold certain standards and impose sanctions if their responsibilities have not been met (Grant and Keohane 2005). Pulled from ideas of democratic governance, the term accountability is seen as a rough substitute for democracy in institutions that are not structured to be democratic but acknowledge that input from those who are affected by their work is important. It is a step further than stakeholder consultation or participatory approaches, which can occur without any changes made to the organization or its work agenda. Accountability is more than simple transparency; it is regulative, including consequences for actions or inactions ("answerability"). It is also constitutive, often seen as a way to force organizations to incorporate diverse voices and views into the design of their work (Mashaw 2006) and to change the power dynamic, making participation meaningful and organizations more effective (Balboa 2015; 2018). Accountability is ex ante when in the form of control over the design and agenda of an institution, or ex poste when in the form of liability for actions taken or omitted. Accountability can also manifest in an actor responding to other actors' concerns or by being responsible in following the rules of the field. These ways of being accountable—control, liability, responsiveness, and responsibility—represent distinct but nuanced ways an organization can demonstrate accountability to a multitude of actors (Koppell 2005).

According to Kramarz and Park (chapter 1, in this volume), objects of accountability have distinct goals for being accountable. The public accountability of government agencies answers primarily to their citizens for the creation of the public good. The private accountability of firms prioritizes return on investment. The voluntary accountability that is associated with nongovernmental organizations and philanthropy focuses on "upholding or diffusing agreed upon moral standards of conduct among self-selected, like-minded individuals" (chapter 1, in this volume). However, the design of ENGOs—the nature of their mission and primary agent of accountability (i.e., biodiversity, clean air, mother earth, or "future generations") means that there is no clarity in "agreed upon moral standards" and individuals are "like-minded" in purpose but not in how they propose to bring about change. How does biodiversity, clean air, or the planet hold an NGO accountable? The answer is: they cannot. Instead, accountability in GEG is a contest of voice and representation. In the absence of a direct mandate by the object of their mission, NGOs pursue distinct and often conflicting ideas of how best to conserve resources. This paper argues that while ENGOs have experienced increased salience as voluntary governors of natural resources, their design, coupled with the absence of voice by their nonhuman and not-yet-human constituencies, amplifies competition among NGOs for funding and agenda space. This competition produces an environmental field riddled with opposing or diverging views on both the appropriate approach to environmental problem-solving and prioritization of accountability relationships. With multiple actors each framing environmental problems differently—preservation, conservation, participatory conservation, or new conservation—they face an increased difficulty in satisfying each other's standards of environmental governance. The result is that balancing accountability demands for ENGOs is problematic.

When asked why accountability seems to be of growing importance to the environmental sector, environment leaders indicated conflicting calls from their agents of accountability (Jepson 2005). They asserted that as ENGOs increase their engagement with corporations, corporate norms of accountability and governance are imprinted on the ENGOs. They also stated that the professionalization of the environmental field has created an uneasy relationship between traditional environmental practitioners and environmental "bureaucrats," each wanting to keep the other in line. With each new participant in environmental governance—corporations, funders, and bureaucrats—comes an increased need to be accountable to that participant. With each new participant comes another, perhaps conflicting idea about how conservation should be done. These conflicting ideas and divergent accountability demands shape the design of these organizations.

ENGOs seem to be interested in answering these multiple competing calls for accountability. They create oversight boards for their work with members from various stakeholder groups. They engage in lengthy processes of stakeholder assessment in the project design phases of their work. They publish information on their process and progress in funder reports, websites, journal articles, and the media. The act of being accountable—of both being transparent in actions and outcomes and answering to a group of stakeholders—often creates an even bigger demand to be accountable. If an actor answers the needs of one group, another group sees the actor's ability to answer and then demands to be heard as well. If an activity is disclosed, stakeholders demand both continued transparency and corrections to any past errors in process. If a shortcoming is disclosed, objects of accountability run the risk of even closer scrutiny by agents of accountability.

As nonprofit organizations, the design of these entities creates competition for funding which generates further dysfunction in the sector. While ENGOs all seek to serve the environment, research on NGO competition indicates that in order to secure their survival, organizations must differentiate themselves from others, creating niches in order to market to funders. Intellectual competitiveness can have positive effects when it generates a broader array of perspectives, analyses, and ideas to inform global institutions like the World Trade Organization (Esty 1998). But as the number of NGOs in a sector increases, coordination and collaboration of these actors is undermined by the competition for contracts, funding, and other resources like staff and board leadership (Aldashev and Verdier 2010; Cooley and Ron 2002; Dolnicar, Irvine, and Lazarevski 2008; Tuckman 1998).

NGOs distinguish themselves through the public goods they offer: the mission, ideology, methodology, geography, or client-base (Aldashev and Verdier 2010). In the global conservation field, a recent exercise to identify the 100 questions of greatest importance to the field demonstrated just how diverse NGO missions could be, while pursuing the same pockets of funding (Sutherland et al. 2009). One indicator of this horizontal differentiation is the "proliferation of priority-setting approaches for conservation over the past decade" (Da Fonseca 2003, 345), each with its own distinct ideas of environmental problem-solving. As stated in the introduction of this chapter, the changes from preservation to traditional conservation to new conservation have created friction between environmental groups. However, even with similar mission statements, major proponent organizations of new conservation each offer global priority-setting models that differ greatly in measure and focus, resulting in different priorities. For example, the WWF's "Global 200" ecoregion approach prioritizes 40.2 percent of the globe while Conservation International's "hotspots" approach prioritizes 13.4 percent. Another top conservation organization, Birdlife International, prioritizes 7.0 percent of the globe in its important bird areas map. Only 3.3 percent of the globe is the priority for all three models (Halpern et al. 2006). Moreover, still other organizations spend substantial amounts of funding in countries not included in any list (Halpern et al. 2006). There is no consensus in the field on the best way to serve the planet, which problematizes the idea that the field is made of "like-minded" organizations holding each other accountable to a common environmental ethic.

ENGOs' funding flows, however, do not demonstrate this diversity. The majority of biodiversity-conservation nonprofits are small-to-medium size, yet a few control a disproportionate share of the resources. For example, TNC controls more than 25 percent of all assets and 16 percent of all revenues of the sector (Armsworth et al. 2012). In the US, only 2 percent of environmental nonprofits have annual budgets over $5 million, yet these few, larger organizations receive more than half of all environmental grants and donations (Montague 2012). This top-heavy distribution of assets and revenue ensures heavy competition for whatever funding is left after these large NGOs secure their share. Moreover, the big three environmental organizations—with their revenues ranging from hundreds of millions to billions of dollars (as stated earlier)—tend to favor the new conservation approach, leaving traditional conservation to smaller or local NGOs (Hance 2016b).

To reduce the threat of being replaced by another organization, NGOs will work with funders to align the NGO mission with that of the funder, either by redirecting the operations of the NGO to align with the funder, or by working with the funder to influence its approach to mission (Domanski 2012). There has been considerable documentation on how NGOs work to influence and direct the field: by changing the normative discourse of conservation (through the creation of these priority models, for example), by informing and lobbying global actors that make the rules and institutions of GEG, and by organizing boycotts and other actions for certain markets (Balboa 2014; Bernstein and Cashore 2000). NGOs also work directly with funders to create regional strategy (which in turn influences the calls for proposals) (Hance 2016b). Many of the big conservation NGO boards include founders of private foundations. As private money grows so too does their influence. In all of these strategies, NGOs become norm champions, promoting a set of approaches and standards that align with their mission, while excluding (to varying degrees) other approaches and standards.

As global conservation becomes a professionalized field, and as our technology allows for real-time understanding of issues and actions, organizations know more and more about each other's activities. ENGO leadership notes that improved communication technologies and cheaper air travel costs have connected actors in conservation more frequently than ever before—making accountability relationships a daily discussion rather than an intermittent one (Jepson 2005). Moreover, the idea of mutual and reputational accountability creates responsibility for NGOs to call each other to account (Balboa 2015; Mitchell and Stroup 2017). However, their horizontal differentiation—manifesting in the various funding priorities; the degrees and requirements of engaging with industry, government agencies, and resource-dependent communities; the uses of natural sciences, social science, and adaptive management; and all of the various approaches raised in the introduction of this chapter for serving the nonhuman and not-yet-human stakeholders—assures no one NGO can ever fully appease the calls to account from other actors. Moreover, as the second half of the accountability trap develops—the maintained pace of environmental degradation despite increased accountability mechanisms—environmental actors are increasingly compelled to call each other to account, creating a feedback loop of accountability and "slow and erratic" progress on environmental goals (Jepson 2005). In this dysfunctional scenario, NGOs are given the difficult choice of either trying to answer the multiple, diverse, and conflicting calls for accountability, or deciding this is a fool's errand and selectively prioritizing accountability agents in order to secure their organizational survival and mission. This chapter asserts that this dynamic of increased competition makes it very unlikely that we will hear of an ENGO that answers the calls for accountability comprehensively while fully achieving its mission.

Three Accountability States for ENGOs

In answering the demands of accountability, ENGOs often fall into a crisis of performance or a crisis of participation. In the crisis of performance, the NGO becomes singularly accountable to its mission, denying the demands of other actors. NGOs in this SAD make temporary strides toward their mission or toward sustaining their organization. However, the NGO cannot avoid the calls for accountability in participation, and progress toward its mission will stall, forming the crisis of performance in SAD. The other side of this accountability dilemma is a crisis of participation. These NGOs develop MAD, working to answer all calls for accountability. This constant pursuit of answering vague, conflicting, and changing demands renders the NGO paralyzed and unable to pursue its mission.

It is important to note how this accountability dilemma reflects voluntary governance's unique design in Kramarz and Park's first tier of governance. Private actors pursue missions (e.g., "to profitably generate goods and services") without falling into the crisis of performance. Indeed, more frequently than not, they are expected to prioritize that one accountability over others. Likewise, the public sector's primary purpose, according to the introduction, is to represent the electorate. Only in the past 40 years have critiques about government's inability to achieve results begun to change how we think of governance. Theoretically, private and public accountability logics have remained fairly static. Only recently have the changing forms of governance blurred the lines between public, private, and voluntary logics of accountability for these actors. For ENGOs, however, the network-based accountability makes these actors more susceptible to the calls from whatever actor speaks loudest at any given time, requiring a flexible amalgamation of accountability approaches. Agents of accountability demand that they focus on both performance and participation, but without acknowledging that the various "participants" might have very different ideas for performance measures. Thus first-tier design issues—changing accountability logics, contested framing of the problem, and network-based accountability—make voluntary governance without dispute increasingly difficult.

Multiple Accountabilities Disorder (MAD)

Koppell's (2005a) MAD reflects the tendency of an organization to be paralyzed by its accountability relationships. In MAD, objects of accountability try to be too accountable (i.e., to too many stakeholders about too many issues and in ways the stakeholders have yet to define or agree upon). Their agents play accountability tug-of-war with the NGO, reducing the organization's efficiency and effectiveness (Koppell 2005a). Managing the demands of multiple stakeholders is difficult for any actor, but the added wrinkle of ENGOs' particular missions means environmental actors often have conflicting ideas of how to solve environmental problems. This makes answering all calls to the satisfaction of each agent extremely difficult.

Traditionally, an accountability bias (Behn 2001) in conservation pushed ENGOs to focus on the outcomes of their work, rather than the processes used to achieve those outcomes (Sawhill 2001). Participatory conservation, however, demands accountability for process, incorporating the needs and desires of resource-dependent communities and other stakeholders. The dual interests in outcomes and process seem at odds with each other, with different organizations focusing on their own prioritization. The urgency of environmental conservation means that taking the time to consult all potential stakeholders in the process might result in extinct species or permanently damaged ecosystems. Moreover, the advent of social media has amplified both the number of potential stakeholders and their accountability demands for ENGOs. All these factors contribute to ENGOs becoming paralyzed by the contradicting demands of MAD and falling into a crisis of participation.

Single Accountability Disorder (SAD)

In SAD, the actor chooses to prioritize its own demands over all others, either through tunnel vision toward its mission or self-preservation of the organization itself (Balboa 2009). When in a SAD state, an organization advances some objectives, but these objectives may not directly fulfill its mission (e.g., greenwashing or mission creep), or may not be sustainable once pressure from external accountability agents comes to bear on the organization. Actors in SAD do not meaningfully incorporate the opinions, expertise, differences, and demands of multiple actors into their work. They selectively incorporate how and to whom they are accountable in order to survive or achieve their mission. These two expressions of SAD reinforce each other. More gains toward the mission will demonstrate organizational effectiveness, which will increase its legitimacy and make it a more durable organization. Maintaining political ties or funding with tangential projects is often done to preserve the organization so that it can eventually advance its mission, especially if the alternative includes destabilizing strategic political ties or jeopardizing the financial health of the organization. After all, if the organization loses financial or political stability, it will never achieve its mission.

To sustain the organization, NGOs rely on many strategies that might seem counter to its mission. So-called mission creep, where an NGO applies for funding that is slightly outside of its mission in order to receive much-needed capital, can temporarily preserve the organization financially (Fowler 1997). By temporarily pursuing funders' objectives over its own mission, the ENGO exhibits a SAD for organizational survival. As the funder pushes for the ENGO to be accountable for the agreed upon outputs and outcomes, the organization's other stakeholders see this as a deprioritization of mission. Not only does this dynamic fulfill Kramarz and Park's trap of increased accountability and decreased environmental gains, it also endangers the ENGO's reputation as a clear agent for its mission in any future efforts.

Much of the attention on "greenwashing" focuses on corporate actions that mislead consumers about the firm's environmental performance (Delmas and Burbano 2011). Still, the debates regarding potential complicity of an ENGO in promoting a firm's green image (whether accurate or not) fall under this category as well (Paddison 2013). ENGOs like the WWF and TNC both work with corporations as part of their new conservation strategy to make industries more sustainable. Traditional conservationists who critique these partnerships accuse these ENGOs of being co-opted by business and deemphasizing both local resource-dependent communities and science (Hance 2016b). Either scenario results in SAD: if the organization has indeed been co-opted and their mission is not being advanced by corporate partnerships, at least the relationship might result in organizational survival in the form of funding (MacDonald 2008). On the other hand, if the organization is truly pressing the corporation to adopt greener practices, then the ENGO is prioritizing its own mission over answering these critical calls for accountability from actors who disagree with the partnership altogether. Either case leaves agents of accountability unsatisfied.

The Relationship between SAD and MAD

An NGO can quickly morph between these dysfunctional accountability states. TNC has been lauded for its fidelity to mission in nonprofit management literature because it will forego popular trends in conservation in order to follow its mission (Kearns 1996). A 2003 Washington Post series illustrated how sticking to one's mission can isolate other stakeholders in the process of conservation (e.g., donors, businesses, landowners, resource-dependent communities, and the public in general), and reduce an organization's efficiency (Ottaway and Stephens 2003; Stephens and Ottaway 2003a–f; Stephens 2003). Indeed, TNC's single-focused interpretation of its mission fortified those who disagreed with it to publicly dispute TNC's legitimacy as a nonprofit, thus illustrating this contestation of ideas on environmental problem-solving. By not anticipating and addressing these conflicts, TNC suffered a crisis of performance with major setbacks and distractions from their mission. When previously ignored stakeholders gained traction in their calls for TNC's accountability, the organization could no longer maintain its SAD state. It had to try to answer the calls for accountability. As a result, TNC used its funds to hire outside counsel, formed an independent governance panel to address the allegations, created new restrictions on its practices, hired a compliance officer, created more oversight policies and procedures, and overhauled its governance structure (TNC 2003). This organization with a reputation for fidelity to mission was "forced to admit that strategies it previously considered vital to accomplishing its mission and that defined it as an institution [were] problematic" (Stephenson and Chaves 2006, 12). The calls for accountability necessitated a change in organizational design, forcing TNC to reconstitute the organization to make it more accountable to various stakeholders. However, with so much effort focused on redesigning the organization and its strategies, the organization transitioned into the crisis of participation in MAD.

Balanced Accountability

The state of balanced accountability is the most difficult to obtain and sustain. To achieve this balanced state, NGOs must convert the competitive environment into a collaborative one, managing the expectations and demands of each stakeholder, and facilitating a network-wide vision for the work it does, in order to make progress toward its unique mission. In balanced accountability, an organization builds into its operations the concerns and ideas of all stakeholders and does not assume that any one process is sufficient for achieving its mission. It is open to learning and willing to change its approach based on an honest exchange of ideas within the network. As an ideal type within a dynamic and changing environment,

NGOs strive to achieve this balanced state, and often experience it not as a sustained state but as moments of balance where there is neither crisis of performance nor crisis of participation. Unlike the competitive environment of MAD that makes incorporating other actors' views into the NGO's operations problematic, the collaborative nature of balanced accountability means participation enhances performance. Moreover, it means that participants understand that their ideas may not be appropriate for each scenario. They may suggest interventions and approaches, but ultimately, the collaborative and communicative relationships between all actors means that actors can feel they have been heard without requiring the project to change completely. Successful interventions result from considering all views and tailoring approaches where appropriate.

Achieving a balanced state for any NGO is no easy task. The existing literature on NGO accountability focuses on its benefits. What better way to serve survivors of a humanitarian crisis than to incorporate their feedback into your service provision (Deloffre 2016)? A project aimed at aiding survivors of gender-based violence surely would benefit from asking the survivors for their views (Dijkzeul 2015). And while the literature often focuses on balancing the relationships between NGOs, clients, funders, and other actors, it fails to discuss the importance of collaboration and competition for balancing accountability. Considering that accountability in voluntary governance is characterized by a mutually agreed upon set of standards or ethics, this is a considerable oversight.

This balance is not, however, impossible. The Locally Managed Marine Area Network (LMMA Network), which is a network of practitioners from a range of organizations, including everything from small, community-based organizations to branches of large ENGOs (like the Wildlife Conservation Society) and universities, demonstrates balance by focusing on community-based conservation while bringing in nonlocal advisors for funding, financial issues, and research methods. Their focus on local practitioners as the drivers for conservation has helped the network engage multiple participants, while demonstrating quantifiable progress toward its vision of "vibrant, resilient, and empowered communities who inherit and maintain healthy, well-managed, and sustainable marine resources and ecosystems" (LMMA Network, 2015). LMMA Network members learn from each other's experiences in community-based conservation but with local agents maintaining authority over their work. While this approach reduces the control nonlocal ENGOs have over the conservation agenda and time-lines, the local focus of the LMMA member organizations creates a cross-learning, cooperative environment that decreases competition among these ENGOs.

The Crisis of Accountability for the International Marinelife Alliance

The story of the International Marinelife Alliance (IMA) in the Philippines is a clear example of an NGO whose initial SAD eventually morphed into a state of MAD with the accompanying crises. The IMA focused on the live reef fish trade in Southeast Asia, where it aimed to eliminate the use of cyanide in fishing and protect reef ecosystems. The IMA's approach combined traditional and new conservation to achieve results in its fight against destructive fishing. The organization trained thousands of fishers in sustainable fishing techniques, created programs to address livelihood issues in fishing communities, connected sustainable fishers with markets that sought sustainable products, and created disincentives for using cya-nide in fishing. Throughout its first 15 years (from 1980 to 1995), the IMA maintained single accountability to itself and its mission. As the program's success brought increased attention and calls for expansion into multiple other countries, the growing number of diverse stakeholders pulled the organization in multiple directions, which made answering these demands while achieving mission impossible. As this case demonstrates, the lack of consensus about the ethical and professional standards of voluntary gover-nance institutions makes balanced accountability elusive.

Founding staff members and leaders of IMA attributed their success to their ability to get things done quickly. Decisions were initially made swiftly by core staff. One informant talked about partnerships and decision-making in IMA's early stages: "the decision-making in a smaller group when you start from scratch is always a lot easier than with a bigger group... [where in a big group] we [could] sit around talking for eight months and then the problem has gotten worse." In contrast, IMA worked for quick action: "the big thing was coming up with an idea, and we started [the programs] even when we didn't have the money because we had a dedi-cated staff who would work to earn the money. The original builders of IMA would do stuff without worrying about getting paid, unlike the people in Washington" (Interview 1, Former IMA Staff, March 2006).

IMA's hallmark program of cyanide detection tests (CDT) and labs exemplified its focus on mission over other actors' requests. The CDT was created in 1991 to offer scientific proof of cyanide fishing in order to raise awareness of the problem, monitor the success of IMA's programs, and enforce regulations against the use of cyanide. IMA used a test procedure created by Dr. R. Sundararajan and approved by the standard-setting body of the American Society of Testing Materials (ASTM) (Holthus 1999; International Marinelife Alliance 1999). Following ASTM recommendations, IMA created the standard operating procedures and determined the equipment needed to create a cyanide detection laboratory (International Marinelife Alliance 1999). After demonstrating the test for the Philippine Bureau of Fisheries and Aquatic Resources (BFAR) in 1991 (Rubec 1997), the first cyanide detection laboratory was established in Quezon City (Metro Manila) under a joint agreement between IMA and BFAR (Pratt 2004). During IMA's heyday, there were six labs throughout the country, fifty cases in the Philippine courts based on positive CDT results (Interview 1, Former IMA Staff, March 2006), and more than 7,000 fish and invertebrates tested for cyanide in the Philippines (Rubec 1997). The labs were central to enforcing the regulations against cyanide fishing and the test results were used in courts to prosecute offenders (Interview 2, Former IMA Staff, November 18, 2005).

In this case, IMA established the labs and focused on achieving its mission without other actors' concerns slowing them down. While the IMA fisheries officers were officially licensed and deputized by BFAR, the government agency required little in return. "With BFAR, it was a one-way street. They never provided anything but money. We did all the work. They never got in the way, never intervened. They never said, 'Do this, don't do that.' We had control of everything" (Interview 1, Former IMA Staff, March 2006). As long as IMA provided the service BFAR needed, not much more was asked of it.

Another example of IMA's SAD was its educational program: The Coral Reef Education for Students (CREST) manuals and kits for Filipino schools (Romero et al. 1995), as well as a Quiz Bowl competition based on this curriculum. These programs were intended to reach the entire community to inform them on reef ecology and the fish trade, and to inspire students to think beyond fishing and aspire to other professions. Aside from the teachers and Palawan State College staff who helped design the curriculum, IMA did not engage partners for implementation. "With the CREST program, they said, 'You have to go to the Department of Education first,' but if we did that, they would have taken three years to study it and nothing would have gotten done. Instead, we went around the back, got it implemented, and then had letters from 37 superintendents of schools saying how great it was and then presented it to the Department of Education, and what could it say? He said, 'Great program. Put our seal on it.' If you start from the beginning, you'll get stopped, same way it is anywhere." (Interview 1, Former IMA Staff, March 2006)

With this program, IMA acquired its own printing press and 25 educational staff members, worked in 1,800 schools, and produced thousands of books per month (Interview 1, Former IMA Staff, March 2006). It was the only ENGO attempting to govern the live reef fish trade, and thus, did not have competing voices critiquing its work or requiring it to account for the process of achieving mission. In true SAD fashion, the organization achieved results without having to answer to others; participation did not slow down the process of achieving mission, nor did it take the precious resources of time or funding away from IMA's objectives.

Expansion and a Conversion to MAD

While the first 15 years of IMA's existence were marked by this single accountability to itself, the organization's success in achieving mission garnered much attention across the globe, which opened it up to more external demands on its operations. This expansion brought into clear relief the crisis of performance within SAD. IMA received requests from governments and other agencies in the Marshall Islands, Solomon Islands, Papua New Guinea, Kiribati, the Carolines and the Marianas, Indonesia, and Hong Kong to create baseline status reports on the trade and to launch similar programs there (IMA 1998). As it expanded, its funding base grew to include funders with varying reporting and programmatic requirements. IMA also started collaborating with other organizations—on publications and outreach with the World Resources Institute, on a program with TNC, and through new board membership on the Marine Aquarium Council. As interest in biodiversity globally was mirrored by the creation of the Convention of Biological Diversity and many other conservation agreements in the 1990s, IMA actually had a track record of doing something toward these conservation ends across national boundaries and sectors. Many government agencies also took an interest in its work—from the previously engaged Philippine agencies to the US Agency for International Development (USAID) and the US Coral Reef Task Force. The expansion of IMA's reach, however, tied the organization to these new actors and their accountability demands. For example:

• Funders required a longer-term comprehensive strategy for IMA in addition to continued results of the type IMA had previously obtained.
• Local fishers wanted to sustain or improve their current living by using sustainable harvest methods.
• Other NGOs demanded scientific review of IMA's cyanide detection and advocated for alternate approaches to making the trade more sustainable.
• Finally, staff wanted a bigger strategic picture of their work, a more participatory decision-making process, and job security.

The addition of these new actors in IMA's work made plain the centralized, quick, and reactionary decision-making that had advanced the organization during its first 15 years of existence. The new stakeholders, however, had different ideas of operations and demanded changes in IMA's *modus operandi*. The strategic plan that staff and funders called for required a change in board membership from a small number of relatives and friends to one that reflected the norms of a professional NGO. These calls for more accountability changed the power dynamic for how IMA achieved its mission. One staff member wrote an email to convince IMA leadership of the need for transition: "In the old days, it was easy—[the founders] did everything, because it was a small organization. But it is not a small organization anymore, it is getting to be a fairly large one with field offices and activities in a lot of places. This demands a different management strategy, as we all know, and we have made a lot of progress moving in that direction" (Source 2, Email Communication, July 18, 2002). No longer could it quickly act to solve a problem: the processes and priorities required by these stakeholders conflicted with what IMA's leaders thought was effective. "They all thought we did things so badly before the strategic plan, but [operating without a strategic plan] worked" (Interview 1, Former IMA Staff, March 2006). While IMA had a specific approach to environmental governance, the growing number of actors in coral reef conservation wanted IMA to follow processes that reflected how they thought the environment and fishing communities might best be served.

Further debates surrounding the CDT laboratory system demonstrated how SAD is not sustainable, since as an organization expands more actors assert their claims for accountability. These debates included the following points:

• Whether there was corruption in the collection of fish samples (Interview 3, Philippine Aquarium Trade Business Owner, March 21, 2006)
• Whether the test was accurate
• If the implementation of the test followed acceptable standard operating procedure
• If testing for cyanide was an appropriate way to deter cyanide fishing

In 1999, the Marine Aquarium Council—an organization created for the certification of sustainably harvested aquarium fish—was asked to perform a peer review of the CDT test (Holthus 1999). This external scientific review listed several criticisms but primarily suggested that the test was neither appropriate nor accurate for the purposes of determining cyanide use in the live reef fish trade (Holthus 1999).

Whether or not these criticisms held water, the debate they engendered is instructive on how SAD can quickly convert into MAD. With little or no oversight, IMA created the labs for cyanide testing throughout the Philippines; implemented an enforcement procedure for collecting and assessing fish catch; and successfully ran the CDT labs from 1992 to 1998. When IMA began partnering with multiple global organizations, these external actors started questioning this approach. "Working with partners, I don't think we gained anything from it. I really thought it set us back. Our partners saw us doing the work, saw us getting the grants and then there was the jealousy thing" (Interview 1, Former IMA Staff, March 2006). As a critique of IMA's entire approach to conservation, one staff member from a competing ENGO claimed, "If we have to test for cyanide, then we've lost already" (Interview 8, Employee, Marine Aquarium Council, March 2006). More important to that competitor was working with fishers to prevent the use of cyanide in the first place and to promote better fish handling techniques. These quotes highlight how accountability is made difficult by NGO competition created by horizontal differentiation with finite resources. They also illustrate IMA's prioritizing its own processes over the demands of other actors. IMA's aversion to taking criticism and to working with partners on improving the CDT displayed not only blind fidelity to its *modus operandi* but also a lack of interest in incorporating the accountability demands of the conservation field (which included peer review and partnerships).

IMA had to redirect substantial resources to answer these multiple calls for accountability. Several staff members were involved in the administrative and political work to facilitate strategic planning, professionalize the organization's leadership, and institutionalize standard processes for decision-making. Founding board members and officers were offended that their dedication to the organization's mission was to be replaced by the nascent interest of individuals who fulfilled the professional norms of boards and leadership. Time and resources were spent in meetings to create these plans and to convince current leadership that the plans were both important and professional (not personal) in nature.

The strong allegations against the CDT process (regardless of the allegations' validity) were detrimental to the legitimacy of the program's major component. Funders who were previously adamant supporters of the labs started hedging their bets with other programs from competing NGOs. And while the agencies that were interested in adopting the cyanide detection laboratories in their countries were still eager to implement IMA's work, IMA staff with the capacity to create these centers were too busy responding to criticisms raised by the Marine Aquarium Council.

With these efforts to respond to demands, to change operations and decision-making processes, and to open up programming to broad scrutiny, the IMA became mired in the crisis of performance that MAD creates. Where previously the organization could ignore other actors in order to achieve its mission of conserving the coral reef ecosystem, this success was short-lived because the organization's expansion opened it up to the scrutiny of a growing number of actors, each with their own ideas of how best to stop destructive fishing. Any changes that resulted from the growing calls for accountability impacted IMA's organizational design and its relationships with other actors, but not to the benefit of the environmental aims the organization set out to achieve.

Conclusions

The crisis of accountability experienced by the IMA is not a new story. With the increasing environmental mandates and decreasing state capacity to implement these programs and regulations, ENGOs have stepped in to fill this governance gap. This has increased the power and publicness of ENGOs, requiring commensurate accountability to ensure that these actors adhere to the norms of their stakeholders in absence of democratic processes. Kramarz and Park state that these ENGOs are designed for "upholding or diffusing agreed upon moral standards of conduct among self-selected, like-minded individuals" (chapter 1, in this volume). The trouble is that, also by design, very few of the stakeholders in environmental governance are "like-minded individuals." ENGO professionals self-select into environmental governance; they are not elected into office because a majority of constituents agree with their approach (like public institution actors). In the absence of a clear mandate, the conservation field in particular is teeming with ideas on how to best serve its nonhuman and not-yet-human stakeholders: from preservation, to traditional conservation, to new conservation. Even within these approaches, there is disagreement about the best way to achieve environmental objectives. The IMA's struggle to be accountable to its peers and other stakeholders while achieving mission is instructive on this dynamic.

This case demonstrates the importance of examining different ways an organization can be accountable: transparency, control, liability, responsibility, and responsiveness (Koppell 2005). Accountability is not merely responding to the demands and complaints of competitors. It is also controlling the design of interventions and maintaining an integrity to mission. It is also about being responsible for upholding the rules of the field and acknowledging that rules might change from time to time and location to location. IMA worked hard to maintain fidelity to mission and control its interventions. It worked to be responsible and uphold scientific norms through the creation of a standardized protocol for testing cyanide in fish, but it was not responsible in upholding the norms of getting local government approval before starting its education project. It prioritized being responsive to local fishing communities over responding to competing NGOs. These relationships and reactions are clear when we analyze IMA as a case study. What, then, might have helped them avoid going MAD? It's hard to say without a broader study of multiple cases, but a few things come to mind. First, this case demonstrates a need for clear understanding of the different ways an organization can show accountability. Discussions of ENGO accountability—both within the sector and from outside agents—that reflect this diversity of approaches to the issue might be more

able to maneuver or understand difference. Second, by using this vocabulary of accountability, ENGOs can manage their relationships with other
actors and explain their prioritization of accountability demands. If IMA
were able to engage with their funders, competitors, partners, local officials,
and fishing communities by stating how they prioritize accountability relationships and why, they might have had more constructive conversations
with their critics and maintained broader support. We won't know in this
particular case, but I write this in the hope that it is useful for other ENGOs
managing their accountability states.

This case, like the others in this book, also demonstrates the importance
of examining accountability through Kramarz and Park's two-tiered analysis to include both the design of the institution and the implementation
of interventions. For public agencies or private industry, the prioritization
seems clearer than for NGOs and other voluntary institutions. As stated
in chapter 1, public agencies hold paramount the representation of the
demos and political parties—both groups with clear ways of making their
desires known and clear mechanisms for sanctioning unwanted behavior.
For private industry, profitability is of primary importance in supplying
goods and services. Here, profitability is easily measured and shareholders can both control future actions and hold the organization liable for
past actions. For ENGOs, however, the goal of upholding moral norms is
complex. Moral norms change. They are contested. And as more actors
are incorporated into the fabric of environmental governance—each with
their own motivations, philosophies, and expectations—these norms
become more contested. Thus, while previous analyses might examine the
second tier of governance, raising questions about the actions of ENGOs,
by examining the first tier of governance this effort demonstrates why
the design of voluntary actors precludes consensus on the second tier of
accountability.

Because of this design, competition in the field of ENGOs has created a
pathological dynamic where organizations with divergent approaches to
environmental governance call each other to account for their approaches,
with no resolution in sight. No one actor can unequivocally demonstrate
that its approach is the best one for achieving environmental objectives,
and differences in approach to serving the nonhuman and not-yet-human
constituents will not be resolved soon. But analyzing the demands of multiple stakeholders through the lens of approaches and philosophies of

conservation, ENGOs might be better equipped to explain their position and approach to funders, members, and other potential partners.

By demonstrating how an ENGO can fall into SAD or MAD, this chapter offers an explanation for Kramarz and Park's accountability trap—which states that ENGOs are increasingly using tools of accountability but without knowing that these processes will bring improved environmental outcomes. This MAD/SAD typology of accountability pathologies illustrates the questions raised when an ENGO must navigate the multitude of accountability demands and determine how best to serve these nonhuman stakeholders. Does it focus solely on its mission—assuming that its mission speaks for the betterment of future generations or biodiversity, but to the detriment of other stakeholder participation? Or does it try to respond to all the demands of stakeholders, even if they do not have the future generation's interest as a priority? And if it does respond to all current stakeholders, will this help it achieve its mission? Does it choose SAD and its crisis of performance, or MAD and its crisis of participation?

Exploring the concepts in this analysis—the two-tiers of accountability of environmental governance; that organizations can demonstrate accountability through transparency, control, liability, responsiveness, and responsibility; that pathologies of accountability can present in this MAD/SAD dichotomy—might not solve the animosity between the Saning'o, the Maasai leader, and the organizations he declared to be his "enemies." Analyzing how new conservation, traditional conservation, and preservation approaches to environmental stewardship conflict in Eastern Africa will surely not end the conflict itself. What this chapter does, however, is shed light on why these conflicts exist and create a vocabulary for deliberating these issues. In doing this, it challenges scholars and practitioners to refine and apply these concepts to other cases. A logical next step would be to compare competition among ENGOs with similar approaches (e.g., multiple new conservation ENGOs) and competition among ENGOs with different approaches (e.g., new conservation and traditional conservation ENGOs) to see how accountability is demanded and upheld, and whether the MAD/SAD dichotomy manifests similarly in different governance networks. Other research could be more experimental, to see if using this analysis in ENGO discussions of accountability changes the competitive nature of voluntary actors. Even more, studying funders and their role in this horizontal differentiation and competition could illuminate broader governance dynamics. This chapter is the first step toward helping voluntary governance actors avoid the accountability trap so that they can convert accountability from an end goal into a means to govern natural resources to serve nonhuman and not-yet-human stakeholders.

Notes

1. Portions of this chapter have been previously published in Cristina M. Balboa, "Mission Interference: How Competition Confounds Accountability for Environmental Nongovernmental Organizations," *Review of Policy Research* 34, no. 1 (2017): 110–131. For a different discussion of accountability in this case study, see Balboa 2018.

2. Conservation International, last updated in 2017, https://www.conservation.org/about/Pages/default.aspx.

3. Wildlife Conservation Society (WCS), last updated in 2018, https://globalinitia tives.wcs.org/Top-Navigation/About-Us/WCS-Vision-Mission-Goal.aspx.

III   Analyzing the Means of Accountability in Global Environmental Governance

5 Hybrid Accountability in Cooperative Initiatives for Global Climate Governance

Oscar Widerberg, Philipp Pattberg, and Lieke Brouwer

Introduction

Few other global environmental issues have witnessed a larger proliferation of new governance initiatives than climate change. Thousands of states, cities, regions, companies, and civil society groups collaborate around climate action. What some have described as a "Cambrian explosion" of governance initiatives (Keohane and Victor 2011, 12) has shifted the center of gravity in global climate governance away from the multilateral state-led response under the United Nations Framework Convention on Climate Change (UNFCCC) toward a polycentric structure (Jordan et al. 2015). This diffusion of authority between public and private institutions poses important accountability challenges for the global climate governance system (Widerberg and Pattberg 2017). Hybrid cooperative initiatives, where public and private actors collaborate on climate action, are particularly interesting. They render traditional conceptualizations of accountability that requires a division of organizations into public or private increasingly difficult to work with (Bäckstrand 2008; chapter 1, in this volume). Consider, for example, the Portfolio Decarbonization Coalition (PDC), a multistakeholder initiative targeting asset managers and holders to decarbonize their portfolios. The initiative is run by the United Nations Environmental Programme (UNEP), together with a Swedish pension fund (AP4), a European asset manager (Amundi), and partnering with an international nongovernmental organization (CDP). In a hybrid constellation such as the PDC that brings public and private actors together, who is ultimately responsible for making sure that the organizations involved live up to their commitments? By what standards should they be held accountable and what sanctions are available if the partners choose not to comply with the rules?

This chapter examines accountability in hybrid climate governance initiatives. It zooms in on what Kramarz and Park call second-tier accountability, at the level of execution of interventions (see chapter 1, in this volume). This chapter discusses processes and standards that initiatives use to measure and evaluate progress; whether sanctions are available to punish noncompliance; and discernable impacts from the initiatives. The chapter presents evidence from four case studies of hybrid cooperative initiatives, based on data from the CONNECT project[1].

The next section presents a brief introduction to cooperative initiatives in global climate governance and their relation to what Kramarz and Park call the the accountability trap (see chapter 1, in this volume). Subsequently, the case study selection is presented as well as short introductions to each case. Next, the chapter presents the analysis of the processes, standards, and sanctions of accountability in the case studies. Finally, the impacts of the initiatives are discussed, and the concluding section summarizes the findings and outlines priorities for future research.

The Rise of Cooperative Initiatives in Climate Governance: An "Accountability Trap"

Cooperative initiatives, social innovations, climate clubs, and *experiments* are among the multiple terms used to describe multistakeholder initiatives where public and private stakeholders collaborate to solve climate-related problems (Widerberg and Stripple 2016). In this chapter, the term cooperative initiatives refers to transnational hybrid initiatives, defined as "institutionalized transboundary interactions between public and private actors, which aim at the provision of collective goods." (Schäferhoff, Campe, and Kaan 2009, 455; see also chapter 1, in this volume). Cooperative initiatives are characterized by transnationality (involving crossborder interactions and nonstate relations); public policy objectives (as opposed to public bads or exclusively private goods); and a network structure (coordination by participating actors rather than coordination by a central hierarchy), where participation is voluntary (Pattberg and Widerberg 2016).

Cooperative initiatives have moved from the fringes into the center of global climate politics. Alternative approaches to the multilateral efforts, including cooperative initiatives, have increasingly been discussed after the failure of the 15th Conference of the Parties (COP) to the UNFCCC in Copenhagen, (Falkner, Stephan, and Vogler 2010; Victor 2011). In the run-up to COP 21 held in Paris in 2015, cooperative initiatives gained increasing attention from the formal climate regime, partly due to the work of the Second Workstream of the Ad Hoc Working Group on the Durban Platform for Enhanced Action (ADP2) to the UNFCCC, which was established in 2011 and tasked with finding ways to enhance pre-2020 climate action. ADP2's challenge was to close the so-called "ambition gap" which had emerged between the pledges made by parties to the UNFCCC and the decarbonization pathway needed to reach the global target of stabilizing global warming to 2°C. Under the supervision and mandate of ADP2, the UNFCCC Secretariat provided two technical reports exploring the potentials in cooperative initiatives and set up a simple database on the UNFCCC homepage, listing a selection of initiatives (Widerberg and Stripple 2016). Several observers hoped that such climate actions by nonparty stakeholders, including cooperative initiatives, could help wedge the ambition gap (UNEP 2015; Blok et al. 2012).

The outcomes of the COP 21 provided unprecedented recognition of nonparty stakeholders and cooperative initiatives in delivering climate action, taking several decisions to increase their capacity (Hale 2016). Governments decided *inter alia* that two high-level champions would be elected to facilitate "the successful execution of existing efforts and the scaling-up and introduction of new or strengthened voluntary efforts, initiatives and coalitions." They encouraged nonparty stakeholders to register their actions in the Non-State Actor Zone on Climate Action (NAZCA), a data platform launched in conjunction with COP 20 in Lima in 2014. And finally, governments decided to convene a high-level event pursuing the Lima-Paris Action Agenda (LPAA), also launched at COP 20, which gave nonstate actors, including multistakeholder climate coalitions, much attention. In the wake of COP 21, several processes (e.g., the Marrakech Partnership for Global Climate Action and the Talanoa Dialogue) have been started to further highlight climate action by nonparty stakeholders and cooperative initiatives. The processes in the UNFCCC aiming to integrate private and hybrid governance initiatives with the existing public regime has also spurred regional and national offsprings. In Sweden and Argentina for instance, governments and civil society groups are launching new initiatives to bring nonstate and subnational climate initiatives closer to the national decision-making processes (Chan, Ellinger, and Widerberg 2018).

In sum, events at both the international, transnational, and national level suggest that cooperative initiatives are gaining further traction as an instrument of choice for addressing climate change.

To what extent are cooperative initiatives having concrete impacts? It is true that a large number and wide variety of cooperative initiatives have been observed and documented in both academic and policy circles (Widerberg, Pattberg, and Kristensen 2016; Bulkeley et al. 2014). For example, the UNEP Climate Initiative Platform contains 222 initiatives to date and the UNFCCC platform NAZCA, established in 2014, showcases 77 cooperative initiatives. Many initiatives engage in actions which, in theory, increase transparency and processes such as creating new standards, recording information on actions and commitments, and publishing progress reports to decision-makers and the general public (Bulkeley et al. 2014; Green 2013). They also generate a baffling amount of data, studies, and reports. The CDP, for instance, records data from over 5,000 companies on climate change, forests, water, and supply chains. The carbon*n* Climate Registry provides a platform for local and subnational governments to report on climate targets and GHG emissions, collecting data from over 600 cities and local governments in more than 60 countries. In theory, cooperative initiatives are thus ameliorating the conditions for holding actors accountable for their activities that have an impact on climate change. By publishing climate commitments of a city or company, for instance, as well as continuously monitoring and reporting on performance, cooperative initiatives provide material for holding actors accountable for their actions. Despite all these cooperative initiatives, however, global greenhouse gas (GHG) emissions keep increasing at a relentless speed, resulting in unprecedented levels of carbon dioxide in the atmosphere (IPCC 2014). So while the possibilities for holding those governing climate change to account have multiplied, the impact on GHG emissions appears nonexistent. This is what Kramarz and Park call the accountability trap, in which the number of processes for accountability increase alongside the "continued deterioration of the environment" (see chapter 1, in this volume). What explains the accountability trap when it comes to climate change? Kramarz and Park develop a two-tier model, focusing on the design of institutions and execution of interventions. Central to their model is the notion that actors have different goals when entering an initiative, as well as different responsibilities and target audiences. For example, a liberal democracy is answerable to its electorate for delivering a public good, a firm to its shareholders to generate return on investments, and a civil society organization (CSO) to uphold moral standards to its followers (see chapter 1, in this volume).

For studying accountability, several analyses have used the concept of "accountability regimes" (Mashaw 2006; Chan and Pattberg 2008). Different accountability regimes can be distinguished through "ideal types" of governance systems that can be divided into public, private, social, or variations thereof (Chan and Pattberg 2008; Mashaw 2006; chapter 1, in this volume). Public actors answer to their citizens through "public accountability regimes" that are hierarchically arranged where "obligations flow up and down hierarchies" (Chan and Pattberg 2008, 105). Private and nongovernmental institutions are linked through "market-based accountability regimes" that are organized around market principles (Mashaw 2006, 122). The third broad category of ideal types are "social accountability regimes" that encompass a wide variety of accountability relationships, from family ties to club membership (Chan and Pattberg 2008, 105). The ideal types and accountability regimes in turn correspond to three actor types: public authorities, firms, and civil society. In public systems, the goal is to provide a public good and to be answerable to an electorate or other political communities; private systems concern economic benefits to consumers and shareholders; and voluntary systems concern commonly "agreed upon moral standards of conduct among self-selected, like-minded individuals" (chapter 1, in this volume). Consequently, different logics lead to different accountability standards, processes, and sanctioning opportunities.

Hybrid cooperative initiatives blur the distinction between public and private institutions. For instance, one of the case studies in this chapter, the Roundtable on Sustainable Biomaterials (RSB) standard, is developed under the auspices of members from the entire supply chain of biomaterials, as well as representatives from diverse groups, such as environmental NGOs (ENGOs), trade unions, and researchers. Bäckstrand (2008, 80) contends that in these cases of networked partnerships, the most applicable types of accountability mechanisms are nonhierarchical and horizontal. These accountability mechanisms are characterized by *reputational accountability*, requiring functioning monitoring mechanisms; *market accountability*, providing signals for rewards or punishment; and *peer accountability*, allowing peers to monitor and assess each other. Bäckstrand further suggests that cooperative initiatives should be accountable to many different actors, state and nonstate, since networked governance arrangements are "neither directly accountable to an electoral base nor do they exhibit clear principal agent relationships" (Benner et al. in Bäckstrand 2008, 82). Bäckstrand, Kramarz, and Park's writings suggest that governance structures characterized by multiple types of actors and networked, horizontal governance modes require us to "unpack" the principal-agent conceptualization of accountability (Bäckstrand 2008, 80). This chapter empirically unpacks the accountability relationship between public and private actors engaged in cooperative initiatives using Kramarz and Park's (Kramarz and Park 2016; see also introductory chapter) second-tier accountability concept, exploring the processes, standards, sanctions, and impacts of accountability. The following section explains the case selection and research approach.

Case Study Selection

Research on cooperative initiatives in global climate governance has increased rapidly, also from an accountability perspective (Widerberg and Pattberg 2017). By creating databases, academics and international organizations are mapping the field of cooperative initiatives in a systematic way (see Widerberg and Stripple 2016 for an overview). NAZCA and the Climate Initiatives Platform for instance, are leveraging the data-gathering efforts by organizations such as CDP and the Covenant of Mayors that focus on specific types of actors such as companies and subnational authorities. Consequently, our understanding of how the landscape of cooperative initiatives is structured has improved tremendously. An interesting observation emerging from the data is that cooperative initiatives often engage directly in creating accountability mechanisms such as standard setting, monitoring, reporting, and publishing. For instance, over 40 percent of the eighty-nine cooperative initiatives collected in the CONNECT project have a "standards and commitments" function, meaning that they require their members to follow certain standards of behavior (e.g., carbon accounting standards) or commit to climate actions (e.g., by publicly stating a carbon reduction target).

This chapter uses a case study approach to investigate what processes and standards initiatives have in place to ensure measures are taken and progress evaluated; what sanctions are used for dealing with misconduct and failure to live up to commitments; and what impacts can be attributed to the initiatives. Case studies allow for going beyond just observing that cooperative initiatives engage in activities related to accountability, and toward exploring how they do so (Yin 2014). To select cases, the chapter starts with a data set of eighty-nine cooperative initiatives gathered in the CONNECT project (Widerberg, Pattberg, and Kristensen 2016). The cooperative initiatives included in the data-set are (1) international and transnational institutions, (2) who not only have the intentionality to steer the policy and behavior of their members or a broader community, (3) but also explicitly mention a common governance goal (4) accomplishable by significant governance functions (Widerberg, Pattberg, and Kristensen 2016). For each cooperative initiative, the data-set includes information on focus area (e.g., urban climate action, climate finance, or energy efficiency), number of members, year of initiations, and various other descriptive statistics. Furthermore, the institutions have been visually mapped using a conceptual model called a "governance triangle," designed by Abbott and Snidal (2009a, 2009b; Abbott 2012). The triangle is divided into seven zones. Zones 1, 2, and 3 comprise institutions with only public, firm, or CSO members. Zones 4, 5, and 6 contain hybrid constellations between two of the three types of actors. Zone 7 contains multistakeholder institutions, where all three types of actors collaborate. Each cooperative initiative is thus situated in the governance triangle depending on its constituent members (public, firm, or CSO). Further, the cooperative initiatives are color coded according to their primary functions, including the following: standard and commitments, operational, information and networking, or financing. Figure 5.1 shows the CONNECT project's version of the climate governance triangle (which is an updated and slightly tweaked version of Abbott, 2012).

This chapter focuses on multistakeholder institutions situated in zone 7, since the primary interest of this chapter is accountability in hybrid constellations where public and private actors cooperate. Moreover, it is reasonable to argue that some cooperative initiatives perform functions that are more relevant for accountability than others. Cooperative initiatives setting up standards and commitments are directly aiming to provide instruments and data which in theory enable holding an organization accountable, or at least monitoring its actions. An institution focusing on information and networking may be less interesting from an accountability perspective since it, in theory, does not suggest an accountability relationship between the members of the institution or to an external constituency.

PUBLIC

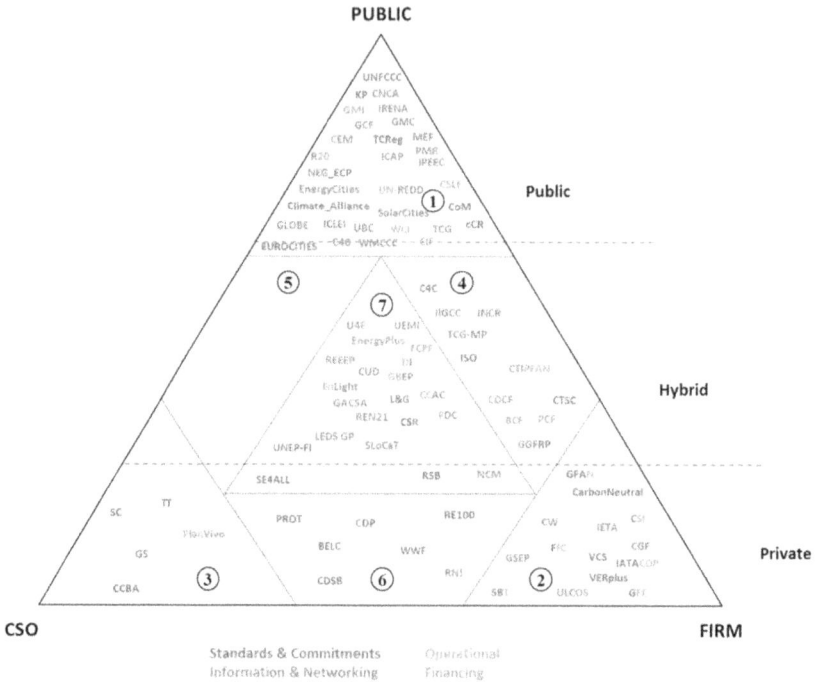

Figure 5.1
Climate governance triangle (published in Widerberg, Pattberg, and Kristensen 2016 and Widerberg and Pattberg 2016, based on Abbott and Snidal, 2009a and b; Abbott, 2012).

The case selection is therefore limited to cooperative initiatives located in zone 7 in the governance triangle and that have standards and commitments as primary functions. Four cases fit these criteria: Lean and Green (L&G); Compact of States and Regions (CSR); UNEP Financial Initiative's Portfolio Decarbonization Coalition (UNEP FI PDC); and the RSB. Due to practical reasons of data gathering, the Sustainable Energy for All (SE4ALL) initiative has been excluded from the study.

Table 5.1 presents the initiatives selected for case studies. All initiatives involve standards and commitments and engage public, CSO, and firm actors in a hybrid form of collaboration. The members are those actors that are formally able to exert influence on the rules, norms, operations, or performance of the initiative, and solely concern organizations (not individuals). The table includes the initiative's name, acronym, starting date,

Table 5.1
Overview of case studies (adjusted from Widerberg, Pattberg & Kristensen, 2016)

Name	Acronym	Start	Members	Participants	Target group	Description
Lean and Green	L&G	2008	1	300	Transport sector	Promotes L&G standard/certification for carbon reduction and cost efficiency
Compact of States and Regions	CSR	2015	4	62	Subnational governments	Collects and publishes data on GHG emissions, reduction targets, and policies
Portfolio Decarbonization Coalition	PDC	2014	4	27	Asset owners and managers	Through disclosure and strategy development, decarbonize investments
Roundtable on Sustainable Biomaterials	RSB	2007	93	92	Biomaterial producers	Using a certification scheme to verify sustainable and ethically sourced biomaterials

number of members[2], number of participants, target group or sector, and a short description of main goals.

The table shows the wide variance across the cases in terms of starting year, number of members, target group, and types of goals. In the following sections, each case is described in more detail:

Lean and Green (L&G) is a transnational cooperative initiative targeting GHG emissions in the transport sector. Started in 2008 by the Dutch-based network Conneckt, it is now active in five countries across three transport sectors: logistics, personal mobility, and inland container shipping. The participating companies and organizations commit to lowering their carbon dioxide (CO_2) emissions by 20 percent in five years. If the target is reached, the company could win the L&G award and becomes eligible for a L&G star, a certification for climate action. The award functions as an indicator for the front-runners in the program, and thus in theory incentivizes other companies to increase their ambitions. The certifications can be used for public relation purposes and are, for instance, portrayed on the trucks of the companies involved in the initiative.

The Compact of States and Regions (CSR) is a cooperative initiative established in September 2014 at the New York Climate Summit that engages subnational governments in providing data on their GHG emissions. CSR is a partnership between five large nonprofit organizations, including the Climate Group, CDP, Regions of Climate Action (R20), and Network of Regional Governments for Sustainable Development (nrg4SD). Also, Local Governments for Sustainability (ICLEI, formerly the International Council for Local Environmental Initiatives), the world's largest initiative for cities and subnational governments, is a supporting partner and provides the carbon*n* Climate Registry (cCR), which is used as the CSR's reporting platform. The main aim of the CSR is to gather data, report, and assess the progress made toward their emission reduction commitments. Despite its recent start, the CSR already collects emissions and commitment data from nearly forty-four subnational governments. Its first aggregate report was released and presented at the COP 21 in Paris.

The United Nations Environmental Programme Finance Initiative (UNEP FI) is a partnership between UNEP and the global finance sector which started in

2003. With nearly 220 members, the initiative focuses on climate finance. Under UNEP FI, the PDC started in 2014 aimed at investors, specifically asset owners and asset managers (UNEP FI 2016a). A key goal for the initiative is to make a carbon footprint measurement and for periodical disclosure to become common practice for investors (UNEP FI 2016a). Currently, the PDC brings together twenty-five investors managing $3.2 trillion in assets, of which decarbonization commitments represent $600 billion (UNEP FI 2016b).

The Roundtable on Sustainable Biomaterials (RSB) is a cooperative initiative which started in 2007, targeting emissions in the biomaterials industry. The industry includes companies engaged in using materials derived from plants or manure, which can be converted and used as an energy source. The RSB gathers stakeholders from all parts of the value chain in the biomaterials industry, as well as civil society (trade unions and rights-based NGOs; social development NGOs; ENGOs), public actors (government, multilateral organizations), and academia. The key instrument is a certification scheme which is provided to companies and organizations producing biomaterials that are sustainable, ethical, and credibly sourced.

For each cooperative initiative, four questions are addressed (also see chapter 1, in this volume):

1. What processes demonstrate accountability?
2. What standards demonstrate accountability?
3. What sanctions are available when there is failure to meet those standards?
4. What impacts do the accountability practices have on reshaping the goals of parties involved in governing the global environment?

Three types of data were collected. First, academic literature and research reports provide a theoretical and practical understanding of hybrid cooperative initiatives in the wider context of environmental and climate governance. Second, home pages and reports by the cooperative initiatives themselves were used. Third, semistructured interviews with 12 representatives from the initiatives themselves, as well as organizations participating in the initiatives, were carried out via telephone or Skype in June and July 2016 (see table 5.2). The next section presents and discusses the results of the case studies.

Table 5.2
Interviews

Initiative	Institution	Respondent Number	Respondent Location	Means	Date
Compact of States and Regions	CSR	R1	UK	Telephone	June 8, 2016
	Newfoundland and Labrador	R2	Canada	Telephone	July 14, 2016
	Newfoundland and Labrador	R3	Canada	Telephone	July 14, 2016
	Baden-Württemberg	R4	Germany	Telephone	July 21, 2016
	Baden-Württemberg	R5	Germany	Telephone	July 21, 2016
Roundtable on Sustainable Biomaterials	RSB	R6	Switzerland	Skype	June 15, 2016
Lean and Green	SkyNRG	R7	The Netherlands	Telephone	July 4, 2016
	Sunchem	R8	South Africa	Skype	July 5, 2016
	L&G	R9	The Netherlands	Skype	June 16, 2016
	L&G	R10	The Netherlands	Skype	June 16, 2016
	Moonen Packaging	R11	The Netherlands	Email	July 20, 2016
UNEP-FI Portfolio Decarbonization Coalition	UNEP FI PDC	R12	France	Telephone	June 27, 2016

Results: Accountability Processes, Standards, Sanctions, and Impacts in Four Cooperative Initiatives

This section discusses "means of accountability," including processes, standards, and sanctions, as well as impacts, across four cooperative initiatives.

Processes

Accountability processes, meaning "through what processes accountability is to be assured" (Mashaw 2006, 118), are likely to be structured differently depending on the constellation of actors. An initiative comprising governments and democratically elected officials, for instance, may face other transparency and procedural demands than a voluntary initiative between companies. Levels of inclusiveness, disclosure, and publicity are likely to differ in public, private, or hybrid settings. For instance, in public governance institutions, accountability processes could mean transparency and public access to data such as budget reviews; in private governance institutions, this could be financial disclosure, auditing reports, following business praxis; and in voluntary initiatives, it could be norm dissemination, lobbying, and information campaigns (see chapter 1, in this volume). In hybrid initiatives, such as those studied in this chapter, it is interesting to examine what accountability processes gain footholds in each initiative.

The accountability processes differ quite substantially across the four cases in terms of levels of detail and rigor. The RSB is perhaps the most advanced in this respect. If a company is to receive an RSB certificate it needs to follow a procedure of application and prepare and be subjected to an audit. Different types of companies, be they smallholders or large scale biomass producers, can choose between different certifications. After notifying the RSB, receiving an approval, and contacting a third-party auditor accredited by the RSB, companies have to prepare for an audit by working their way through an extensive checklist using tools provided by the RSB. If the auditor considers the company ready, it receives the certification. Depending on their risk level, RSB participants are periodically evaluated (every year or every two years) depending on their risk score (Roundtable on Sustainable Biomaterials, 2017). L&G also provides a certification and an award. Organizations are expected to provide a plan of action, which is evaluated by a third-party auditor (TNO 2015). The plan receives a grade arranged on a three-point scale (green, orange, or red) depending on its quality. Red indicates that the entire plan must be rewritten, something which is allowed up to three times. If the plan is given a green grade, the L&G award is given. If the plan is not approved, it gets an orange grade for improvement, or if it needs to be redone entirely, it gets a red grade. The company then has five years to execute the plan; if they are successful, they receive an L&G star, which corresponds to a certificate. A second star can be obtained through an enhanced plan with more elaborate CO_2 monitoring (Connekt 2017).

In contrast to RSB and L&G, accountability is demonstrated in the CSR and the PDC by information disclosure. Commitments and progress made are published annually in the CSR disclosure reports, providing detailed information on the goals and actions by cities and regions. Similarly, the PDC relies on the commitments their participants make and their decarbonization strategies in the annual report of the Portfolio (UNEP FI and CDP 2015).

A distinction regarding accountability processes can thus be made between the RSB and the L&G, which have certification-based processes, and the CSR and PDC, which have disclosure-based processes. Certification-based approaches have different accountability process logics than disclosure-based approaches. The certification-based approaches have detailed safeguards ensuring that their target companies comply with certain standards. In particular, the third-party verification system is a powerful tool for distancing the cooperative initiative itself from the actual process of accountability (see chapter 3, in this volume). For disclosure-based approaches, such as in CSR and PDC, the key to change is disclosing information about the behaviors and accomplishments of the participating actors to a third party, for instance, the public (Mitchell 2011).

Standards

Standards for accountability refers to the yardstick by which agents are held to account. In climate governance, an impact-level yardstick would be GHG emissions; however, few cooperative initiatives are collecting such data, or engage in governance mechanisms that only indirectly are expected to reduce emissions (Widerberg and Stripple, 2016). Hence, beyond direct GHG emissions reductions, for public governance institutions, standards for accountability could be legislation, policy instruments, or monitoring.

For private governance institutions, it could be prices, environmental, social, or other governance standards and benchmarks, and availability of products. Finally, for voluntary initiatives, it could be the uptake of a certain norm by the target group (chapter 1, in this volume). In hybrid initiatives, not all these standards are available to the group as a whole. For instance, a company cannot always be held accountable by the same yardstick as a subnational government.

Across the four cases, the certification-based cooperative initiatives differ distinctively from the disclosure-based approaches when it comes to standards. The certification-based approaches both have highly developed and detailed standards for which to hold the organizations in question to account. The RSB employs specific standards that are based on 12 principles going beyond GHG emissions, including the following: legality—the laws and regulations that apply are adhered to; human and labor rights—these rights are not violated and decent work and workers' wellbeing is being promoted; and land rights—respecting traditional land rights of local and indigenous communities. GHG emissions should be significantly reduced compared to fossil fuel use. Counted across the whole life cycle, the RSB requires 50 percent lower life-cycle GHG emissions than a fossil fuel baseline. L&G also have detailed standards for assessment; however, the focus is entirely on reduction of CO_2 emissions. The level of detail in the plans submitted by the companies is key to receiving a favorable recommendation from the auditor. Organizations aiming for the first L&G star have to adhere to the standard of a minimum greenhouse gas emissions reduction of 20 percent, to be achieved within a maximum of five years.

On the other hand, the disclosure-based cooperative initiatives have far less rigid systems and standards for accountability. The CSR expects participants to report a public commitment to reduce their greenhouse gas emissions to the Compact with regionwide inventory data on an annual basis. There are no requirements as to the level of ambition of targets or progress toward those targets. Asset owners and managers taking part in the PDC are requested to have made a climate-related disclosure pledge, decide on a decarbonization strategy, and to submit a timeframe and percentage of the assets managed. Furthermore, the PDC requires a board-level commitment to the initiative.

Sanctions

Sanctions for accountability refers to what happens in cases of noncompliance, i.e., when a partner in a cooperative initiative fails to live up to its commitments or the spirit of the cooperation. While a public actor can be punished by an electorate (at least in liberal democracies), companies can be punished by stock markets or consumers, and CSOs can lose reputation or members, it is less clear what the stakes are for partners in hybrid cooperative initiatives. The sanctions have to either be streamlined, finding a common denominator for all types of partners, or differentiated, where each type of partner is treated with a different sanction in case of noncompliance.

For the certification-based cooperative initiatives, the most severe sanctions for not complying with the standards are straightforward: namely, the loss of the certificate. If a participant to the RSB does not live up to the criteria at an audit, violations are categorized as major, which need to be resolved quickly, or minor, for which there is more time to resolve them (RSB 2016). If infractions are not resolved, the RSB certificate of an organization is suspended and their publication on the RSB website removed until a future audit proves satisfactory. The RSB suspends organizations that demonstrate severe noncompliance at an audit, as well as organizations that demonstrate a smaller noncompliance but do not repair the infraction within a given time frame (dependent on the infraction). The suspension is withdrawn only when every noncompliance is closed. The audit reports are published, all certified organizations are published, and the RSB certificate is withdrawn if an organization is noncompliant.

L&G has a similar sanction of companies. In the worst-case scenario of noncompliance, they are forced to stop using the certificate. In L&G, if a plan of action is not approved, the organization does not receive the L&G award or second star but has to revise and resubmit the plan. There is no procedure in case a plan of action is not approved at the third submission because, as one respondent put it: "If a plan of action is orange [up for revision], I have never encountered a situation in which it is not green [approved] at the third attempt. Or the party really is not trying, but there's money involved, so parties really do their best to get their plan of action green." (Interview R9).

The rules, however, appear to be applied quite strictly. If, for the attainment of the first star, an organization does not achieve the 20 percent reduction of greenhouse gas emissions within a period of five years, the star is not granted. The organization consequently has the possibility to start anew, or to leave the initiative. In the hypothetical case that an organization decides to leave L&G, it is not allowed to use their logo and promotional material anymore, whether on the their website or in other communications.

For the disclosure-based cooperative initiatives, exclusion is the heaviest sanction available. In the CSR, if a previously participating state or region does not disclose their regionwide greenhouse gas inventory data, it will be excluded from the disclosure report. There are no sanctions from the initiative regarding the (lack of) progress that states and regions make, or whether or not they achieve the targets they have committed to. The PDC has yet to encounter a situation in which a participant fails to live up to their reporting obligation, and it would be up to the steering committee to determine what would happen if, after repeatedly asking the asset manager or owner to report, they did not comply (Interview R12). The initiative does not apply any sanctions regarding the attaining of targets, as one respondent stated: "We're not going to punish or exclude a member for being unsuccessful" (Interview R12). This demonstrates that the PDC values the appearance of commitment to their goals more than the actual achievement of results.

Beyond being excluded from an initiative, reputational damage is a central sanctioning mechanism in all four cases. Being in noncompliance with an initiative's goals or the self-stated commitments (for example, on a homepage), could have a series of (hypothetical) effects. For market actors, reputational damage could lead to a decrease in business opportunities as individual consumers, public authorities (through procurement guidelines), and companies are increasingly factoring sustainability into their purchasing decisions. For disclosure-based initiatives, the public response is an important ingredient for effectiveness. A member to the CSR argued, "What we do is we make available that data, in a very nice way, in English, and we produce disclosure reports. And then it's up to other organizations or up to academics, media, citizens, civil society, to hold their states accountable." (Interview R1). As Mitchell (2011) argues, transparency is most influential on behavior when it is linked to social sanctions, such as public outrage when environmentally harmful behaviors become known. Changing social norms could also have positive effects, as a respondent from a subnational authority in Canada argued, "We're looking at our competitors, economically and geographically and otherwise, and no one wants to be the laggard, no one wants to be doing nothing while everyone else is doing something. It becomes, by doing benchmarking like this, it almost sets it up to become a race for the top, rather than a race to the bottom. You want to be a leader." (Interview R2). The PDC counts on a combined public and private sanctioning mechanism where consumers and other societal actors punish a company through reputational damage (e.g., loss in business opportunities) but also engage shareholders in the company's behavior. The level of publicity a company gains from joining or committing to a cooperative initiative is thus a double-edged sword. As one interviewee from PDC argues,

Because it's becoming so high level, organizations know that people are going to be watching them. A lot of institutions that have made a commitment have actually announced it with a lot of fanfare...And none of these institutions have made their announcement until they had outlined their strategy and put the strategy in place. Because they know that they are going to be held accountable to those commitments. So, to be honest, I actually don't think the scenario will exist [in which the actors do not make good on their commitments], just because the commitments are made at such as a high level. No one wants to look like they have failed. Or that they haven't come through on those commitments. (Interview R12).

This suggests that actors participating in one of the hybrid voluntary initiatives are unlikely to be sanctioned, since they usually join when they already have a plan and know they will succeed, and are furthermore apprehensive of reputational damage. On the other hand, the initiatives are unlikely to apply serious sanctions to participants failing to meet their criteria, as they strive to preserve them as members and retain or regain their commitment.

Impacts

The final, and for many observers the most important, aspect of cooperative initiatives, is whether any tangible impacts can be attributed to the initiative. Also called *output accountability*, this type of accountability focuses on whether the cooperative initiative has reached its goals and can account for its impacts (see chapter 1, in this volume). On the whole, there is little data on the ex post effects of cooperative initiatives (Widerberg and Stripple

2016). It is also important to note that most cooperative initiatives are not envisaging direct environmental impacts from their actions, but rather focus on indirect impacts such as reduced energy intensity or uptake of renewables, or even more indirect indicators such as disclosure levels or reporting to a data repository. In some cases, there is no clear causal link between successful implementation of accountability procedures and standards, and environmental impacts.

Evaluation research in general is quite skeptical about the capability of drawing straight causal lines between an environmental institution and effects on the environment, due to the many confounding factors influencing the causal chain (Miles et al. 2001). Yet, Kramarz and Park rightly notice that despite the many accountability mechanisms in place, there seems to be no significant effect on the environment as a whole. However, this does not mean that individual progress has not been made. In the four cases analyzed in this chapter, tangible effects are found: holders of the first L&G star have reduced their emissions by a minimum of 20 percent compared to their base measurement, and some have widely exceeded this target. For example, Moonen Packaging reduced its GHG emissions by 50 percent. Actors from the initiatives hope that through their arrangement, the participating institutions are held accountable, and this will result in significant impacts. While the CSR requires participating subnational governments to set targets and report on progress, the relatively nascent start of the initiative makes is difficult to assess progress. Furthermore, it may in any case prove difficult to attribute any emission reductions to the Compact directly. This also applies, to some extent, to results achieved by members of L&G and the PDC. Several factors are at work for these actors, legislation increasingly comes into play, and it remains to be investigated how public pressure and market demands would have affected the actors without being channeled by the initiatives.

In the end, there are clear cases when private actors have been punished for not abiding by the spirit of cooperative initiatives. Consider, for example, the case of Shell, a fossil fuel company, who were forced to leave the influential climate lobby group Prince of Wales Corporate Leaders Group (CLG) amid concerns over its strategy to drill for oil in the Arctic, which went against the spirit and goals of the CLG (Stacey 2015). Similarly, Volkswagen's cheating on emissions tests on about 11 million diesel cars and the ensuing legal actions saw its stock price plummet (at least temporarily) from a year high of roughly 253 euros in April 2015 to 92 euros in October 2015, equal to a drop of 63 percent (Google Finance). Moreover, processes for accountability are external to the procedures of the cooperative initiative. For example, in 2015, when Volkswagen's large-scale cheating on emissions tests was revealed, the company's four climate pledges on the NAZCA platform were duly removed.

Conclusions

Climate change governance is an issue area haunted by the accountability trap, where processes and standards for holding stakeholders accountable proliferate without any visible reduction in the total amount of GHG emissions. This chapter focuses on second-tier accountability, studying the processes, standards, sanctions, and impacts in four cases of multistakeholder cooperative initiatives engaged in climate action. One can make a distinction between the RSB and the L&G, which are certification-based initiatives, and the CSR and PDC, which are disclosure-based initiatives. The cases show how the "logics of action" (see chapter 1, in this volume) in the initiatives revolve around the use of common standards and reporting formats. Certification-based initiatives, in particular the RSB, have a more rigorous process and detailed standards in place than the disclosure-based initiatives; for instance, the certification-based initiatives require third-party verification for the certificates.

At the impact level, there is some (self-reported) evidence that the organizations that are part of cooperative initiatives are changing their behavior. For instance, some transport companies in the L&G initiative have reduced their GHG emissions substantially. Tying the reductions to the influence of the cooperative initiative, however, remains a methodological challenge for the future. Moreover, none of the four initiatives have sanctioning mechanisms in place, beyond withdrawing memberships, certifications, or the right to use logos for branding. It is also unclear to what extent such sanctioning mechanisms have been used and what their effects have been. In sum, this chapter is congruent with the description of the "accountability trap" in the introductory chapter of this volume by suggesting that while parts of second-tier accountability (primarily processes, standards, and sanctions) can be described in detail, it remains difficult to link the outputs of the various initiatives to their environmental outcomes.

In the context of accountability, more research on sanctions and their various effects on actors in cooperative initiatives would be particularly useful to better understand to what extent they play a role in accountability as a "regulative mean."

Notes

1. Coping with Fragmentation: Assessing and Reforming the Current Architecture of Global Environmental Governance, http://fragmentation.eu.

2. *Members* refers to those actors with governing capacity, i.e., rulemaking functions in the cooperative initiatives. *Participants* are those actors that are rule takers.

6 Navigating Contested Accountability Logics in Nonstate Certification for Fisheries Sustainability

Lars H. Gulbrandsen and Graeme Auld

Introduction

Transnational nonstate certification programs—a form of private-voluntary governance, as defined in this volume—set standards for responsible business practices against which companies may be audited to verify compliance.[1] Companies that wish to gain access to the potential market benefits certification provides must pass a compliance assessment conducted by an independent audit organization that itself must be accredited to perform audits for the certification program.

Many environmental groups have supported certification. They have worked in partnership with companies and other stakeholders to establish these programs. They have helped to develop program standards. Moreover, they serve to encourage companies to participate in the hope of holding companies responsible for their operations' environmental and social impacts. Using so-called naming-and-shaming campaigns to target companies near to end-consumer markets—like supermarkets and retailers—these groups have engendered demand for certification. The environmental purchasing commitments made by these targeted companies have helped expand uptake of certification through global supply chains.

This role played by environmental groups, however, complicates the accountability relations of this form of private-voluntary governance. Certification programs, and their accredited auditors, serve as an accountability mechanism for those buyers that seek assurances that their suppliers are meeting environmental standards. In this way, certification serves as a market assurance scheme to guard against fraud and facilitate credible transactions in features of goods and services—the sustainability of how they were produced, for instance—that would otherwise remain invisible.

However, the demand for these assurances in large part flows from the campaigning pressures of environmental groups. These buyers and environmental groups, moreover, claim to advance consumer and citizen interests, respectively—with businesses trying to assuage consumer disquiet about the environmental and social practices of a company's supply chain, and environmental groups claiming to champion the broader public interest of environmental conservation. All told, the relationships among the certification program, accredited auditors, environmental and social groups, and the users and targets of a program's rules, as well as governments, the general public, and other stakeholders, are rarely straightforward.

This volume seeks to understand such complex relations in the context of global environmental governance (GEG) by analytically distinguishing two tiers of accountability—one that centers on problem framing, goals, solutions, and institutional design; and another that focuses on the execution of these institutional solutions. Our chapter focuses on the second tier; however, we argue that, for at least two reasons, the two tiers of accountability are tightly connected in practice, particularly with nascent private-voluntary governance. First, private-voluntary governance gains authority from external audiences, who determine whether the rules and actions devised by the governance institution are legitimate and ought to be deferred to. Second, disagreements among these external audiences over problem framing and appropriate goals are key to examine in order to understand the nature of accountability for these institutions. As the evaluations of these programs' external audiences are the foundation for claims to legitimacy, the character of such a community is significant for how accountability functions with private-voluntary certification programs (Black 2008; Cashore 2002). End-of-pipe accountability cannot therefore be entirely separated from critical outside judgments about whether the private-voluntary program has framed the problem in the right way and is tackling appropriate goals.

To advance an analysis of accountability in this context, we follow the editors' (see chapter 1, in this volume) use of Grant and Keohane's (2005, 29) definition of accountability as instances when "some actors have the right to hold other actors to a set of standards, to judge whether they have filled their responsibilities in light of those standards, and to impose sanctions if they determine that those responsibilities have not been met." We also adopt Keohane's (2003) definition of two accountability logics: an internal logic centered on ensuring that participating producers comply with the program's requirements; and an external logic wherein the program responds to the competing demands of environmental groups, academics, businesses, governments, and public(s) for accountability against varied normative principles. This external logic links the execution of the program's solutions back to Tier 1 considerations about the appropriate problem framing and goals.

Following organizational scholars (Oliver 1991) and principal-agent theorists (Mattli and Büthe 2005), we highlight that a multiplicity of stakeholder demands—stakeholders who are all vying to be principals that control the certification agent—create strategic opportunities for a certification program to choose the normative ends it aims to advance, the calls for accountability it needs to address, and how to address them. But the choices are not limitless. Power relations where stakeholders provide essential resources—such as buy-in from certain actors, funding, and expertise—to a certification program matter as they are likely to shape what external accountability demands are most salient to a program (Black 2008; Oliver 1991). Hence, when the boundaries of a certification program's global community are unclear and evolving, calls for more or deeper stakeholder participation (e.g., Bäckstrand 2008; Abbott and Snidal 2009) are unlikely to lessen the contested politics of accountability surrounding these governance institutions. Rather, they may only facilitate greater accountability to stakeholders that are already relatively influential—that is, stakeholders with whom a program has a dependent relationship due to the resources these stakeholders provide (Oliver 1991). It also means a program may be even less likely to be accountable to critical outside audiences for protecting the environment or the public good, as compared to the interests of specific and influential external constituents. On the other hand, critical outside audiences are not powerless. Careful examination of their activities highlights that private-voluntary programs are frequently reminded of their Tier 1 decisions about goals and how these may fall short of the aims of helping disempowered stakeholders and improving environmental outcomes.

To detail this argument, we examine the Marine Stewardship Council (MSC), an initiative that sets standards for certifying responsible capture fisheries. As evolving governance institutions, we argue that programs like the MSC face three accountability-related decisions on an ongoing basis—what goals (or normative principles) will the program advance, who will have access to influence the program's decisions, and what accountability mechanisms (e.g., standards and processes) should it adopt to signal the credibility of its intent to reach its goals. The question of what goals to advance relates to this volume's interest in the standards that determine accountability; ultimately, a program's goals matter for its potential on-the-ground impacts. This volume's interest in the processes that demonstrate accountability and the available means for sanctioning poor performance underlie the second and third questions.

Tracing the MSC's operations reveals the logics of internal and external accountability, along with the contestation between these two, as the program has defined its goals for advancing sustainable fisheries and determined which actors can influence its internal governance processes. We observe a fundamental misalignment for the MSC because it claims to advance fisheries sustainability but has given limited access to environmental groups that also intend to advance this normative end. The salience of this misalignment is heightened by the demand-generating role that environmental groups play for the MSC. Aligning with the logic of internal accountability, the program has attempted to address varied critiques voiced by its external stakeholders by strengthening its assessment and objections procedures. All the while, some environmental groups have decoupled their campaigns from directly supporting the MSC, to minimize the MSC's potential negative impacts on their other actions for advancing sustainable fisheries. In this way, they may deprive the MSC of a key resource—demand for the program's services—in an attempt to underscore why the MSC ought to be accountable to their concerns. Hence, to understand the MSC's accountability relations, we need to consider rival processes like market and information campaigns undertaken by other actors. Following the logic of external accountability, these processes are often attempts to hold the MSC to account.

Our analysis proceeds in three parts. First, we review analytical approaches to investigating accountability in nonstate certification programs, paying particular attention to the distinction between internal and external accountability. Second, we examine three facets of the MSC's history that illustrate the program's evolving internal and external accountability relations. Third, we discuss the key tensions that emerged because of a perceived misalignment between the goals the MSC advances and which actors are granted governance influence, and how the MSC attempted to ease those tensions by reforming its assessment and objections procedures. Hence, our chapter contributes to this volume by investigating how decisions at the Tier 1 level (i.e., who accounts to whom and for what) can influence Tier 2 accountability, specifically the standards and processes of a nonstate certification program.

Accountability in Nonstate Certification

Global governance faces an accountability deficit when measured against liberal democratic norms and associated mechanisms of accountability—in this volume referred to as *public accountability*. This deficit applies both to intergovernmental organizations (IGOs) and transnational governance schemes like nonstate certification (Rosenau 2000, 192; Grant and Keohane 2005).

Given this shortcoming and recognizing the dramatic rise in transnational "new" governance, attention has turned to other accountability mechanisms. Certain scholars argue that wide representation of stakeholders is a precondition for accountable transnational governance (Bäckstrand 2008). Others note the great diversity among modes of representation and emphasize the importance of understanding the consequences of differing levels and types of stakeholder engagement (Fransen and Kolk 2007; Abbott and Snidal 2009). According to these scholars, more needs to be understood about how nonstate governors make decisions about stakeholder engagement and how these decisions affect the governors' activities and broader efforts to hold different actors responsible for environmental and social harms.

The participation of environmental groups can be critical for nonstate certification programs (Cashore 2002). Relations with these groups provide a newly formed program with legitimacy by association. Other actors—particularly auditors, academics, businesses, and funders—provide additional symbolic, epistemic, and material resources to new certification initiatives to legitimate their role as global governors (Cashore et al. 2004; Boström 2006). A key question then, is this: how do these relations vary over time as a certification program develops its own basis of legitimacy and hence gains autonomy from its initial, and potentially varied, principals that advance diverse normative positions on appropriate problem framing and institutional goals.

Multistakeholder relations can provide an organization with more decision-making flexibility (Mattli and Büthe 2005; Oliver 1991; Black 2008). A multiplicity of demands allows the organization to perform selective accommodations, addressing those concerns that are in its own interest to address while ignoring more challenging stakeholder demands. Yet, external stakeholders are not all equal. Some, like funders or businesses, have greater significance given the fact that the program's financial and operational survival may rely on their support. Hence, to understand accountability relations for nonstate certification, we need to understand how different stakeholder relations, and the differing power relations these involve, matter. Such differences will condition what accountability processes stakeholders can access and demand, and what sanctions they can wield in instances where they perceive performance is lacking. Arguably, following Black's (2008) analysis, these differences will matter even more given the polycentric nature of transnational governance; that is, the multiple sites in which regulation occurs at the transnational level. In the absence of a clear prioritization of global norms and standards, the terms of accountability for nonstate certification programs are likely to be even more ambiguous and subject to debate. The key point here in relation to Keohane and Grant's (2005) understanding of accountability—and this volume's notion of Tier 1 accountability—is that who has the right to hold a certification program to account is neither clear cut nor static.

To account for this ambiguity and dynamism, we focus on the distinction between internal and external accountability (Keohane 2003). These respective forms of accountability have their own logics, understood as theories for how particular substantive and procedural rules lead to certain ends (Auld, Renckens, and Cashore, 2015). The logic of *internal accountability* rests on the idea that institutionalized relations are critical, including those between producers and certifiers, between certifiers and accreditation organizations, and among a program's governance bodies like its board, secretariat, and technical or stakeholder committees. Rules governing these internal relations are a means for achieving environmental and social outcomes, and for ensuring that the program is a credible and reputable governor. Indeed, the logic of internal accountability is based on Weberian ideas of technocratic effectiveness—sometimes termed bureaucratic accountability systems (Romzek and Dubnick 1987).

Concerning this volume's notion of Tier 2 accountability, most certification programs delegate auditing to independent certifiers that are typically accredited by, and answerable to, accreditation bodies, which in turn are accountable to the certification programs. The certifiers issue certificates to producers that comply with the standards, audit performance through regular inspections, and may penalize noncompliant producers by suspending their certificates. Although participation is voluntary, producers must consent to regular inspections and accept the consequences of noncompliance. In these ways, producers are held accountable for their performance to the certifier, and ultimately to the certification program. Sanctions operate on the basis of the threat of an annulled certificate due to some nonconformance with the program's standards.

The logic of *external accountability*, by contrast, centers on the idea that enhancing responsiveness or answerability to markets and stakeholders outside the certification program is key for ensuring that a program accomplishes its goals (Gulbrandsen 2008). Moreover, such outside accountability is an end unto itself, in which stakeholder views ought to be considered and acted upon, not merely collected for instrumental purposes. Certification, and a program's label, serves as assurance for consumers, retailers, and other buyers seeking information about a product's social and environmental attributes. External accountability also aligns with democratic norms that those affected—directly or indirectly—by a program's activities ought to have influence over the program's decisions (Gulbrandsen 2008; Black 2008; Koenig-Archibugi and Macdonald 2017). Accountability thus involves both consumers' or retailers' right to exit to another provider and an option to voice concerns wherein they can ask questions and demand answers (Mulgan 2000, 586–589). Following this logic, certification programs and certified producers must recognize that they are answerable to external communities. Failure to do so may result in sanctions such as material and symbolic losses of goodwill, credibility, and trust from the marketplace and relevant stakeholders.

The idea that a program is embedded within, and reliant on, some external community is central to the logic of external accountability. Some scholars have suggested ideas for the boundaries of such communities and ways in which programs might become more legitimate. Bernstein and Cashore (2007), for instance, posit that the global supply chain targeted by a nonstate certification program serves as "lines on the map" that delineate a political community from which a program seeks legitimacy (see Black 2008). Similarly, one can understand the basis for a governance program's accountability as arising from social spaces denoted by a community's boundaries (Kramarz and Park 2016) wherein normative principles are intersubjectively generated over time. Such ideas are consistent with the argument that stakeholder engagement is a precondition for accountable transnational governance (Bäckstrand 2008). It is through these external relations, in other words, that private-voluntary governance initiatives are potentially held accountable for Tier 1 decisions about problem framing and institutional goals.

However, while evidence exists that a community is forming around the work of nonstate certification (Bartley and Smith 2010), some researchers note the absence of certain ties (Fransen, Schalk, and Auld 2016) and persistent tensions between different organizing logics for private governance (Auld, Renckens, and Cashore 2015; Haedicke 2016; Obach 2015). Indeed, as Black (2008) notes, because of the diversity of communities underlying polycentric regimes, one of their defining features is the persistent competition over what substantive and procedural normative principles ought to be pursued. Through what procedures should sustainability be demonstrated? Should sustainability encompass social and environmental objectives? In the absence of convergence to common beliefs among a program's audience on the right answers to these questions, the logics of internal and external accountability will likely operate at cross-purposes, creating the possibility that internal accountability rises while external accountability declines.

Moreover, the lines between the communities involved in internal and external accountability relations are often blurred. Büthe (2012) reminds us that actors may relate to a certification program in several ways: they may use a standard, be a stakeholder with interest in a program's work, or be the target of the program's rules. These internal-external boundaries evolve, just as who has the right to vote in democratic states has changed over time. This is important because delineating who is in and out affects the normative principles against which a certification program will be measured. Narrowly focusing on interests within seafood markets and the fisheries supply chain, for instance, may neglect global-commons concerns arising about ocean systems. This problem is not unique to nonstate certification. Stakeholder processes run by governments make decisions about who has a legitimate interest in a process or set of decisions, and the boundaries can be hotly contested (Gibson 2012). Thus, it is useful to examine questions of how, to whom, and against what norms the MSC is held to account through the lens of the contested logics of internal and external accountability.

Accountability of the Evolving Marine Stewardship Council

We examine the MSC's evolving internal and external accountability relations by tracing three facets of the program's history—the 2004 release of a commissioned review of the MSC (the Wildhavens report), the lead up to the 2008 changes to the MSC's assessment methodology, and the evolution of the program's objections procedure. We do not claim that these are the only facets of the MSC's history that matter for accountability. However, we do suggest that they are useful as illustrative probes for examining the interaction between internal and external logics of accountability within private-voluntary governance, and more specifically for revealing how Tier 1 accountability decisions (on who accounts to whom and for what) influenced Tier 2 accountability (the standards and processes that demonstrate accountability). As context, we detail three accountability-related features of the MSC's processes and standards—governance as it relates to what actors have influence over the program, the program's overall goals, and its standards and assessment process to elucidate internal accountability mechanisms.

The MSC began in 1996 as a partnership of the World Wide Fund for Nature (WWF) and the Unilever corporation. By 1999, it was an independent nongovernmental organization (NGO) governed by a board of trustees, with the assistance of a secretariat (known as the MSC executive) that facilitated the program's work. Thus, internal accountability centers on the board of trustees; they are ultimately responsible for the actions of the organization, which includes the performance of fisheries carrying the MSC label. Initially, the board's work was complemented by a standards council, national working groups, and an advisory board. The advisory board resembled a membership body with three chambers—one for those making a living from fisheries, one for governments and NGOs, and one for educational, social, and consumer interests. Following a governance review in 2001 (partly in response to concerns about limited stakeholder involvement in the program's governance), the standards council was replaced by a technical advisory board that was tasked with providing advice on standards, chain of custody, and logo licensing. The stakeholder council, which replaced the advisory board, was designed to represent broader stakeholder interests and provide guidance to the board of trustees. Two of its members were also to serve on the board. The stakeholder council still serves as the main process for stakeholder input for the MSC, with the board of trustees retaining final decision-making authority (Auld 2014, 192; Gulbrandsen 2010, 120). Finally, funders—primarily trusts and foundations—were responsible for covering the majority of the program's early operating budget. Over the years, however, logo-licensing fees have grown to contribute a larger share, lessening the program's reliance on grants.

The program's standard and assessment process has also engaged stakeholders. The program's fisheries standards—known as the MSC principles and criteria—were developed through a stakeholder consultation process between 1996 and 1999 (Fowler and Heap 2000, 140). Whereas some stakeholders argued in favor of wide standards that addressed both environmental and social issues, the MSC decided to keep them narrower, focusing primarily on environmental issues and fishing operations. Agreement was reached on three principles addressing the health of the target fish stocks, the ecosystem impacts of the fishery, and the performance of the fishery management regime. Together they were meant to represent a standard for sustainable fisheries. A review of these standards took place in 2013 and 2014, and a new standard became operational in April 2015. Thus, the program's performance and its accountability to its own goals hinges to a degree on judgments about the sustainability of certified fisheries. The early decision not to address social issues in the principles and criteria of the program meant that issues like fishing rights, the needs of fishworkers, and the wellbeing of fishing communities were excluded from such judgments.

A final piece of the MSC's internal accountability regime centers on the assessment process. Accredited certification bodies conduct the MSC assessment process. These certifiers appoint expert assessment teams that evaluate if applicant fisheries meet the MSC standard. The team usually consists of a stock assessment expert, a fisheries biologist, and a fisheries management expert. Assessments are a transparent process in which stakeholder input is actively sought and evaluated, reports are open to stakeholder comments, and certifiers must demonstrate that consideration has been given to such comments in their final report. Importantly, in the original assessment procedure, the assessment team developed fishery-specific interpretations of the MSC principles and criteria. As we detail later in this chapter, this changed with the new assessment methodology introduced in 2008.

The Wildhavens Report

In January 2004, the Wildhavens report was released as an assessment of the MSC's efforts to promote sustainable fisheries. It provided a vivid illustration of the blurred boundaries between the program's internal and external accountability relations and the importance of funders as a force behind external pressure on the MSC. Commissioned by the Homeland Foundation, the Oak Foundation, and the Pew Charitable Trusts, the report examined four case study fisheries (two that had been certified and two undergoing assessments) of the twenty fisheries under assessment or already certified. It also reviewed the performance of the MSC as a governance organization (Highleyman et al. 2004, i).

By interviewing forty-two stakeholders (including individuals involved in MSC governance as well as those external to it) and reviewing myriad documents, the Wildhavens report captured and amplified the concerns of external stakeholders, particularly environmental groups focused on ocean and fisheries conservation (Auld and Renckens 2017). These concerns focused on limited stakeholder involvement in the program's governance and the purported failings of the MSC's internal accountability mechanisms for overseeing the certifiers' assessment work. All told, the report illuminated early instances where outside stakeholders (funders and environmental groups) used the MSC's purported goals—a Tier 1 decision—as a benchmark to call for accountability and sought to contain what the MSC undertook to ensure it did not interfere with other attempts to advance sustainable fisheries. Calling out the MSC for perceived shortcomings is more easily understood when we account for the other initiatives environmental groups and funders were supporting to advance fisheries sustainability. In this respect, the polycentric nature of fisheries regulation gave these groups other interventions to support that, depending on the performance of the MSC, may be viewed as more likely to advance improved fisheries management and benefits for ocean ecosystems.

As a new program, there was understandable ambiguity about to whom it was accountable. One of the program's first initiatives—drafting standards—did widely engage external stakeholders with workshops held in various countries between 1996 and 1997 (Fowler and Heap 2000). While the Wildhavens report noted concerns about the MSC voiced during the discussions, it also supported the transparent, consensus-oriented nature of the standard-drafting process. This supportive tone was in contrast to how the report characterized MSC's governance problems. Invoking norms underlying the logic of external accountability, the authors opined that "the Board in a consortium organization understands that its right to govern is premised on achieving the goals of its diverse stakeholders. A lack of accountability will alienate stakeholders and risks defusing a results-oriented culture" (Highleyman et al. 2004, 16). In other words, many external stakeholders felt the MSC ought to be accountable to their interests, and arguably the expectation that it would do so was reinforced by the broad participation in its standards drafting work. Indeed, in an exchange among MSC critics and supporters, a WWF official involved in launching the MSC wrote a letter to readers of SAMUDRA (a periodical of the International Collective in Support of Fishworkers) responding to concerns about the program's potential negative impacts on small-scale fisheries and neglect for social development issues. The letter explained that stakeholders were critical and taken seriously by the MSC, and it urged groups to have "a voice in the governance and development of the MSC" (Sutton 1998, 30). Arguably, these urgings influenced stakeholder expectations about the problem framing and goals of the MSC as the first fisheries entered full assessments. They also reflected the MSC's early need to receive material and symbolic support from external stakeholders.

The MSC was sensitive to these comments (e.g., MSC 2004b), but appeasing competing interests about what goals it ought to address was tricky, which arguably provided the program a growing level of autonomy from certain demands. A point of debate was how the MSC ought to characterize the performance of certified fisheries. The Wildhavens report noted that many environmental groups opposed the use of the term *sustainable*; they felt that it connoted an achieved state, not an aspiration. The MSC considered this issue during a joint meeting of the stakeholder council and the technical advisory board on May 27, 2004 (MSC 2004a). At the meeting, representatives of retailers, processors, and fisheries supported retaining the term *sustainable*, seeing it as an aspirational goal. Environmental groups disagreed, arguing that sustainability should be viewed as an end point (MSC 2004a). Meeting attendees, with the exception of one unnamed stakeholder council member, agreed that the MSC should retain the sustainable terminology but create a clearer public statement of what the term meant for the program (MSC 2004a).

Early controversy over the performance of certified fisheries further illustrates the uncertain and evolving internal-external boundaries and struggles among groups to hold the MSC to account for their preferred problem framings and goals. With the fisheries assessments, accountability relations were complicated by the procedural norm of independent audits (i.e., not performed by MSC). Certifiers initially had the discretion to translate the MSC principles and criteria into operational scoring for individual fisheries. This became problematic when stakeholders disagreed with the conclusions the certifiers drew about early applicant fisheries. Three of the four fisheries examined in the Wildhavens report were controversial: the New Zealand hoki fishery, the South Georgia toothfish fishery, and the Alaskan Eastern Bering Sea and Aleutian Islands pollock fishery (Alaskan pollock). Various groups appealed the certifications of these fisheries, but all certification decisions were upheld. As we will discuss, this signaled to many groups that outside strategies of accountability would be important. Indeed, environmental groups in these case study fisheries worried that the MSC might curtail their other efforts to advance sustainable fisheries. For instance, Greenpeace targeted the Alaskan pollock fishery before the MSC audit and viewed an MSC endorsement as problematic, because it lessened the Greenpeace campaign's bite. Moreover, Alaska Oceans Program, another environmental group concerned about the pollock fishery, ended its engagement with the MSC because the group felt the MSC had been insufficiently attentive to its concerns (Auld 2014).

The Alaskan pollock fishery also warned groups that the MSC might undermine government regulations. Part of the concern arose because existing US fisheries legislation provided environmental groups a certain degree of influence—particularly through the courts—over US fisheries management activities. The Wildhavens report noted that since 1998 environmental groups had successfully won four court cases against the US government claiming that the pollock fishery was not complying with the Endangered Species Act and the National Environmental Policy Act. The pollock case also followed debates over the reauthorization of the Fisheries Conservation and Management Act, which led to the 1996 Magnuson-Stevens Act, which required a ten-year plan for rebuilding stocks defined as overfished by an annual assessment of the National Marine Fisheries Service (Rosenberg et al. 2006). Although the new provisions did not address all the objectives of NGOs working on fisheries issues, there was a general sense that the new act was an improvement (Akhtar 1996). In other words, stakeholders not only felt the MSC limited their influence over its decisions, they also saw it as a potential form of greenwashing that distracted attention from legal noncompliance. The comparative potential of different interventions—a key feature of polycentric regimes—is therefore a key feature of understanding the accountability relations forming around MSC as a nonstate certification program.

The Fisheries Assessment Methodology

Our next case—reforms to the fisheries assessment methodology—traces the MSC's efforts to bolster its internal accountability mechanisms to assuage stakeholder demands. The Wildhavens report enumerated several problems with the assessment process. It called for improvements to transparency, stakeholder engagement, peer review, explanations for the reasoning behind assessment decisions, and interpretation guidance for the certifiers developed through a consensus-based process involving the technical advisory board (TAB) and the stakeholder council (Highleyman et al. 2004).

The MSC tackled these challenges through a larger reform process. On the assessment issue, the board of trustees provided renewed support to an ongoing project (the operational interpretation project) that was tackling the consistency and quality of assessments (MSC 2004b). This gathered momentum in 2005 with a joint project of the MSC executive and the TAB, which informed discussions at a June 2005 TAB meeting that reviewed the proposed work of the quality and consistency project (formerly the operational interpretation project) on, among other things, a new assessment tree and an operational interpretation of the standard (MSC 2005b).

In August 2005, the quality and consistency project released a rationale for its work, explaining that "the MSC has not provided CBs [certification bodies] with specific guidance requiring use of mandatory narrative or quantitative descriptions of the PIs [performance indicators] and SGs [scoring guideposts] that should be applied across fisheries … the MSC and its technical advisory board (TAB) realized that this circumstance creates the possibility for variable and inconsistent results in applying the standard with respect to the underlying intent of the Principles and Criteria" (MSC 2005a). As a corrective, the project emphasized four things. First, it intended to give MSC greater oversight over the certifiers, particularly during the assessment process. Second, it explained that the existing MSC standard lacked a sufficient narrative to guide certifiers as they developed assessment trees. Third, it saw its role as doing a house cleaning of the assessment tree structures based on experience gained. Finally, the project recognized that certifiers needed better guidance on what "measurable performance indicators and benchmarks for scoring would improve quality and consistency of fisheries assessments" (MSC 2005a). In other words, it sought to reduce the discretion of the certifiers, bolstering the strength of the MSC's internal accountability mechanism. Whereas the certifiers had initially lent credibility to the program due to their preexisting auditing expertise, the logic of internal accountability implied the need for greater oversight to ensure the MSC solidified its own reputation.

Notably, while the quality and consistency project received attention, the TAB also discussed the concerns of applicant fisheries about the varied, and often lengthy, assessment process. The TAB indicated it would investigate the matter (MSC 2005b), and International Policy Director Chris Grieve followed up with a memo to stakeholders, certifiers, and fisheries indicating that assessment length was being considered and comments were welcome (Grieve 2005). As with the debates over the program's use of the term sustainable, the issue of assessment length highlighted that fisheries were concerned about the assessment process but for different reasons than NGOs (as captured in the Wildhavens report). Such competing interests complicate questions of to whom the MSC ought to be accountable and for what—in this case, inconsistent scoring with implications for *effectiveness* (whether certification improves fishery management and practices), or lengthy assessments with implications for *efficiency* (achieving such improvements at minimal costs).

These various interests became more central as the MSC initiated a process that engaged stakeholders on questions about changing the assessment methodology. The process' first phase involved five regional workshops in

April and May of 2006 that heard from forty-eight individuals representing various interests. Another forty-one people were invited to expert workshops (MSC 2006b). Many problems with the interpretation of the MSC standard were aired. General problems included the varied circumstance of fisheries, the need for consistency, and what was the best assessment methods given the high data variability and uncertainty for some fisheries (MSC 2006c).

The process led to a new fisheries assessment methodology that was implemented in July 2008 (MSC 2008). The MSC claimed the changes addressed applicants' need for quicker assessments and stakeholders' concerns about consistency (MSC 2009). However, the changes more clearly limited the certifiers' discretion. The default assessment tree and associated performance indicators became mandatory for all fisheries entering full assessment after July 28, 2008. Deviations were only permissible if an assessment team received written approval from the MSC's senior fisheries assessment manager (MSC 2008). In this way, the MSC responded to external pressure by exerting more control over the assessment process. This strategic reaction, moreover, illustrates how multiple stakeholder demands strengthened the MSC's position *vis-à-vis* the certifiers, in part reversing the power relation wherein the MSC had drawn on certifiers' expertise as an initial basis for its credibility and authority. The process also illustrated the relative influence of different external stakeholders. While the Wildhavens report had engaged many more environmental groups and academics as interviewees, participants in the quality and consistency project were disproportionately representatives of fisheries businesses and governments (Auld and Renckens 2017).

The Evolving Objections Procedure

Turning to our final case, opportunities to lodge complaints have been in place since the MSC launched, but a formal objections procedure was first introduced in 2001 and has since undergone several revisions. More than anywhere else, the lines between internal and external are clearly delineated: only stakeholders involved in or consulted during the assessment process may object to the certifier's decision. Even for those stakeholders, however, the costs and complexities of the objections procedure may constitute a barrier for using it to enhance internal accountability.

The first approach for complaints and dispute resolution gave the certifiers the role of specifying and implementing policy and procedures for handling disputes. An unresolved dispute could then be referred to the MSC. The objection to the New Zealand hoki fishery was a critical early test for this approach. It exposed serious shortcomings, including that the approach lacked a time limit for submitting a complaint; guidance regarding the scope and handling of a complaint; and a timetable for the processing and determination of a complaint (Leadbitter and Ward 2003, 81).

Stakeholders began discussing solutions in early 2001, even before the hoki decision was finalized. In October 2001, the MSC adopted an initial objections procedure. It was not applied to the still-active hoki dispute and it imposed a time window of fifteen working days after the release of the final certification report in which a complaint could be lodged. Hence, older fisheries like the Western Australia rock lobster fishery, which critics alleged did not meet the MSC principles and criteria (Sutton 2003), were not eligible. In July 2002, while the hoki complaint continued, the board of trustees adopted an objections procedure for use in all subsequent assessments. Any dispute a certifier could not resolve would be referred to the board of trustees, which would establish a dispute panel chaired by a board member with no interest in the fishery. At least two "eminent scientists" were also to be appointed to advise the panel (Leadbitter and Ward 2003, 82).

Features of the 2002 objections procedure lay the foundation for subsequent objection proceedings. One feature was an initial review by the MSC objections panel chair to determine if the objection was "patently frivolous or otherwise spurious," in which case the panel would not consider the objection (MSC 2010a, section 4.2.4.3). In a second feature, the objection panel could either allow the certifier's determination to stand or remand it to the certifier with instructions "to consider significant procedural issues or information omitted or inadequately considered in the assessment" (MSC 2010a, section 4.2.4.11). The certifier had to respond to the objections panel chair in full detail to the matters specified in the remand. The objections panel could then accept the certifier's response or remand again and make a final decision. Another important requirement was that at least one objection panel member needed experience as an MSC fishery assessor or peer reviewer (Brown, Agnew, and Martin 2016). Objectors had to pay a fee to the MSC, but it was refundable if the objection was upheld.

The 2005 adoption of the Food and Agriculture Organization (FAO) guidelines for the ecolabeling of fish and fisheries products from marine capture fisheries (FAO 2005) was the next impetus for changes to the MSC's objections procedure (Gulbrandsen 2010, 128). The FAO guidelines addressed most aspects of fisheries certification, including "resolution of complaints and appeals." And although they were nonbinding, the guidelines did exert normative influence over the MSC to comply with their provisions in the structure of its internal accountability mechanisms.

In choosing to comply with the FAO guidelines (MSC 2006a), the MSC changed two aspects of the objections procedure (Brown, Agnew, and Martin 2016). First, in accordance with the guidelines (section 147), the MSC specified that the objector would pay for the objections process to a cap of £15,000 (US$ 19,700 as of July 24, 2018), although objectors with financial constraints were eligible for exceptions. Second, the MSC made the objections procedure independent of the program (consistent with section 148), which meant that MSC could no longer have a board member as chair or member of the objections panel. Hence, the board of trustees appointed an independent adjudicator (now a roster of adjudicators) to replace the objections panel.

The next impetus for change came from the stakeholder council, which began calling for major overhauls in 2007. The board of trustees responded by instructing the MSC executive to review the objections procedure and recommend changes. In 2010, the board adopted a revised procedure that institutionalized the office of an independent adjudicator, with the adjudicator appointed by the board of trustees for a three-year period with possible renewal (MSC 2010b, 4.3.1). The revised procedure clarified its role as determining "whether the certification body made an error that materially affected the outcome of its Determination"—it was not to review and rescore the subject fishery (MSC 2010b, 4.2.1). However, the 2010 revisions altered the remand process such that changes to scoring could occur. The adjudicator could ask the certifier to reconsider its determination in light of the objector's concerns. This process would then repeat until the adjudicator accepted the certifier's changes or upheld the complaint.

As previously mentioned, the objector covers the cost of an objection process, which the MSC reports only funds the legal process, not MSC's internal staff costs or costs to the fishery and the certifier (Brown, Agnew, and Martin 2016). However, stakeholders and fisheries scientists maintained that these costs still posed a barrier to submitting formal appeals (Jacquet et al. 2010), in effect limiting stakeholder access to a key internal accountability mechanism. Following these critiques, in August 2010 the MSC lowered the capped cost to £5,000 (US$ 6,600 as of July 24, 2018) (MSC 2010b), and since then, about 10 percent of objectors have had the fee waived because of financial hardship (Brown, Agnew, and Martin 2016). The procedure has remained closed to parties that did not participate in the assessment process, underscoring the point that the lines between internal and external accountability are clear.

Discussion

The MSC's evolving accountability relations highlight that key tensions can exist when there is a perceived misalignment between the goals a certification program advances and which actors are granted governance influence. This is particularly the case because the MSC's activities and those of environmental groups pushing companies to change their seafood purchasing practices have been tightly intertwined. Demand for MSC certification has risen as a direct result of campaigns by groups such as Greenpeace, bolstering the significance of these groups as stakeholders for which the MSC ought to account. However, these groups have been frequent critics of the MSC's approach to improving the state of global fisheries. In other words, Tier 1 decisions about problem framing and goals have been central to the MSC's accountability relations.

How has the MSC navigated this misalignment? Though the program could reconsider its goals to lessen the inconsistency perceived by environmental groups, it has not done so. The MSC has, on the other hand, incrementally moved toward greater inclusion, granting critical stakeholders greater access to its decision-making through the creation of the stakeholder council. Processes like the quality and consistency project also sought broad stakeholder input to improve the assessment methodology, even if business and government interests were the dominant participants (Auld and Renckens 2017). Moreover, reforms stopped short of wholesale governance changes. Rather than create a membership body with decision-making authority, the MSC has chosen to inform stakeholders of its activities and draw on their expertise and concerns when needed to make individual assessments credible (Auld and Gulbrandsen 2010). It has enhanced outreach to stakeholders but remains committed to its centralized and streamlined approach to governance and stakeholder involvement. Arguably this undergirds stakeholders' perception that the opportunities for voice are relatively weak. Hence, we do observe a misalignment because the MSC claims to advance fisheries sustainability but has given limited access to stakeholders (environmental organizations) that support this normative end. This misalignment is salient because of the role many environmental groups have played in fostering demand for the services the MSC performs.

In such cases, greater attention arguably falls on the third solution—internal accountability mechanisms. The MSC has focused on enhancing the credibility of the fisheries assessment process and improving the opportunities for holding certifiers to account for certification determinations, efforts rooted in the logic of internal accountability. Indeed, telling changes to the objections procedure occurred when the FAO released its guidelines. The MSC chose to conform to these norms even though doing so clearly exacerbated tensions with external stakeholders over who should pay the costs of an objection (Howes 2006). The objections procedure has thus evolved through several revisions to become a sophisticated and institutionalized system that resembles a public regulatory regime with legal provisions for administrative review where questions of standing (who can sue) and the degree of deference to the lawmaker and implementing agency are key features affecting the performance of such accountability mechanisms (Howlett 2000).

Still, internal accountability mechanisms that adhere to the procedural norms of an effective bureaucracy and the separation of standard setting from auditing do not necessarily provide stakeholders influence over assessment outcomes. Indeed, environmental and social stakeholders have complained that fishery certifiers do not adequately address their concerns and are too attentive to the needs of the fishing industry. The significant authority delegated by MSC to the certifiers arguably comes at the expense of the ability of stakeholders to affect decisions. The assessment process is paid for by the applicant fishery, which, in the process, becomes the certifier's client. Because expert assessment teams appointed by the certifier score applicant fisheries and determine certification outcomes, they have considerable decision-making power. However, apart from being accredited by an independent organization, certifiers and the expert assessment teams they appoint are not directly accountable to external stakeholders or to the public(s). The persistent roles and significance of these actors highlight the potentially asymmetric power relations within the MSC's community, which implies that some accountability relations are more important for the program than others (Boström 2006; Black 2008).

Thus, from the perspective of those outside the organization—particularly environmental groups—the calculus appears to focus on the possible negative interactions of an unaccountable nonstate certification program with other forms of governance like government regulations or direct market campaigns that target the purchasing behavior of supermarkets and retailers. This is an expected dynamic in the context of polycentric regimes (Black 2008) where forum shopping is a strategic option that allows groups to support institutions that best advance their preferred problem framings and institutional goals (Alter and Meunier 2009). The Wildhavens report documented these concerns for the Alaskan pollock fishery. More recently, seafood buyer guides published by various groups (e.g., the Monterey Bay Aquarium) and watchdog reports on the environmental performance of supermarkets (e.g., Greenpeace) often disagree with the MSC on how to evaluate the sustainability of specific fisheries (Auld and Cashore 2013). Some of these groups initially attempted to change the MSC: for example, by calling on the program to not claim fisheries were sustainable, or not to grant certificates to controversial fisheries. However, they have since sought to influence fisheries using their own direct market campaigns—a form of market accountability—to ensure greater consistency with the problem framings and normative ends they seek to advance. They have also turned to and supported academic evaluations to point out shortcomings in the program and its claimed performance as an environmental steward.

The rationale for this move to support alternative mechanisms is apparent in the history of the objections procedure too. The procedure has been criticized for its expense, limited openness to stakeholder participation, and track record (Christian et al. 2013). Out of more than 300 fishery assessments (including reassessments) by the end of 2015, the objections process has been triggered thirty-one times as a result of accepted objections from environmental groups and other stakeholders, including industry associations representing certified fisheries. Only two of the accepted objections against the thirty-one fishery assessments were upheld and the fishery's

certification denied as a result (MSC 2015a, b)—those of the Faroese North-
east Atlantic mackerel (January 2011) and the Echebastar Indian Ocean
tuna fishery (November 2015).

The MSC claims these critiques misunderstand the procedure's aims
(Gutierrez and Agnew 2013; Brown, Agnew, and Martin 2016). The independent adjudicator must consider whether the certifier made a serious
procedural error or arbitrary or unreasonable scoring decision based on the
evidence available to it. The process is not designed to rescore the fishery,
but it can and does often identify and require fisheries to implement further improvements to their practices in order to become certified. However,
some stakeholders find it hard to accept that a procedural examination
process would not be required to sometimes provide for a de novo review.
This is one reason why certain groups want the objection procedure to
include the option for a full reassessment. Despite such calls, the MSC has
not acquiesced, maintaining that the purpose of the objection procedure is
to provide a review process that is consistent with the standard of appellate
review of administrative decisions in most countries and with complaints
procedures in other certification programs (Brown, Agnew, and Martin
2016). As a consequence, however, some environmental groups that initially supported the MSC have dismissed the program and turned to other
market accountability mechanisms to advance their normative ends. For
these stakeholders, the MSC's objections procedure only serves to enhance
internal accountability to a process, not external accountability for the content of decisions or to stakeholders who share MSC's goal of fisheries sustainability. Withholding their support and backing their own campaigns is
one available means to sanction the MSC in the hopes that it will improve
its future performance.

Conclusions

Just as Keohane (2003) argued in the case of international organizations, we
maintain that accountability in voluntary-private governance is informed
by logics of internal and external accountability. Emerging nonstate certification programs—a form of private-voluntary governance—have the added
challenge of operating with poorly delineated and often contested boundaries of their external audiences, a defining feature of polycentric regimes
(Black 2008). Accounting for these boundaries clarifies the contestation

between internal and external accountability that occurs as certification programs determine what goals to advance and which actors to give access to their internal governance processes.

We have observed a misalignment because the MSC claims to advance fisheries sustainability but has given limited access to environmental groups that feel they too are advancing this end. The misalignment is particularly salient because these environmental groups, through their naming-and-shaming campaigns, have materially helped the MSC by engendering demand for certified seafood (see also chapter 3, in this volume). However, rather than fully open its governance processes to environmental groups, the MSC has attempted to resolve the misalignment by bolstering internal accountability mechanisms like the fisheries assessment methodology and the program's objections procedure. In this way, the program has staked its reputation more on the alignment of its procedures with the norms of bureaucratic expertise. These efforts resulted in advanced accountability mechanisms that resemble public sector mechanisms central in administrative law—monitoring, reporting and verification, enforcement, adjudication, and dispute resolution (see Meidinger 2006).

This approach has come with costs. We have observed that elaborate internal accountability mechanisms do not necessarily provide stakeholders with influence over fisheries assessments, as the process is based on expert evaluation of stakeholder input, not a stakeholder negotiation process. NGOs and other stakeholders can appeal certification decisions, but objections are costly and rarely lead to certification denial. The question thus remains whether the objections procedure has value for those who believe that because of inflated scores, loose interpretation of MSC's criteria, and great flexibility in scoring by expert assessment teams, the MSC certifies controversial and unsustainable fisheries. This is a critical question because the objections procedure is the only internal sanctioning mechanism that stakeholders can use to directly hold certifiers to account for scoring of fisheries and decisions, the outcomes of which have implications for whether the MSC is helping to promote sustainable fisheries.

When considering external accountability, some observers argue that the MSC has chosen a path that could undermine credibility and trust in the program unless it changes its goals or grants environmental groups more influence. Others have called on the program to drop the use of sustainability as a claim, or else to explain to consumers what aspects of sustainability

MSC certification does not cover. Such calls have thus far met with little success. Thus, some environmental groups have distanced themselves from the program and sought to advance fisheries sustainability through their own direct market accountability mechanisms, such as seafood buyer guides. They also appear to assess the MSC more in relation to governance mechanisms such as fisheries regulations and court cases in order to minimize the negative impacts the MSC could have on other actions addressing fisheries sustainability.

These outside strategies, in other words, are efforts to hold the MSC to account for its Tier 1 decisions, and they underscore our argument that Tier 2 accountability is significantly affected by the critical judgments of outside audiences about whether a private-voluntary program has been set up to address the right problem framing and goals. Put differently, environmental groups that have been critical of the MSC have not forgotten their original concerns about the goals the program sought to address; rather, they attempt to use the MSC's internal accountability mechanisms, and their own direct market accountability mechanisms, to constantly remind the program and the fisheries sector of these critiques.

In nonstate certification, problems of inclusion and exclusion may arise out of difficulties in establishing the boundaries of external communities; that is, determining to whom the certification program ought to be accountable. Private governors may also use inclusion and exclusion instrumentally to ensure desired outcomes in rulemaking processes. Such strategies may have unforeseen consequences, however. This chapter shows that a narrowing of participation in one venue can lead excluded stakeholders to pursue other mechanisms to seek accountability. Hence, it is critical to recognize the interdependence of decisions about how, to whom, and against what norms certification programs are held to account.

When a program does not address misalignment or inconsistency by changing its goals or normative principles or by granting actors greater influence over the program, those actors are likely to engage in rival processes to hold the program accountable and to pursue their objectives. Examining such dynamics is a key area for future research on the accountability of private governance, not only in the case of fisheries certification but also for a wide range of market-based sustainability certification programs. Indeed, given the rise of polycentric governance arrangements, we need to be asking whether the interactions of diverse governance arrangements, not the single efforts of one private-voluntary program, are leading to improved environmental outcomes.

Note

1. This chapter represents a significantly revised and extended version of Lars H. Gulbrandsen and Graeme Auld, "Contested Accountability Logics in Evolving Non-state Certification for Fisheries Sustainability," *Global Environmental Politics* 16, no. 2 (2016): 42–60. We contributed as equal lead authors on this chapter.

7 Accountability in Public-Voluntary Governance: The Case of Illegal Wildlife Trade

Lorraine Elliott and William H. Schaedla

Introduction

In their introductory chapter to this volume and elsewhere, Kramarz and Park (2016; also see chapter 1 in this volume) discuss a range of hybrid institutions and arrangements in global environmental governance (GEG). In particular, they focus on the paradoxical rise of accountability mechanisms which have not been accompanied by corresponding environmental gains. This problem is ubiquitous; it occurs across a multitude of different issue areas. Our interest here is in hybrid institutions and arrangements that straddle public and voluntary sectors, the former constituted particularly by states and state agencies, and the latter by nongovernmental organizations (NGOs) or what Biermann and Pattberg (2012) refer to as agents beyond the state. In these arrangements, accountability standards and measures of their effectiveness are—by nature of the players and external forces involved—frequently framed in terms of environmental outcomes.

There is an extensive literature on NGO engagement in GEG, exploring their various roles as advocates and lobbyists, as voices of dissent, as agenda setters, as service deliverers, and as participants in and reporters of international negotiations on rule systems and regulations. In these roles, NGOs (voluntary sites of authority) have constructed, or have had delegated to them, a range of relationships with governments and agents of the state more generally. Issues regarding accountability in such contexts are explored in depth in other chapters in this volume with a focus on questions of representation and transparency (see chapter 4, in this volume). The examples of "public-voluntary" or hybrid governance that we explore in this chapter raise similar questions about the ways that participants define standards of accountability, ascertain compliance, and impose sanctions on recusant parties (see Grant and Keohane 2005, 29). Our examples of these hybrid governance arrangements also entail substantial blurring of the lines between actors' assumed areas of public and/or voluntary responsibility and authority factors that tend to confound straightforward assessment of accountability.

As Bäckstrand suggests, the "concept of accountability should be redefined to fit the elusive character of … hybrid governance structures" (2006, 293). We are interested first in how accountability functions, or should function, for the individual participants in hybrid arrangements. We also give thought to accountability at the point of hybridity or boundary spanning between actors, when the distinction between the state (public) and NGO (voluntary) blurs over the very kinds of activities that are assumed to be the prerogative of the modern state.[1] In this regard, hybridity can be understood as more than the mix of actors, though that is our main focus. Rather, hybridity is also constituted by the mechanisms of interaction and the blurring of logics of action.

Our focal area for this investigation of public-voluntary hybrid governance is the fight against illegal wildlife trade. In this policy space, there are any number of the more usual and conventionally understood interactions between governments, intergovernmental organizations (IGOs), and NGOs. For example, NGOs are actively present at international negotiations under treaties such as the 1973 Convention on the International Trade in Endangered Species of Wild Fauna and Flora (CITES; about which more later). They lobby, work with delegations, circulate informal proposals, disseminate the results of their own research investigations, and maintain a close, critical eye on compliance. NGOs have been central to the development of protection and anti-trafficking campaigns, often in partnership with, or with support from, government authorities.[2]

Our specific interest, however, is in the accountability issues that arise when NGOs become involved with governments and IGOs in the kinds of activities that are more often reserved for, and indeed are assumed to be, the bailiwick of the state—policing and enforcement. In effect, hybridity is not just about the actors involved but is also about relaxing assumptions about distinct logics of action associated with public and voluntary roles. Our analysis is related primarily to the second tier of GEG—the execution of environmental interventions as defined in Kramarz and Park's chapter in this volume.

As the CITES Secretariat has observed, "in recent years, non-governmental organizations (NGOs) have begun to play an increasingly significant role in the delivery of enforcement-related training and in developing enforcement strategies at national and sub-national level" (CITES 2010, 3). This suite of roles can be interpreted as an expanded version of advocacy and service delivery, a kind of supply-side voluntarism. But it may also be demand driven. As Smith and Klaas (2015, 20) point out, "the diversity and complexity of environmental crimes ... require advanced skills, expertise and extensive surveillance ... and are most effectively dealt with when cooperation exists between all or many relevant actors [including] NGOs, governments [and] the police." Relevant government (public) authorities involved in enforcement and prosecution are often lacking in all of these areas.

Cooperative activities involving NGOs are often undertaken in close and sometimes formally constituted relationships with governments, agencies, and IGOs. Governance is therefore "practiced [as] a negotiated process" (Jordan 2005, 5–6) between public and voluntary spheres of authority. We provide a more detailed narrative of this activity in the second substantive section of this chapter. But as we explain there, what WWF refers to as "long-standing partnerships ... working closely with law enforcement" (McLellan and Allan 2015, 3) can take a number of hybrid governance forms. These range from the conventional to the covert. NGOs train and build capacity among enforcement officers or related professionals such as prosecutors and the judiciary. They may be involved in managing and analyzing confidential (usually state-based) data. They may also provide various kinds of operational and enforcement support in areas such as surveillance, intelligence gathering, logistics for undercover operations, and inputs to criminal prosecutions.

These hybrid forms of engagement and governance are not always formalized through devices such as memoranda of understanding. Indeed, in some cases, where the focus is on covert activities, they are not even openly public. NGOs have been central to policy advances and operational successes in the fight against illegal wildlife trade. In this regard, they contribute to strengthening "public sector governance, capacity, and institutions" (Nelson 2007, 30). White refers to this as a form of role displacement in which "NGOs end up doing what should be done by formal state agencies," often (he argues) because those agencies find it easier to have the NGOs do that work (2012, 11). Despite its willingness to work with NGOs, the CITES Secretariat has at times also been critical of these kinds of relationships, drawing attention to what it perceives as (unspecified) situations in which "government agencies appear to have almost abdicated their statutory and constitutional roles to NGOs" (2010, 3).[3]

We begin this chapter by exploring what these various public-voluntary practices and relationships mean about accountability in general. Our analysis is informed by the six accountability questions identified by Kramarz and Park (chapter 1, in this volume). Consequently, we explore the apparently simple (first-tier) design questions, "accountability to whom and for what?" As we note, in public-voluntary hybrid arrangements, these questions focus on accountability between actors, accountability of such actors to their individual constituencies, and accountability of the hybrid arrangements themselves. We also give thought to benchmarks of accountability—or what Kramarz and Park (chapter 1, in this volume) refer to as second-tier processes, standards, and sanctions of input and output accountability. We explore these second-tier processes through ideas about organizational predictability, internal (or horizontal) peer-to-peer accountability, and vertical or upward/downward accountability in service delivery situations.

In subsequent sections of the chapter, we take CITES and its processes as a focus for this analysis. It is the key piece of international law through which governments who are parties to the agreement—now numbering 183—work individually and cooperatively to regulate legal wildlife trade and take action to restrict or control trade for species that are endangered, or that are likely to be endangered, by such trade.[4] CITES is fundamentally a conservation agreement, not a crime or law enforcement treaty. In effect, the fight against wildlife trafficking is a means to a biodiversity conservation end. As we argue in the concluding section of the chapter, this can complicate judgments about effectiveness as a form of output accountability.

Capturing Hybrid Accountability

Grant and Keohane define accountability as a situation in which "some actors have the right to hold other actors to a set of standards, to judge whether they have filled their responsibilities in light of those standards, and to impose sanctions if they determine that those responsibilities have not been met" (2005, 29). Yet, as Ebrahim points out, "accountability is a complex and dynamic concept" (2003, 815). Kramarz and Park also observe that hybrid institutions create "more complexity for understanding accountability relationships and responsibilities for effective environmental action" (2016, 10). In simple terms, and in line with Grant and Keohane's approach, accountability requires actors to be "answerable for their actions and the consequences that follow from them" (Korach 2006, 196). In a public-voluntary hybrid arrangement, the challenge lies in determining which actors have the right to hold others accountable and on what basis (first-tier accountability), and who sets standards and who judges whether those standards have been met (second-tier, regulative accountability).

We focus here on the idea that accountability is not just a relationship between actors. Rather, accountability to process (input accountability), and assumptions about what constitute legitimate spheres of action for actors, dominate the hybrid arrangements that span public and voluntary sectors. On the question of representation and constituency, often argued to be a core accountability metric for whether NGOs are legitimate actors in global governance, we take our lead from Charnovitz who argues that there are a number of governance contexts "that have nothing to do with representing anyone in particular." These arise, he suggests, when NGOs act as "sources of information and expertise," when they are delivering services, and when they are "standing up for a core value" (2006, 26), or, as Kramarz and Park describe it, functioning as norm champions. As we explore in this chapter, these activities are directly applicable to the ways that NGOs engage in hybrid practices focused on enforcement and the illegal wildlife trade.

Two themes at the core of accountability standards and processes for both state/public and NGO/voluntary activity in GEG broadly—and more specifically in the issue area of illegal wildlife trade and enforcement— focus on integrity and impact. Each comes with a bundle of overlapping assumptions about the normative or constitutive content of accountability and expectations about appropriate regulatory mechanisms for holding accountable both individual actors and the arrangements between and among them. Taken together, they anticipate a mix of first- and second-tier questions about "effectiveness, ... organizational reliability and legitimacy" (Jordan 2005, 7).

Taking the latter of Jordan's points first, questions about legitimacy focus on external accountability (Kramarz and Park's first-tier questions about who is held to account and to whom) and the "rightfulness" of individual actors and the kinds of hybrid arrangements that we explore in this chapter. In effect, do these actors—and therefore arrangements between and among them—have the right and/or the responsibility to act? Second, are those actions "desirable, proper or appropriate" (Suchman 1995, 574)? In the regulative context of GEG, the standards of accountability that establish the authority for public actors can be legally grounded in the provisions of treaty law, in decisions of state parties, or set out in the terms of specific contracts. It can also be derived from past practice and credible expertise. Yet as we note elsewhere in this chapter, these questions become more complicated when NGOs become formal and often equal and active partners with governments and IGOs at intervention points along the enforcement chain. These issues are further complicated by the fact of a wide variation in where and how NGOs operate in such hybrid partnerships. International NGOs (INGOs) typically have access to more significant levels of funding and are able to negotiate more effectively with governments and IGOs. Invariably, they are also better at accessing and mobilizing the kind of technical expertise that is required for successful hybrid enforcement activities. However, the combination of global priorities and demands for accountability to international donors may defeat efforts to localize their approaches. As a result, they may be less well placed than local NGOs when it comes to understanding the local contexts and needs (chapter 4, in this volume) central to effective outcomes in the fight against illegal wildlife trade.

As Jordan points out (as mentioned earlier) accountability is also understood to derive from, or to be measured as, a function of organizational reliability, a factor in Kramarz and Park's input second-tier, regulative accountability. In institutional terms, this is often reduced to a focus on internal practices such as management and financial arrangements. Jordan and van Tuijl add to this the "efficiency of operations and working within legal confines in a transparent manner" (2006, 2). Our analysis touches on this intrasystem accountability as it relates to the legal structures underlying hybrid arrangements and the behaviors of parties to those agreements. This is akin to the standards of accountability for public agents that Kramarz and Park identify, but in a hybrid arrangement it can also frame standards for NGOs in terms of contractual obligations that define desired conduct. Accountability also relates to the kinds of questions that donors ask of entities (such as NGOs) that they have contracted and funded for service delivery in a hybrid context. This brings a focus on multidirectional accountability and the complexities of scale to an analysis of accountability in hybrid governance. Such arrangements are sometimes described in terms of upward accountability from service providers to donors, or downward accountability from service providers to the third-party recipients of donor specified services (for example, developing country beneficiaries of international aid programs). These kinds of upward-downward first-tier accountability considerations also apply to our cases, particularly in the formal contractual arrangements such as those between the wildlife trade monitoring NGO, TRAFFIC and CITES, or between TRAFFIC and the European Commission in which public agents also have obligations (such as reporting and providing data) to NGOs.

Finally, accountability is embedded in questions about effectiveness which Kramarz and Park (chapter 1, in this volume) explain as outcome, or external accountability. This is about being "answerable for performance to key stakeholders" (Brown et al., cited in Nelson 2007, 17). At a minimal level, these are questions that "usually have to do with the quality and quantity of services offered" (Jordan 2005, 7) and underpin judgments about whether responsibilities have been fulfilled and whether sanctions are in order. In the context of policing and enforcement actions and arrangements against the illegal wildlife trade, effectiveness—for which actors are held accountable—can easily be stretched to include the contribution that "services" make directly or indirectly to effective interdiction and prosecution, or to reducing demand and supply, or to ensuring compliance with legal and regulatory frameworks.

Kramarz and Park (2016, 10) suggest that hybrid arrangements which straddle more than one type of governance logic tend to preference "particular goals that shape not only what they are accountable for but also how." Biermann et al. (2009) posit that various kinds of hybrid arrangements may result in conflictive goals and outcomes that pose a potential obstacle to effective environmental action. The hybrid governance examples that we examine later in this chapter are perhaps more akin to what Biermann et al. refer to as cooperative and synergistic fragmentation. The former is marked by "different institutions and decision-making procedures that are loosely integrated" while the latter "provides for effective and detailed general principles that regulate … policies in distinct yet substantially integrated institutional arrangements" (Biermann et al. 2009, 20). In the fight against illegal wildlife trade, the development of formal hybrid arrangements between public and voluntary actors take advantage of what could be described as governance economies of scale, pooling efforts and taking advantage of the synergies that can arise from different kinds of expertise and capacity brought together in the pursuit of strategic collaboration and effective outcomes. The way in which accountability is defined and managed—and whether those definitions and accountability values are shared by the relevant parties—can be a key factor in how well hybrid or fragmented arrangements deliver effective outcomes. We return to this issue of effectiveness and the role of accountability mechanisms in such outcomes later in the chapter.

CITES and TRAFFIC

One of the longest-standing public-voluntary relationships on wildlife trade related issues exists between CITES and the international NGO, TRAF-FIC. TRAFFIC is a network arrangement, established in 1976 by the Species Survival Commission of the International Union for Conservation of Nature (IUCN, itself a hybrid institution) in an agreement with the non-governmental organization, WWF.[5] The entry into force of CITES in 1975 was a major factor in the decision to establish TRAFFIC. The organization is focused on wildlife trade monitoring as the basis for the development of effective conservation policies and programs. TRAFFIC, and its parent IUCN, contribute to the scientific rigor and precautionary approach of CITES through analyses of proposals to amend the CITES appendices, technical support for national-level scientific authorities, and training for what is known as the *Non-Detriment Finding process*.[6]

In 1999, the CITES Secretariat and TRAFFIC signed a memorandum of understanding (MoU) to establish a "formal mechanism for collaboration between the two agencies" (CITES/TRAFFIC 1999, 1). That MoU recognized the "similarity of mandates and complementary roles" and past collaborations. It suggested, therefore, that it would be mutually advantageous for the two organizations to work together, in a structured collaborative partnership, to strengthen the implementation and enforcement of the Convention, particularly in the area of capacity building. While the MoU clearly establishes a hybrid governance arrangement straddling the public and voluntary sectors, it makes no specific mention of accountability. However, it does contain provisions that mesh with the approach to accountability that we have outlined earlier in this chapter, and the framework that Kramarz and Park outline in chapter 1 of this volume.

TRAFFIC's technical expertise is recognized as the basis for its participation in the partnership, along with its role in developing joint activities and advancing efforts to build implementation and enforcement capacity among CITES parties. Indeed, the regional and national offices of the TRAFFIC network are designated CITES Capacity Building Collaborating Centres. Areas of mutual interest are to be identified by the partners jointly and are to be subject to periodic review. Indeed, mutual approval, coordination, and consultation are at the core of the accountability relationship between the CITES Secretariat and TRAFFIC. There is to be a workplan that is agreed upon each year. Each partner is expected to keep the other informed of its respective policy approaches and activities. In this respect, internal accountability is understood in horizontal terms and is to be achieved through structured reporting and transparency.

Public-Voluntary Hybrid Accountability between CITES and NGOs

CITES anticipates a variety of roles for NGOs. Although the Convention is not strictly speaking a UN Convention, it follows United Nations Economic and Social Council (UN ECOSOC) practices for accrediting nongovernmental organizations at Conferences of the Parties (COP).[7] Article XI(7) includes international and national NGOs among those bodies or agencies "technically qualified in protection, conservation or management of wild fauna and flora" who can request to be represented at COPs.[8] The Convention also notes that the Secretariat may be assisted by such "technically qualified" nongovernmental bodies to the "extent and in the manner ... consider[ed] appropriate" (Article XII(1)). The Secretariat "has no *specific* investigative or enforcement authority as part of its mandate and has no powers to conduct investigations at national level" (CITES 2004, 2; emphasis added).

The parties also anticipate active compliance and enforcement roles for NGOs in forms that constitute the kinds of public-voluntary hybrid arrangements that Kramarz and Park identify in chapter 1 as environmental interventions. Guidance from the Secretariat states that "the NGO community has a vital role to play in supporting wildlife law enforcement efforts" (CITES 2010, 3, paragraph 26). The relevant COP resolution (Conf. 11.3 Rev. CoP16) provides that, where appropriate, parties should "evaluate and utilize for enforcement purposes, information from non-governmental sources while maintaining standards of confidentiality" (CITES 2013, 6). It suggests that CITES Management Authorities, which are established by each party to meet its obligations under the Convention, should coordinate (inter alia) "where appropriate [with] sectoral non-governmental organizations, by arranging training activities and joint meetings, and facilitating the exchange of information" (CITES 2013, 5). Annex 3 to that resolution notes that wildlife law enforcement units might "establish appropriate links" with NGOs that could "offer relevant information, expert advice and assistance" (CITES 2013, annex 3, 4) though it says nothing about what form such links might take. The annex also recognizes that NGOs undertake "research or trade surveys that might involve a covert element" (CITES 2013, annex 3, 4).

In summary, the Secretariat and the parties have anticipated (hybrid) relationships with, and roles for, NGOs in areas such as law enforcement training and capacity building; funding; and the provision of information and expert advice, including that which might come from covert operations. Two caveats are warranted here. First, through seeking to define the boundaries of what might be considered appropriate, the Secretariat and the parties have also outlined constraints on NGOs and on their working relationships with them. The Secretariat advises parties that NGOs "should not be allowed access to intelligence or to engage in any operational activity without appropriate legislative authority as well as the agreement of ... prosecution authorities" (CITES 2013, 4).[9] It continues that "NGOs ... should not be allowed to undertake activities that rest more properly with government agencies, e.g. covert operations or the maintenance of databases on crime and criminals" (CITES 2013, 4). While these constraints are intended to keep voluntary sector actions subordinate to public sector leadership in environmental enforcement, actual practice is flexible. As we explore later in this chapter, "support" varies widely under hybrid arrangements. As a result, participant perceptions of accountability also vary.

We turn now to examine two of the three areas of public-voluntary hybrid engagement that we identified earlier—training and capacity building, and the provision of information and expert advice—to examine how the complexities of accountability are both understood and managed. We then examine how NGOs, governments, and IGOs have worked together on operational aspects of enforcement practice, which adds complexity to the discourse and practice of accountability. As explained previously, our focus is primarily on the second-tier, regulative frame that Kramarz and Park outline in chapter 1.

Training and Capacity Building

As noted previously, enforcement-related training and capacity building constitutes one of the key sectors in which CITES (used in this sense as a collective noun that includes the Convention, various resolutions and decisions adopted by the parties, and the Secretariat) anticipates a legitimate role for nongovernmental organizations. CITES is not alone in this regard. Individual governments and IGOs such as the World Customs Organization (WCO) have also called on NGOs for training expertise. A comprehensive treatment of such programs is beyond the scope of this chapter, but an illustrative list provides insight into the ways they function. In some cases, the nature of NGO support is confined to training government officials. In other cases, NGOs actually support the placement of such officials at enforcement sites. TRAFFIC has delivered training programs to the Ecuadorian military on combating wildlife crime; contributed to CITES-enforcement workshops for forest police officers in China; and worked in collaboration with the International Criminal Police Organization (INTERPOL) and the United Nations Office on Drugs and Crime (UNODC) to deliver regional training on wildlife and forest crime in Cameroon. The International Fund for Animal Welfare (IFAW) has conducted training for game wardens in Trinidad and Tobago; delivered elephant antipoaching and wildlife crime training in various countries in Africa, as well as India and Bhutan; and worked with United Arab Emirates (UAE) authorities to deliver wildlife trafficking prevention workshops to UAE customs officers. The Wildlife Conservation Society (WCS) has collaborated with Chinese CITES Management Authority to deliver training for customs officers to support frontline enforcement efforts; worked in conjunction with the US Embassy to provide training to US military forces in Afghanistan to help reduce illegal trade; and cooperated with national agencies in hosting an interagency field mission for border enforcement officers from Laos, China, and Vietnam. Freeland Foundation has developed an extensive suite of training and capacity building courses for wildlife crime investigators under its Protected-Area Operational and Tactical Enforcement Conservation Training/Detection of Environmental Crime Training (PROTECT/DETECT) program. Freeland's contribution to training and capacity building grew from its role as a lead implementing partner of Asia's Regional Response to Endangered Species Trafficking (ARREST), which was funded by the US Agency for International Development (USAID).[10]

Training and capacity building activities fit broadly within the concept of hybrid governance in that they straddle public and voluntary sectors. They typically function through contractual or grant-type arrangements associated with specific service delivery, rather than more formal partnership arrangements such as those established under memoranda of understanding. Accountability mechanisms in these arrangements, such as requirements for reporting, auditing, and outcomes (or key performance indicators) are managed under the terms of individual awards and contracts between the relevant NGO and the party that commissions training or capacity building activities. In this regard, the questions "accountable to whom, and for what?" will deliver clear answers that are set out in each specific contractual arrangement.[11] Our other key metrics of effectiveness and legitimacy, as measures of upward-downward and external accountability, respectively, are relevant here as well. Indeed, they may well be crucial in a context in which NGOs—as organizations that are neither state-based nor established under legislative authority—deliver training to government agencies and agents, since such actions go to the heart of state prerogatives in law enforcement and investigation. The CITES Enforcement Expert Group has expressed some concern about the "delivery of enforcement related training by non-governmental organizations," arguing that "this should only be conducted by suitably experienced enforcement officers" (2009, paragraph 12.g).[12] INTERPOL, on the other hand, has argued that "of necessity" its efforts in this regard required "working closely with 'non-police' law enforcement agencies," such as NGOs, "particularly in support or capacity building initiatives" (Nellemann, Redmond, and Refisch 2010, 67).[13]

In the face of disputes about whether NGOs should be involved in enforcement training and capacity building, standards or measures of accountability function through the credibility, expertise, and competence of both the trainers and the programs that they deliver. In response to the question "accountable to whom," and complementing the upward accountability to those with whom a contract exists, this constitutes a form of "downward accountability to [those] who are being served" (Nelson 2007, 16) or, in this case, those who are being trained. One measure of effectiveness therefore relates to how well training activities bridge upward-downward accountability; that is, accountability between the NGO and those who fund or contract training (on the one hand), and between the NGO and those who are trained (on the other). These issues of credibility and expertise take on an extra dimension in the context of the battle against the illegal wildlife trade and outcome accountability. Enforcement officers are those who are or who will be involved in frontline operations which may involve covert activity, surveillance, interdiction, and arrest in often dangerous circumstances. Consequently, training is not simply a matter of imparting information and knowledge. It is also about effective preparation for potentially dangerous or life-threatening situations.

Information and Expert Advice: ETIS and EU-TWIX

Under the broad terms of the MoU described earlier in this chapter, TRAFFIC is contracted to manage for CITES a key law enforcement data collection and analysis tool—the Elephant Trade Information System (ETIS).[14] It constitutes a hybrid governance arrangement, straddling the state and intergovernmental public sector represented by CITES and the voluntary sector represented by TRAFFIC. ETIS is mandated to measure, record, and report on levels and trends in illegal elephant killing, and the trade in ivory and other elephant specimens since 1989.[15] CITES parties are expected to report all seizures of illegal elephant ivory within their territories to TRAFFIC or to the Secretariat. ETIS also maintains subsidiary information on law enforcement effort and efficiency, rates of reporting, legal and illegal elephant product markets, governance issues, background economic data, and other factors.

Data collection goes beyond simple information gathering and reporting. Under this hybrid governance arrangement, TRAFFIC has the authority to seek information from relevant national agencies if parties report cases without providing the detail required in the data collection forms. TRAFFIC's analysis of the data is integrated into decision-making on trade, management, protection, and enforcement. TRAFFIC is expected to undertake a number of other tasks in conjunction with its ETIS responsibilities. For example, as well as collecting and analyzing data, it is to assist parties in "ensuring data quality and consistency, and providing tools and training in data collection, data utilization and information management" (CITES 2013, 6).

The mechanisms and standards of accountability are not spelled out in any specific detail. Nevertheless, the direction of accountability might be deduced as mainly one-directional (upward) since TRAFFIC is held accountable to the CITES Secretariat and parties through standards relating to oversight and reporting.[16] Oversight is managed through an independent technical advisory group (TAG) involving range state representatives, global experts, and co-opted experts from IUCN's Species Survival Commission.[17] The ETIS reporting requirements are multidimensional. TRAFFIC is required to "produce a comprehensive analytical report with full explanatory and interpretive notes prior to each meeting of the Conference of the Parties."[18] This analytical transparency holds TRAFFIC accountable for the scientific credibility of its ETIS findings. Such credibility is important given claims that the ETIS analyses "have had an immense impact … [on] CITES policy and interventions for elephants" (TRAFFIC 2012, 2). This reporting requirement also constitutes accountability measured and achieved through contracted task fulfilment. TRAFFIC recognizes these reports as meeting its obligations to CITES (Milliken et al. 2016, 3) and CITES, in turn, accepts them as part of its own public reporting requirements. Therefore, the credibility of the ETIS process also has implications for the accountability of CITES parties to their own constituents. In effect, the CITES compliance mechanism rests on independent analysis and data, rather than primarily or exclusively on self-reporting by the parties.

The ETIS reports also include cluster analyses "to identify those countries/territories most prominently implicated in the illicit trade in ivory" (Milliken 2016, 11). In effect, the NGO (voluntary sector) partner in this hybrid arrangement is identifying for the Secretariat (public/state sector) those countries of primary concern "which the Parties could consider for inclusion in the CITES oversight process to address illegal trade in ivory" (Milliken 2016, 18). This too has consequences for the parties themselves by way of what could be considered an informal sanctioning process if they fail to meet the public standards established through the Convention.

European Union Trade in Wildlife Information Exchange

TRAFFIC has had a lead role in another CITES-related information and communication tool that straddles public and voluntary sectors in its contribution to illegal wildlife trade governance and enforcement mechanisms. In 2004, TRAFFIC joined with the Belgian Federal Police, Belgian Customs, and the Belgium CITES management authority to obtain funding from the European Commission to establish an "Internet-based, secure access platform." The system is designed to make "EU-wide CITES seizures data available to wildlife law enforcement officials across the EU [European Union]" (Sacré 2016, 479).[19] TRAFFIC administers it on behalf of the other partners. TRAFFIC also develops detailed trend analyses of the seizure data for enforcement officials. As with ETIS, the broader goals of the European Union Trade in Wildlife Information Exchange (EU-TWIX), which help to define outcome accountability, go beyond data collection. It contributes to a suite of mechanisms that are designed to "help national law enforcers in the EU to undertake risk analysis and to better coordinate joint investigations" (IUCN 2007, 6) to meet their public accountability obligations under the European Wildlife Trade Regulations. Unlike ETIS, EU-TWIX is not a single database. The main components are a confidential mailing list and an access-restricted repository of EU-wide seizure data which is reported by European Union member states and non-EU participants in the TWIX.[20] The mailing list is used daily by European officials for purposes such as sharing CITES alerts and stolen specimen alerts, seeking assistance with species identification, and helping to identify requirements for further training (see Sacré 2016, 481–483). EU-related seizure data from the WCO's Customs Enforcement Network is also transferred to EU-TWIX. In this context, then, an NGO has access to law enforcement data that would normally only be available to officials from government and intergovernmental agencies.[21]

The processes and standards of accountability for EU-TWIX are similar to those that apply under ETIS: the existence of an advisory mechanism, task fulfilment, and credibility of output and outcomes. EU-TWIX is overseen by an advisory group consisting of officials from six CITES management authorities in EU countries that also functions as a decision board. Evidence from the advisory group and TRAFFIC suggests that this hybrid arrangement is seen as accountable by its constituency. By the time of its ten-year anniversary in late 2015, 840 wildlife law enforcement officials from more than 100 European enforcement agencies were connected to and making use of EU-TWIX (TRAFFIC 2015). According to the advisory group, EU-TWIX is a "functioning and useful system" that "produces results" (CITES 2010, 2). TRAFFIC reports that several criminal investigations have been instigated each year as a direct result of the enforcement-related messages exchanged by officials through EU-TWIX (TRAFFIC 2015). The credibility of the EU-TWIX as a hybrid arrangement—and particularly TRAFFIC's role in it—can also be measured in the fact that the governance model has been used as the basis for other enforcement databases such as Tigernet (a collaboration between TRAFFIC and India's National Tiger Conservation Authority) and AFRICA-TWIX (hosted by the Central Africa Forest Commission and managed by TRAFFIC). In this context, the taking-up of the program can be seen as evidence that voluntary (i.e., NGO) standards are being met.

While our discussion in this section has focused on the relationship between CITES, CITES-related processes, and TRAFFIC, this kind of hybrid governance and enforcement arrangement is not unique in the anti-wildlife-trafficking sector. In October 2013, TRAFFIC entered into a memorandum of understanding with the WCO to formalize an existing cooperative relationship to bolster responses to illegal trade in protected animals and plants (see WCO 2013). Under the terms of this MoU, WCO and TRAFFIC agreed to pool their capacity building efforts with a particular focus on training materials and activities. They also agreed to enhance their information exchange. The WCO agreed to provide TRAFFIC with Customs seizure data for the two databases discussed previously (ETIS and EU-TWIX), and TRAFFIC committed to assisting the WCO in identifying gaps in enforcement and detecting new threats. In contrast to the caution expressed by the CITES Secretariat (as noted previously) about the boundaries for NGO contributions to policing and enforcement, the WCO seemed more welcoming. The press release announcing the MoU noted that TRAFFIC's "expertise, experience of effective strategies and technical resources ... have already been put to good use by the WCO" (WCO 2013). The WCO entered into a similar formalized relationship with the WCS, signing a MoU in January 2016 to "exchange information, collaborate on policy decisions, and cooperate in multiple ways to stop illegal wildlife trade" (WCS 2016). The WCO's use of similar agreements with different NGOs is an interesting development that could be taken as a proliferation of the public-voluntary hybrid governance model in an enforcement context. On the other hand, the potential for expansion of such arrangements is probably limited. Both agreements were contingent on participation by a skilled NGO with proven technical capacity. Despite proven accountability processes and standards for structuring and managing the hybrid governance arrangements, access to secure information is the exception rather than the rule. Programs like those of TRAFFIC and WCS remain rare in practice. Governments and IGOs have remained cautious about instantiating a generic norm that might facilitate NGO access to confidential data.

Operational Engagement

Hybrid practices in operational aspects of wildlife law enforcement which bring together government authorities, IGOs, and NGOs in various permutations have been most controversial in practical and accountability terms. The CITES Secretariat has argued that "such organizations should ensure that the methods they use are legal and ethical" to avoid compromising investigations by law enforcement agencies or rendering information inadmissible in court (CITES 2004, 2–3). The Secretariat has also worried that "the correct balance is not being struck" (2010, 3) between the investigative responsibilities of states and those that they delegate to NGOs. This concern with method and balance frames both the purpose of accountability (accountable for what) and the measures of accountability when NGOs adopt or are delegated responsibilities in the operational enforcement space.

As we discuss in more detail here, that straddling of the public and voluntary sectors can take a number of forms. Some arise from specific agreements between NGOs and governments and/or IGOs. Some are part of longer-term enforcement campaigns. NGOs also undertake independent undercover investigative and surveillance operations which generate findings about "environmental harm and offender wrongdoing" as White puts it (2012, 7) that can then be disseminated to public authorities either through open-source publication or through less public personal contacts. These constitute assumed rather than delegated responsibilities in a hybrid context (see Charnovitz 2006). Despite disapproval from some within the enforcement community, independent NGO operations (particularly those undertaken by organizations experienced in this field) are rarely amateur or cavalier in their planning or execution. Indeed, the individuals involved often have professional policing and law enforcement backgrounds. As Simmons (cited in Gemmill and Bamidele-Izu 2002, 92) notes, in operational contexts NGOs are often crucial to "mak[ing] the impossible possible by doing what governments cannot or will not do."

In this section we explore three broad categories of hybrid enforcement operations and the accountability issues that they raise. First, we touch briefly on independent operational investigations undertaken by NGOs. Second, we provide a brief overview of the kind of operational support that NGOs provide to other nonstate actors. Although this functions outside the public-voluntary boundaries of this chapter, we include it as part of the broader enforcement context. Finally we explore the different ways in which NGOs have worked collaboratively with government authorities and intergovernmental agencies, often at the behest of the latter, in operational nodes along the enforcement chain. We address the issue of operational effectiveness in the concluding section.

Investigative Activities

Independent investigative activities are undertaken by a number of NGOs. These vary widely in the ways they are conducted. Some are highly cooperative arrangements, with the voluntary actors acting as functional extensions of public offices. Freeland Foundation, for example, has worked closely with various police forces in Southeast Asia under the USAID-sponsored ARREST program to improve regional and national curricula on wildlife crime (Freeland 2016). The mechanics of this approach include close collaboration with government agencies and the execution of actual investigative activities in the course of training and capacity building programs. Wildlife Alliance, which operates primarily in Cambodia, takes a similar embedded approach, providing "technical assistance for investigations" (Wildlife Alliance 2016) for the Wildlife Rapid Rescue Team (WRRT) that it established and continues to fund. The WRRT includes Cambodian Forestry Administration personnel, members of the country's judicial police, military police from the Royale Gendarmerie, and two embedded Wildlife Alliance staff.

TRAFFIC's approach to its investigative work depends on the country involved. As already noted, its TWIX projects are conducted in close association with government agencies. Yet the organization has also been a pioneer in independent investigations of illegal wildlife trade. It has produced hundreds of watchdog-type papers and publications since it was founded. Its investigations and tip-offs have resulted in significant seizures by wildlife enforcement agencies. The same agencies have also turned to TRAFFIC to assist in enforcement-related analyses of seized specimens and illicit documentation (see, for example, Raza and Chauhan 2012; Pantel and Anak 2010).

Other voluntary organizations take a very different approach. The Environmental Investigation Agency (EIA) describes itself as "an independent campaigning organisation" (EIA 2016). EIA identifies "diligent, carefully planned undercover investigations" as being at the heart of its work in the campaign against illegal wildlife trade.[22] Its investigators, some of whom have law enforcement backgrounds, use techniques such as hidden filming, establishing "front" companies, and identifying criminal groups to follow leads and gather credible evidence. Its investigative activities into illegal wildlife trade are conducted without direct collaboration with government agencies, in part because EIA maintains a strong focus on outing corruption in the public sphere.[23] A few examples will be useful. In 2014, an EIA team, working with Education for Nature Vietnam (ENV) conducted undercover investigations in the Golden Triangle Special Economic Zone in Laos to document illicit wildlife products, including those deriving from captive-bred tigers (EIA 2015a). In June 2015, EIA investigators posed as timber buyers in order to evaluate the illicit timber trade between Yunnan and Myanmar (EIA 2015b). An undercover investigation of Japanese ivory traders revealed fraud and corruption, including within the agency tasked to manage Japan's ivory tusk registration scheme (EIA 2016).

Some of these investigative activities by voluntary organizations involve reporting accountability from NGOs as service providers to public national agencies. All place a high premium on some version of outcome accountability. That is, they derive legitimacy from how well they actually expose—and curtail—wildlife trafficking activities. It is interesting that the most important validation in this process seems to come from peer-to-peer interactions, a form of accountability to social networks that Kramarz and Park identify as common for the voluntary sector. Different organizations follow up and check one another's work. For example, TRAFFIC and EIA regularly cite each other's research (EIA 2015a, 22; Stoner and Pervushina 2013, 40). Wildlife Alliance notes on its website that the WRRT team was recognized by TRAFFIC as "the leading example in anti-wildlife trafficking law enforcement" with a "high level of sustained enforcement and efficacious seizure" (Wildlife Alliance 2016).

Operational Support

Depending on context, operational support can also be subject to differing accountability measures. Here again, the ARREST program provides insight. The program included needs assessments and subsequent material support to public sector organizations (police, wildlife, and customs agencies) in Asia. Freeland played an intermediary role in the process, with upward accountability to USAID through its grant award and downward accountability to national agency clients in support of their counter wildlife crime efforts. However, there was a disconnect in this approach when it came to weapons training. USAID is subject to strict rules prohibiting the purchase or use of firearms. When Freeland's country-level "clients" requested such training, the organization sought additional inputs from the United States Department of Justice International Criminal Investigative Training Assistance Program (ICITAP). ICITAP is empowered to work directly with enforcement agencies. By bringing them to bear on key activities, Freeland was able to maintain accountability to both its clients, and its bottom-line (outcome/external accountability) mission to secure resilient ecosystems (Bowman, personal communication 2016).

Such workarounds are common in public-voluntary hybrid actions against wildlife crime. In Operation Unicornis, WWF worked closely with Nepalese government authorities to increase security posts within protected areas and to engage former army and police personnel to patrol vulnerable locations outside those areas (WWF 2008). Likewise, the International Fund for Animal Welfare had a key role in the preparation for INTERPOL's Operation Worthy, a three month long transnational operation undertaken in 2012 and targeted at the illegal ivory trade.[24] IFAW sponsored pre-operational training in search and seizure techniques for officers from the participating countries. A follow-up enforcement operation in 2015— Operation Worthy II—was supported by IFAW and the Wildcat Foundation. All these examples point to a strong focus on effectiveness on the part of voluntary organizations involved in operational and investigative support.

Conclusion

Smith and Klaas have pointed out that "the ways in which [NGOs] behave and the roles they assume" in environmental crime enforcement "raise important questions regarding accountability and expertise"' (2015, 20). Jordan and van Tuijl are more specific in identifying those questions. They ask, "[W]hat roles are valid for NGOs to play?" "[W]hich responsibilities should be clearly articulated as part of these roles?" and "[T]o whom should NGOs be accountable?" (2006, 1).

In this context, the editors of this volume set us the task of answering a number of questions related to hybrid governance that straddles the voluntary and public sectors: What process demonstrates accountability; what standards demonstrate accountability? What sanctions are available when there is failure to meet those standards? What is the impact of accountability practices on reshaping the goals of parties involved in governing the global environment? Our focus has been on the fight against the illegal wildlife trade and on the ways in which the apparently clear boundaries between NGO and state actors are blurred and crossed in activities related to wildlife law enforcement. As Bäckstrand points out, these kinds of hybrid governance arrangements often "escape traditional models of ... accountability" (2006, 292). We suggest they may also escape traditional delineations between public and voluntary sectors. When NGOs act as regular proxies or capacity-building agencies for governments and intergovernmental bodies, the identities of individual actors are likely to be less important than the ways and means of their interactions. States may adopt voluntary or private modalities, while NGOs may become functionally public entities.

To some extent, the framework of multidirectional accountability introduced here for hybrid public-voluntary arrangements, and its ideas about organizational reliability, effectiveness, and legitimacy, is little different from those that apply in other governance arrangements. Accountability is demonstrated through processes that involve reporting, targets, management, evaluation, oversight, and mutual recognition in formal and informal hybrid arrangements. The standards are embedded in, and measured by, the credibility and cogency of scientific output, the reliability of information and training, the efficacy of operational support, and the validity of investigative outcomes. As we have explored here, this is not just a one-way relationship in which NGOs are accountable to IGOs and state agencies. In many cases, NGOs expect, and indeed require, credible inputs from their public sector partners to enhance and strengthen their own contributions to counter illegal wildlife-trade enforcement actions. Hybrid governance arrangements operating to counter the illegal wildlife trade require that all parties—including states and their agencies—are transparent and noncorrupt. In some cases, the standards and process of accountability in these hybrid arrangements hew to those more associated with voluntary actors and governance arrangements. This is the case in the WWF Unicornis example. The government of Nepal has long been content to accept NGO management of such projects. As a result, NGOs can exert some influence over project planning and execution. In other arrangements, such as the examples involving INTERPOL, accountability is more skewed toward public contractual standards because INTERPOL is strict about the way it engages NGOs.

The nature of accountability sanctions in this hybrid space, and particularly as it applies to wildlife trade enforcement, has both a formal and informal dimension. Kramarz and Park (2016, 6) identify sanctions as actions to "punish a lack of transparency, answerability, or compliance." In the cases and practices that we have explored here, punitive action can take the form of what Bäckstrand et al. call the "ultimate sanction" of removing the agent, whether state or nonstate, from its position (2012, 139). Yet it is not always clear what "removal" might mean in the hybrid context examined in this chapter. It can mean withdrawal of program funding from NGOs if they fail to deliver on training programs or data management and analysis, or if they fail to meet reporting requirements. However, in many cases there are extensive "sunk costs" involved that make financial sanctions difficult. The specialized nature of wildlife law enforcement may also limit viable partnership options.

The relationship, therefore, is not necessarily as one-sided as it might seem. NGOs also have the option of publicly refusing to work with government agencies with poor credibility or histories of corruption. As we explored earlier in our discussion of TRAFFIC and CITES, "naming-and-shaming" sanctions can be powerful, particularly when they are embedded in formal hybrid arrangements. At first blush, naming and shaming may seem like a clear example of a voluntary accountability sanction. Yet such accountability tactics also function in the public relationships between states. Parties to CITES regularly disclose embarrassing information about one another in the form of trade data and reports. These actions may be functionally indistinguishable from those of NGOs, even in cases where NGOs are not involved.

This begs questions about whether acknowledged partnerships are necessary definitors of hybrid governance. When government agencies employ tactics or standards developed by NGOs, they are essentially hybridizing themselves. To complicate matters, states also rely on and work with NGO partners to accumulate trade information. These arrangements may be formal (and acknowledged) or informal (and not acknowledged). Either way, they tend to make states more voluntary and NGOs more public in the ways they operate. In such arrangements, NGO involvement effectively becomes a proxy for public accountability.

The relationship between accountability standards and processes, on the one hand, and the effectiveness of governance arrangements on the other, is unclear. In the case of CITES, increasing hybridization between public and voluntary accountability has altered implementation practices, but it has not resulted in specific textual changes to the treaty. As we have explored in this chapter, NGOs have gone from being monitors and observers of treaty compliance (this was TRAFFIC's original role) to coordinators and capacity creators. Their engagement has also helped set new professional standards for data collection and enforcement. As we noted, there has been some transfer of best practice accountability standards and processes between public and voluntary agencies. On the other hand, hybrid arrangements can also enable governments to outsource and potentially abdicate public accountability by failing to provide resources that would ensure that training is operationalized internally.

How different accountability standards arising from hybrid governance arrangements relate to effectiveness remains an open question. This would likely be assessed in terms of diminishing illegal wildlife trade and the impact that reduction has on biodiversity conservation. It would be complicated by the fact that illegal wildlife trade constitutes a moving target in terms of what species are traded, what forms the trades take (live, dead, derivatives), where they are sourced, how they are trafficked, and where they end up.

We can say intuitively that collaboration between governments, IGOs, and NGOs has resulted in a much greater awareness of the illegal wildlife trade. Yet as Wandesforde-Smith (2016, 375) points out, the government and public interest generated by hybrid programs are much easier to measure than their actual impacts on interdictions, arrests, and prosecutions. Evidence suggests that interdictions and arrests have gone up and it might be reasonable to assume that training, capacity building, and operational cooperation between the public and voluntary sectors has been a factor in the increase. Enforcement agencies have confirmed that processes such as the exchange of confidential information through hybrid arrangements such as EU-TWIX has helped with investigations (see Sacré 2016, for example).

As we do not know, and cannot know, how much illegal wildlife trade is undetected, we cannot make definitive claims to "effectiveness" at reducing it. It is also difficult to say with certainty whether the kinds of hybrid arrangements we have explored here have affected broader conservation outcomes. Biodiversity has continued to decline globally since the inception of CITES and the rise of public-voluntary support for conservation objectives. Many species have become more endangered. Others have shown increases in numbers, but not necessarily as a clear result of CITES actions or the hybrid arrangements explored in this chapter.

The fight against illegal wildlife trade confounds a straightforward assessment of any relationship between accountability frameworks and environmental outcomes. The underlying assumption is that working together will (somehow) lead to better environmental outcomes. Yet hybrid public-voluntary relationships are highly variable. They may range from longstanding, formally structured interactions, to situations where one party simply adopts the modalities of another. As we have demonstrated here, accountability across these arrangements is correspondingly wide-ranging.

Notes

1. We are conscious, of course, that in the security sector in particular there is a long history of "state agency" being delegated to nonstate actors, though often those who function more in the private rather than voluntary sectors.

2. In 2015, for example, the WWF Wildlife Crime Initiative launched a demand reduction campaign focusing on rhino horn with the support of the Vietnamese CITES management authority. WWF's Zero Poaching Framework, developed on the back of the Tigers Alive Initiative, has been endorsed by all thirteen tiger range

states. Elisabeth McLellan and Crawford Allan, *Wildlife Crime Initiative Annual Update 2015* (Gland: WWF and TRAFFIC, 2015), 9.

3. Ironically, government officials and NGO representatives often express similar sentiments. One of us (Schaedla) has worked extensively on NGO "augmentation" of government enforcement activities in Southeast Asia. Government participants in these arrangements regularly expressed concerns that the NGOs lacked legal authority to conduct enforcement work. Yet their concerns usually took a back seat to more pressing needs for the efficacy boost provided by NGO material support and technical skills. NGO partners likewise worried about undermining individual legal cases and the long-term efficacy of enforcement agencies, but nevertheless continued the support on the grounds that the engagements were necessary to prevent species extinctions.

4. At time of writing, more than 35,000 species are protected from over-exploitation through trade under CITES rules. Approximately 5,600 of those are animal species: the remainder, about 30,000, are plant species.

5. At the time of the agreement, WWF was known collectively as the World Wildlife Fund. As the present time, however, only the United States Office and its subsidiaries refer to themselves by this acronym. The remaining WWF offices identify as the World Wide Fund for Nature.

6. CITES Non-Detriment Findings (NDFs) are required under Articles III and IV of the Convention. The wording stipulates that national scientific authorities must conduct assessments of species proposed for trade to ensure the proposed exports do not adversely impact populations.

7. The Convention, sometimes also known as the *Washington Convention,* was not negotiated under UN auspices. However the United Nations Environment Programme (UNEP) in Geneva hosts the CITES Secretariat.

8. The ECOSOC Credentialing Arrangements require that NGOs "shall be of recognized standing within the particular field of its competence or of a representative character." Steve Charnovitz, "Accountability of Non-governmental Organizations in Global Governance," in *NGO Accountability: Politics, Principles and Innovation*, ed. Lisa Jordan and Peter van Tuijl (London, UK: Earthscan, 2006), 24.

9. In their discussion of networks, NGOs, and the fight against environmental crime, Smith and Klaas pick up on this idea of legislative authority in their description of NGOs as "non-legal" actors. Lucy Smith and Katharina Klaas, *Networks and NGOs Relevant to Fighting Environmental Crime* (Berlin, Germany: Ecologic Institute, 2015), iii.

10. All PROTECT/DETECT curricula are accredited by the American Council on Education (ACE) (PROTECT/DETECT, 2017). ACE represents nearly 1,800 higher learning institutions, and is the largest college and university accreditation body in the

United States; see http://www.acenet.edu/about-ace/pages/default.aspx. It provides college credit for PROTECT/DETECT courses, and allows the credits to transfer across institutions. Training programs on offer from different NGOs are ostensibly comparable. Most cover similar topics and nearly all entail some form of external review or accreditation. However, offerings by one NGO are seldom recognized by others, and it is left largely to donors and agencies receiving training to make judgments about their equivalency.

11. It is notable that many of these NGOs employ highly qualified professional staff who are responsible for contract management and financial transparency and accountability.

12. These general observations were motivated by its discussion of INTERPOL's Project Oasis, a capacity building initiative in Africa.

13. In this particular report at least, the CITES Enforcement Expert Group was somewhat inconsistent in its approach to NGOs. In later sections of the report it noted that it had found "particularly useful a check list of actions ... developed by TRAFFIC for the Wildlife Trade Enforcement Group of the European Union" (2009, paragraph 14). It also welcomed a submission by the Environmental Investigation Agency—a "non-governmental organization"—and "encouraged the CITES Secretariat to take account of the submission as it prepared for the tiger conservation strategy workshop" (2009, paragraph 18).

14. ETIS was a development of the Bad Ivory Database System (BIDS) that TRAFFIC established in 1992.

15. By January 2016, the ETIS database held 24,636 seizure records of ivory and elephant products. Tom Milliken, Fiona M. Underwood, Robert W. Burn, and Louisa Sangalakula, *The Elephant Trade Information System (ETIS) and the Illicit Trade in Ivory*, the report to the 17th meeting of the Conference of the Parties to CITES, CoP17 Doc. 57.6 (Rev.1) Annex, May 27, 2016, 3.

16. It is worth noting that TRAFFIC did subject its BIDS database, the forerunner of ETIS, to an external evaluation process as a step in the development of a more sophisticated monitoring tool.

17. TAG minutes are publicly available on the CITES website.

18. Reports must include an overview of the methods used for data analysis. Transparency on models and calculations has been further enhanced through the publication of open-access articles. See, for example, Fiona M. Underwood, Robert W. Burn, and Tom Milliken, "Dissecting the Illegal Ivory Trade: an Analysis of Ivory Seizures Data," *PLOS ONE* 8, no. 10 (2013): 1–12.

19. Although known as an EU tool, enforcement agencies in 36 European countries (that is, more than the 28 EU countries) have access to this information and communication system. So too do officials from the European Commission, the CITES

Secretariat, INTERPOL, UNODC, the WCO, Eurojust, Europol and the EU Network for the Implementation and Enforcement of Environmental Law.

20. It also contains a number of directories that enable users to find contact information for relevant experts.

21. Under the TWIX arrangement, TRAFFIC is the legal owner of the database platform but not the data itself. See, Convention on International Trade in Endangered Species (CITES) of Wild Fauna and Flora. Enforcement "Matters and the Development of a Global Seizures Database." Fifteenth meeting of the Conference of the Parties Doha (Qatar), March 13–25, 2010, CoP15 Inf. 37, 3.

22. Environmental Investigation Agency, "About Us," last updated in 2018, https://eia-international.org/about-eia. EIA also undertakes investigations on the illegal timber trade, the black market in ozone depleting substances, and electronic waste (e-waste).

23. Investigators from the organization have been excluded from Cambodia and denied visas because of their work in the country (EIA 2005).

24. "INTERPOL's Largest Operation Combating Illegal Ivory Trafficking Targets Criminal Syndicates," *Interpol Media Release*, June 19, 2012, https://www.interpol.int/News-and-media/News/2012/PR049.

IV Conclusion

8 Does Accountability Matter for Global Environmental Governance?

Susan Park and Teresa Kramarz

Introduction

The volume began with the recognition that both global environmental governance (GEG) and attendant accountability mechanisms have flourished over the past two decades. *Accountability* has become a buzzword in global governance and, as this volume shows, accountability processes have emerged in a variety of contexts where actors attempt to govern the impact we have on the biosphere. Yet this has led to a trap: there has been a growth of accountability mechanisms for holding those governing the global environment to account, built on the assumption that this will improve governance and therefore environmental outcomes—while environmental degradation continues relentlessly. The purpose of this volume was to probe how actors governing the earth's systems are using accountability, and whether accountability mechanisms can improve global environmental outcomes. Our point of departure was that accountability is a means to an end, and as such must be measured against its dual promise: improving environmental outcomes and being responsive to stakeholders affected by environmental problems. As we described in chapter 1 of this volume, this promise of accountability is derived from the claims and standards set by actors in and with authority for governing the global environment.

In that chapter, we proposed that scholars of accountability must investigate the goals of the multiple actors engaged in public, private, voluntary, and hybrid global environmental institutions. Given the multiplicity of actors in GEG, we must recognize that they have different goals guiding their actions, which determine to whom and for what an account must be rendered. This is important considering that accountability is often understood as "public" accountability, or where citizens are able to hold their representatives to account within a democratic context. That a variety of actors at the global level have different goals for which they render an account to different audiences influences the framing of their environmental priorities and how their accountability is devised and measured. We provided a theoretical framework for tracing how ideal-type public, private, and voluntary governance institutions prioritize different goals: the provision of public goods, profitmaking social welfare, and spreading moral conduct. In practice, there are also attempts to deliver more than one of these goals in hybrid governance arrangements.

Identifying the normative goals of those who have authority to shape the rules of environmental governance is important because it structures the interventions they instigate to address environmental problems. It also influences the accountability procedures that they establish to hold themselves accountable for those interventions. We argue that accountability mechanisms often fall short of delivering the intended environmental outcomes because environmental goals are subservient to prior and more important goals held by different types of environmental governors across these institutions. When there are competing interests, environmental goals take a back seat to public goods, profit, or moral conduct. The contributors of this volume examine how those governing the global environment are attempting to be accountable and to what effect. Each chapter identifies the normative goals that guide different accountability mechanisms by analyzing who is being held to account, to whom, and for what.

The theoretical framework established in the introduction proposed interrogating environmental accountability at two tiers of governance: the design, and the execution of environmental interventions. As we suspected, authority holders may be held to account for their actions without necessarily mitigating negative environmental impacts. Authority holders are held to account through existing governance institutions that bias goals such as short-term economic gains over environmental ones. This is because those establishing GEG are not held to account for the first tier of governance: where problems are framed, priorities identified, and solutions devised. The current literature tends to apply accountability to established governing processes rather than investigate whether, for what, and to whom those in authority were answerable in designing any given environmental intervention. This is vital because the risk of applying accountability purely to functional concerns of verification, measurement, and compliance obviates the analytically prior questions that determine which accountability mechanisms matter for improved environmental outcomes.

For this reason, the first half of the volume assesses how the goals of GEG shape accountability processes by interrogating the design of governing institutions that address environmental problems. In doing so public, private, and voluntary governance arrangements are investigated in terms of how they were created to address environmental issues. The second half of the volume reviews how accountability procedures work in holding authority holders to account for delivering on their promises. Here, the contributors identify the different standards, processes, and sanctions of accountability for hybrid governance arrangements. In other words, they assess whether or not the accountability procedures created by those governing the environment are actually helping to stem further environmental deterioration. Throughout all of the chapters we question whether there is a feedback loop from the design of institutions to the creation of accountability mechanisms, and whether the operation of the accountability mechanisms at Tier 2 of governance reconstitutes the goals of GEG institutions at Tier 1.

This concluding chapter is structured in four parts. First, we survey the different normative priorities of public, private, and voluntary governance for holding those in authority to account for their environmental impact. Here, we analyze the different accountability demands placed on public, private, voluntary, and hybrid environmental governors. We also document how new accountability relationships are being forged between actors that may not have existed previously and how this intersects with the self-directed accountability processes which we have taken as of primary importance in the first chapter (see chapter 1, in this volume, figure 1.3). Second, we question whether the globality of governing the environment creates accountability gaps or whether holding multiple governors to account in each step of an increasingly global accountability chain is an effective and meaningful tool for environmental action. Third, we review the findings of the chapters within the volume to question whether accountability procedures are being used as feedback loops for redesigning institutions to further improve their impact on the environment. Fourth, we return to the original provocation of this volume and examine ways to redress the accountability trap. Based on the evidence provided throughout this volume, we argue that so long as accountability is viewed through the lens of compliance and enforcement, rather than learning, the accountability trap will remain at both tiers of GEG and for all types of governance arrangements.

Who Governs?

As described in chapter 1, our theoretical framework is informed by a constructivist understanding of international relations in which accountability emerges as a relational concept that is defined intersubjectively by social actors who constitute and regulate its practice. Accountability is practiced differently in a variety of institutional contexts. Although this is a result of both agents and structures, a foundational premise of our volume is that the logic of action that animates different institutional arrangements addressing environmental problems matters greatly. This constitutive argument focuses on how the structure of GEG institutions reflect public, private, and voluntary actors that have different goals, with corresponding responsibilities to target audiences. These goals delimit the options considered when designing environmental interventions that are deemed appropriate. In other words, they have a constitutive effect on actors' understanding of the purpose of accountability in the first place. To reiterate the theoretical argument: public, private, and voluntary logics of action generate specific governance goals which influence for what and how different actors are held responsible in environmental institutions. This determines how their actions are rendered to a relevant community at two tiers of governance. The first tier is the original design of governance institutions, where problems are framed, priorities identified, and solutions devised. The second tier of GEG is the execution of environmental interventions where verification, measurement, and compliance are evaluated. We therefore premised that other types of accountability exist beyond public accountability. For instance, corporations are evaluated on market accountability, and voluntary actors are held to account for meeting shared understandings of appropriate behavior. We proposed that environmental governors internalize a need to act and render an account of their actions based on bureaucratic, utilitarian, or moral standards. These standards may lead to important governance dysfunctions rather than curbing environmental degradation.

Hybrid GEG arrangements raise difficulties in terms of accountability. How accountability processes, standards, and sanctions are determined and implemented is opaque, and it can be difficult to know who to hold to account, to whom, and for what. We contend that there is a hierarchy of goals in hybrid arrangements, and that a case-by-case analysis reveals the prioritization of certain public goods, profit and social welfare, and the spread of moral behavior. Benchmarks of accountability in public, private, voluntary, and hybrid governance arrangements are discussed in relation to the findings of the chapters.

Public Governance

The standard benchmark for what constitutes accountability is rooted in democracy. Public officials are held to account through democratic elections and bureaucratic procedures (Rubin 2006, 76–77). Public officials and bureaucrats respond to public demands for addressing environmental problems by establishing and upholding legislation and international agreements. The execution of public accountability focuses on holding signatory states responsible to treaties, protocols, and agreements between states, while delegating the monitoring of many of these agreements to international organizations.

Chapter 2, by Aarti Gupta and Harro van Asselt, investigates how states are held to account for meeting agreed upon carbon reduction targets through the United Nations Framework Convention on Climate Change (UNFCCC). International treatymaking privileges demonstrating accountability through increasing transparency and disclosing information. Under the 2015 Paris Agreement, states have committed to holding each other to account for their carbon reductions through a "pledge and review" procedure that facilitates greater transparency. This was a distinct shift from the "targets and timetable" model that had been in place under the 1997 Kyoto Protocol. In order to be effective, states have agreed to hold each other to account for reducing their climate impact through non-legally-binding nationally determined contributions (NDCs). This means that transparency is understood as a vital component of accountability, because it is a tool that allows the monitoring of states' compliance in meeting their commitments. The Paris Agreement provides the prospect of greater accountability through its "enhanced transparency framework," which commits states to new reporting and review requirements.

Underpinning this commitment to addressing climate change through the UNFCCC, and fundamental to the conception of public accountability, is an adherence to state sovereignty. This ultimately means that concerned stakeholders and the biosphere are reliant on states providing accurate information on their actions to reduce carbon emissions and that shaming rather than coercion from other states is the means that will induce greater action. The UNFCCC process has continued to grapple with how to address inequalities between states for setting climate commitments. While the norm of common but differentiated responsibilities is entrenched within the UNFCCC, the normative bias of public accountability remains fraught over the UNFCCC's handling of the notion of sovereign equality in the face of states' inequality with regard to responsibility and burden sharing. For now, this means that states continue to determine whether their climate commitments are "fair" for their electorates and compared with other states' commitments. Hanging the success of the UNFCCC for reducing global warming on the enhanced transparency framework demonstrates the extent to which public accountability is normatively biased toward state sovereignty (and the logic of representation for the provision of competing public goods at the national level) over global environmental protection.

Private Governance

Private governance is now a major feature of GEG. The primary goal of private governance is to maintain profitability for shareholders while abiding by rules designed to maximize social welfare. While consumers and shareholders hold producers and suppliers accountable for meeting regulatory and social standards of appropriate business practice, this has been grafted onto market practices that generate profit. Thus, environmental issues have been incorporated into market transactions, which constrains profit making but does not make environmentalism an authoritative goal in its own right. As outlined in chapter 1, the processes of accountability have been included in the business model by adapting organizational practices, as supplements in supply chains, and included in logistical decision making, annual financial reports, and extra certification schemes. Standards that demonstrate accountability include the price, availability, and ease of access to desired goods and services within the scope of acceptable business practices. Added onto these are social and environmental benchmarks. Failure to meet these standards could result in litigation, as well as reputation and profit loss.

In chapter 3, Hamish van der Ven traced the increasing attempts at governing the environmental impact of global value chains. This is not a traditional form of governance, such as an international environmental treaty between states. Nor is it a voluntary commitment to specific standards formed around voluntary guidelines based on an industry or product, such as the International Council of Chemical Association's Responsible Care program (Vogel 2008, 269). However, a purely private GEG institution can be identified through regularized attempts to limit certain practices that negatively impact the environment. The chapter maps how the various corporate actors within global value chains are being held to account. Primarily driven by concerned nongovernment organizations (NGOs), corporations, particularly "lead firms," are attempting to be accountable to consumers. Yet this is not a case of producers and suppliers of goods being held accountable directly by either NGOs or consumers; instead, they are being held accountable to third-party certifiers of environmental standards (Cashore, Newsom, and Auld 2004).

Third-party certifiers, such as independent conformance assessment bodies (CABs), provide "club goods" that benefit corporations while providing independent analysis of whether a firm is meeting its environmental standards (Prakash and Potoski 2010). However, the relationship remains conflicted. As van der Ven points out, CABs must hold companies to account for meeting certain standards, otherwise CABs will not be viewed as legitimate by stakeholders such as NGOs. On the other hand, the standards must not be too stringent, otherwise no company will be able to meet their standards and companies will choose other certification schemes to pay to voluntarily follow (see also chapters 5 and 6 of this volume).

Problematically, CABs direct accountability relationship is with the producer and supplier, while the normative priority remains that the corporation adhere to survival and profit over environmental standards. As van der Ven demonstrates, at each level of the supply chain there are accountability procedures in place, but the private contractual relationship of that accountability undermines the ability to uphold environmental standards. In global value chains, lead firms may change contracts with producers or suppliers for economic reasons which could undermine or even sever contracts with companies that are strong environmental performers.

Do private governors adhere to a different form of accountability? Or should we speak of the increasing "publicness" of corporations (Freeman 2006, 83–86)? It is clear that some of the processes for holding private governors to account do seem to be similar to those holding public actors to account for the provision of public goods such as the health of the biosphere. In public and private accountability, the disclosure of information is vital for being able to determine whether or not actors are doing as they say they are doing—although types of disclosure differ between public and private sectors. Yet accountability sanctions for public versus private sector governors are not the same: international treaties and domestic law on the one hand, compared with voluntary guidelines determined largely by companies and (some) domestic law on the other. Although the force of the sanctions remains different, they share the prospect of legal action: public actors may be kicked out of office while firms may face reputation loss, consumer boycotts, and economic losses. The fundamental distinction between public and private actors is the problem of holding private actors to account for public goods when their primary normative commitment is fitness of the firm as measured by profit. While contractual relationships between the state and corporations may hold private actors to account for public goods, frequently this does not align with the normative commitment to uphold environmental standards within the timeframe necessary for ecosystem health (see Rosenberg 2017; Balboa 2016).

Voluntary Governance

Voluntary governance accountability for global environmental benefits is much less commonly discussed than public or private governance. As illustrated in van der Ven's chapter on accountability in global value chains, environmental NGOs (ENGOs) can also create governance arrangements— although this may not fit traditional understandings of global governance. In chapter 1, we identified Carbon Action Rationing Groups (CRAGs) that seek to extend selfless carbon-reducing behavior through self-monitoring and shaming, but we can also point to the rise of ENGOs in specific issue areas to identify how they are increasingly constituting the rules for governing the environment.

In chapter 4, Cristina Balboa looks at the role of conservation NGOs in identifying specific practices for protecting the biosphere. Voluntary actors such as ENGOs are held to account for constructing ethical frames and socializing a standard of acceptable conduct to hold others and themselves accountable. The processes voluntary actors use to demonstrate their accountability is to provide information of their practices and engage in campaigns, lobbying, and marketing to spread their ideas. The standards of accountability to which they are held is determined by their social networks. Failure to be responsible and answerable for spreading new ideas and ethical frameworks could lead to reputation loss, or being "named and shamed," leading to a loss of brand influence and materially undermining the operation of the organization or association.

Balboa's chapter reveals the problems inherent in having no agreement among conservation NGOs over how to govern the biosphere. Here, competing ENGOs debate whether a conservation, new conservation, or preservation approach is best and where to biophysically focus their attention. Thus, there is no accountability for how large ENGOs choose to address environmental degradation at the design stage of environmental governance. This is vitally important considering the increasingly monopolistic organization of ENGOs globally.

Of course, ENGOs face pressure to be accountable, not just to each other, but to donors through contractual relationships, members and supporters through their normative commitments and actions, and governments for their legal status (this is discussed more a little later in the chapter). For Balboa, ENGOs therefore face an internal crisis: they can single mindedly continue to address environmental degradation following their normative commitment (whether it be new conservation or preservation), or they can attempt to be accountable to a range of stakeholders who may question that given approach, which in turn may lead to a redirection of organizational resources. Balboa, following Koppell (2006), frames this as deliberating between a single accountability disorder (SAD) versus a multiple accountability disorder (MAD). A third way, she argues, is possible: a balanced state that seeks to offset being accountable to a range of stakeholders while remaining "true to mission." This precarious position is intrinsic to being an NGO: it is dependent on establishing and agreeing on moral ethical frames that others will take up. Rather than meeting the terms of office or the bottom line, ENGOs must be relevant, competent, and persuasive to competing audiences to continue to govern the environment.

Beyond self-imposed social standards, the voluntary sector is important because it continues to demand public regulation over environmentally degrading practices and to hold private actors to account. Being able to hold actors in positions of authority responsible and answerable for their actions is to determine what broader social goals matter and what are the legitimate grounds for making authority holders accountable. This stems from social networks as a site of "meaning-making" regarding what constitutes acceptable behavior. As chapter 3 demonstrates, voluntary accountability can bring actors together into a hierarchical authority relationship where none before existed, such as prompting the creation of CABs for suppliers and producers.

Lorraine Elliott and William Schaedla's chapter on the relationship between ENGOs and states also demonstrates how voluntary governors can create proxies for public accountability measures. Both reveal how ENGOs wield their legitimacy and gain authority over corporations and the state. This role fundamentally relies on the moral authority of NGOs above the perception of power derived from public office or the pursuit of survival and profit of market actors. For this reason, voluntary actors are held to a distinct form of accountability.

Hybrid Governance

GEG is more than just any single public, private, or voluntary institution attempting to address a specific environmental problem. Environmental action is characterized by wide, deep, and hybrid relationships between actors from different types of institutions, who come together to jointly design rules and implement activities to address the ongoing deterioration of the earth's systems. In this volume, we have highlighted how divergent logics of action between these institutions have an impact on the resulting types of accountability that they generate. In chapter 1, we mapped three ideal-type institutions: public, private, and voluntary. For each of these, we described their primary purpose, the main actors subject to accountability, stakeholders to whom accountability is owed, and the normative priorities, processes, standards and sanctions. However, as previously mentioned hybrid GEG arrangements raise difficulties in terms of accountability. How accountability processes, standards, and sanctions are determined and implemented is opaque, and it can be difficult to know who to hold to account, to whom, and for what.

As noted in chapter 5, by Oscar Widerberg, Philipp Pattberg, and Lieke Brouwer, mapping the accountability of the various actors that comprise hybrid GEG arrangements is complex in the sense of identifying who is accountable to whom and for what. It becomes more complicated when actors have to negotiate the processes, standards, and sanctions for demonstrating accountability without a clear sense of how other actors are working toward protecting the environment. Across the four cases discussed there—Lean and Green (L&G), the Compact of States and Regions (CSR), the Portfolio Decarbonization Coalition (PDC), and the Roundtable on Sustainable Biofuels (RSB)—there is a wide variety of processes, standards, and sanctions for demonstrating accountability with no clear sense of which, if any, are the most optimal for meeting their objectives. For all of the cases examined, it remains unclear how much their actions contribute to reducing global emissions.

Chapter 7, by Elliott and Schaedla, illustrates how the voluntary guidelines established by ENGOs have been taken up by states to become the means of ensuring verification, monitoring, and compliance for the illegal wildlife trade. In this case, states and international organizations adopt ENGO processes and standards of accountability without a clear interrogation of to whom and for what ENGOs were accountable in designing them. In contrast, in chapter 4, Balboa shows that ENGOs are holding themselves to account to a variety of stakeholders for a range of goals beyond the functional delivery of any discreet set of agreed upon goods.

We therefore question whether hybrid initiatives necessarily offer the global environment something greater than the sum of their parts. The contributions in this volume suggest that they do not create a distinct, pro-environmental logic of action that supersedes the individual purposes of the institutional actors who comprise them. As chapter 6, by Lars Gulbrandsen and Graeme Auld, demonstrates, hybrid governance arrangements such as the Marine Stewardship Council (MSC) become sites for contestation of competing institutional purposes and logics of action. The MSC, a nonstate certification initiative comprised of private and voluntary actors, must navigate the dual agendas of profit and sustainability. Actors from the voluntary sector are concerned with the limited access and influence they have in promoting their agenda of environmental standards within this hybrid institution, which they are helping generate demand for while contributing to profit for certified fisheries.

This illustrates how the dual purposes of profit and moral conduct are not wedded into one broader logic of action under the MSC umbrella. Instead, these individual purposes present themselves as two separate legs on which the hybrid institution is built. This leads to a negotiation over to whom and for what the hybrid arrangement is accountable. In this case, the accountability mechanism of this hybrid governance arrangement must struggle with delivering something greater than the sum of its parts. Under conditions of competing purposes, to whom and for what matters most in hybrid governing arrangements? Do the various private-voluntary initiatives under the UNFCCC, or the MSC, hew to market standards of accountability? Are they able to balance market and public or voluntary standards? Multiple accountability relationships compete due to different logics of action, determining what goals matter most.

Chapter 3, by van der Ven, describes precisely how the private purposes of rent seekers become all-encompassing in the accountability of global value chains, subsuming environmental goals. Hence, it is crucial to identify and reveal the hierarchy of values for which each GEG institution holds itself accountable. One of the key contributions of this volume is to provide an analytical framework and empirical account of the variation that exists among different accountability arrangements, given the distinctive goals and means that characterize public, private, voluntary, and hybrid governance institutions.

The Multiple Accountabilities of Global Environmental Governance

Our volume analyzes the multiple accountabilities that emerge in the context of globalization. The theoretical framework identified in the introduction mapped out the key questions of accountability for institutions operating under public, private, and voluntary logics of action: whom, for what, to whom, and what standards, processes and sanctions are used to show accountability (Marshaw 2006)? We developed a table of the goals and means of accountability according to these three traditional types of governance institutions (see figure 1.3 in chapter 1), which provides an analytical map defining ideal-type accountability systems based on the logics of action of public, private, and voluntary sectors. Mapping accountability in this fashion allows us to investigate within and across arrangements in two specific ways. Within each governance institution, we are able to identify the accountability obligations between actors based on their priorities, and the tools used to demonstrate and implement accountability. Across institutional types, we are able to identify the nature and extent of mixing and borrowing from different systems of accountability in any given environmental initiative.

Applying the framework to the empirical chapters reveals a pattern of continuity with the environmental accountability established in figure 1.3, as well as departures from it. The chapters demonstrate that public, private, and voluntary actors hold their main purpose, and who is held to account, as a constant in the constitutive first tier of governance. For example, public actors are defined by their main purpose (to represent) and elected officials and civil servants are those to be held to account. The chapters in this volume show that these features of representation and accountability by public officials remain constant even when public actors become part of public-private or private-voluntary institutions. However, other aspects of the accountability systems listed in figure 1.3 become unmoored.

Throughout this volume, our contributors demonstrate that actors are not limited to the supposedly traditional accountability relationships that we mapped in chapter 1. This is pertinent in terms of whom they hold themselves accountable to, as well as for what, and through which means they demonstrate that accountability. Balboa's chapter illustrates that NGOs struggle deeply with the questions of to whom and for what they should hold themselves accountable. In practice, accountability relationships are more networked and webbed than the table of ideal types denotes. Owing, in part, to the increasingly hybrid nature of GEG, there are now multiple accountability relationships between public, private, and voluntary actors (Kuyper and Backstrand 2016), which brings actors together in variations of hierarchical and horizontal relationships where no such codependencies had previously existed (Gulbrandsen 2008). Some scholars have mapped these relationships according to a principal-agent model approach to accountability (see Rosenberg 2017, as well as chapter 4 in this volume), or how principals and contracted agents are being held accountable through those relationships. Of course, this is just one way to examine the accountability relationships between multiple actors in GEG; there need not be a contract for an accountability relationship to exist.

For example, corporate actors in the public-voluntary agreements identified by Wideberg, Pattberg, and Brouwer in chapter 5 under the polycentric UNFCCC umbrella may now be held to account by ENGOs trying to trace whether or not these commitments are being upheld. Unlike the principal-agent model, where principals delegate to agents to undertake tasks on their behalf as identified by a contract, these relationships are nonlinear.

They are nonlinear in the sense that these actors may be held to account by different actors for separate things. In the case of the UNFCCC voluntary initiatives, transport companies may be held to account by their shareholders for the impact their voluntary pledge has on their bottom line and reputation, while the company is being held to account for meeting its pledge to L&G, and L&G must demonstrate that its actions are consistent with carbon reductions in accordance with the UNFCCC. Moreover, the company is also in an accountability relationship with its consumers, the states in which it operates, and civil society groups that are affected by its operations. These are not linear in the sense of only being unidirectional pathways for holding the company, certification system, and UNFCCC to account. Rather, they are webbed, meaning that these accountability relationships overlap, and come from a variety of directions and compete in terms of demanding actor's attention.

Balboa's chapter on ENGOs demonstrates this complexity for how voluntary actors seek to hold themselves and each other to account, while simultaneously being held accountable by donors and governments as well. The evidence points to mongrelized systems of accountability that mix and match obligations to different stakeholders without necessarily prioritizing environment outcomes or the welfare of those most vulnerable to environmental deterioration in the resulting arrangements. Furthermore, as Gulbrandsen and Auld note, calls from scholars for greater or deeper relationships of accountability in nontraditional modes of governance are unlikely to result in more democratic modes of accountability (see chapter 6 in this volume; see also Bäckstrand 2008 and Abbot and Snidal 2009). Consistent with our analytical propositions in chapter 1, they find that the divergent goals that multiple actors bring into hybrid governance arrangements sets the stage for greater contestation of who and what to account for. However, in cases like the MSC, this only results in greater accountability to actors who were already influential.

The privateness or publicness of any given actor engaged in environmental governance is no longer wholly defined by its institutional identity. For example, NGO behavior may operate according to its institutional governance type, but it may also diverge from it. Traditional voluntary governance includes an NGO demanding accountability to prioritize ethical frames, by relying on information campaigns and resorting to naming and shaming as a sanction for failing to meet accountability standards.

Chapter 6, by Gulbrandsen and Auld, epitomizes this approach. It describes the traditional tactic of naming and shaming by environmental groups to force private firms to seek certification for the environmental and social impact of their operations. But they may also go beyond this in terms of their normative priority at the constitutive tier of governance. In contrast, in Elliott and Schaedla's chapter, NGOs become proxies of public accountability. They highlight how states and NGOs work together as partners to accumulate embarrassing information on other states' illegal trade, then use the mechanism of naming and shaming against each other as parties to CITES. This means that NGOs are responding to regulatory demands, upholding and obeying the law, not abusing powers, and serving the public interest. These are activities that we have traditionally identified as the normative priority of public accountability.

We see this also occurring in private governance. Chapter 5, by Widerberg, Pattberg, and Brouwer, shows how private actors seek to establish public standards of accountability through voluntary initiatives that fit under the UNFCCC umbrella. The variance in goals and means deployed by public, private, and voluntary actors requires scholars to conceptualize hybridity in broader terms, which go beyond the institutional identity of a given actor. The nature of hybridity in GEG is nuanced and transcends the institutional identities of the actors that comprise new governance initiatives. The hybrid governance cases analyzed by our contributors suggest a need to delve deeper into the transactional quality of the relationships between actors.

For example, in chapter 3, one could argue that private corporations are taking on public roles and trying to promote environmental standards, yet the mechanisms of accountability are not hybrid but remain market oriented. In this chapter, a market for virtue exists for purchase between consumers and suppliers. In chapter 6, this market exists between fishing producers and individual consumers, and in chapter 5, it is between carbon emitters. Yet, in none of these cases are private actors doing the governing by themselves.

Learning from Practice: Accountability as a Feedback Tool

As we discussed previously, the chapters in this volume uncover both expected and unexpected features of traditional accountability systems in

GEG. Some of the behavior documented in the chapters diverges from the theoretical expectations laid out in chapter 1, while other accountability relationships, such as the hybridized relationships highlighted, are not explicitly addressed therein. What is most revealing, however, is that mechanisms of accountability discussed across all the chapters are still primarily designed as tools for monitoring and sanctioning unwanted actions. This upholds a particular conception of accountability based on verification, measurement, and compliance, whether it be for public, private, voluntary, or hybrid governance. Although the sanctions for noncompliance vary in intensity and type, the field as a whole tends to view accountability as control and compliance rather than learning.

We argue that a narrow approach to accountability as compliance remains a fundamental obstacle to obtaining meaningful environmental action (Kramarz and Park 2016). In chapter 1, we differentiated between two tiers of governance. The first tier comprised the actors and decisions involved in the design of environmental interventions while the second tier concerned itself with the mechanisms of execution of these interventions. We proposed, and our contributors illustrated in the empirical cases, that there are foundational questions related to accountability in both tiers of governance, but scholars and practitioners to date have tended to focus on accountability when dealing with implementation concerns. As we conclude this volume, we return to this proposition and draw out the link between Tier 1 "constitutive" and Tier 2 "regulative" components of accountability in GEG. We examined earlier whether the connections between the two run only in one direction or both ways. In other words, the constitutive rules creating GEG institutions frame environmental problems in certain ways, which delimit how environmental accountability is understood. That connection is clear. Less clear is whether regulative accountability procedures and mechanisms feed back into recalibrating the design of GEG institutions.

Can accountability become a tool for feedback and learning to better achieve these goals? Ebrahim (2005) characterizes the lack of organizational learning as one of the key myopias inherent in prevailing conceptions of accountability in service oriented sectors. According to Ebrahim (2003), the absence of learning is a feature of the functional approach to accountability, which aligns with our description of Tier 2 regulative governance questions. Raggo (2014) conducted in-depth interviews on accountability with 150 leaders of transnational NGOs and found that learning was the least important aspect of respondent organization's accountability strategies. More recent scholarship is starting to look at conditions where accountability could lead to organizational learning. For example, the analysis of workplace learning from Shilemanns and Smulders (2015, 248) finds that "organizational learning may thrive under the condition of multiple accountability and generally requires a combination of control *and* critical feedback."

One of the most important limitations of current accountability mechanisms within GEG is the missed opportunity of feedback to adapt the design of institutions or interventions so that these become more effective in addressing the environmental outcomes they were ostensibly set up to achieve. The focus remains on short-term performance outputs rather than on long-term transformational outcomes. Some of the chapters in this volume attest to this truncated relationship between accountability and learning for improved design and implementation of environmental interventions.

The continued reliance on accountability as a tool of command and control proves to be a gating factor in its promise to improve environmental governance. Gulbrandsen and Auld go one step further in chapter 6, suggesting that ignoring feedback and remaining tone deaf in the practice of implementing environmental interventions, like the MSC, can push excluded stakeholders to seek rival processes that promote their own objectives. This undermines the MSC's certification system and its potential impact on sustainable fisheries, further fragments environmental governance, and endangers further duplication of efforts.

Furthermore, cases like the MSC show that learning from NGO demands for greater accountability translated into bolstering internal consultation procedures rather than granting influence over decision making to these stakeholders. In this sense, the MSC "learned" how to better manage its stakeholders rather than better respond to the nature of their claims. It would be hard to argue that, in providing consultative rather than adjudicative influence to stakeholders, the MSC procured either of the goals that accountability mechanisms were set up to achieve: improved environmental outcomes and responsiveness to stakeholders affected by environmental problems. This example suggests that future research on accountability and learning must be sensitive to the analytical distinction between procedural versus substantive dimensions of learning.

An important exception to the claim that there is a truncated relationship between accountability and learning is Gupta and van Asselt's chapter 2, which finds some potential for feedback loops in the UNFCCC's transparency mechanism. This chapter looks at the question of whether the operationalization of an enhanced transparency framework, a key component of accountability, can be transformative and spur environmental change. The authors are interested in investigating under what conditions transparency may do more than reveal and begin to shape pro-environmental action by parties to the Convention. They argue that the practice of disclosing contributions to reduce greenhouse gas emissions may serve as a feedback loop to ratchet up ambitions. In this case, the authors find that, at least theoretically, there is potential for the implementation of transparency initiatives to contribute to the quality of future environmental commitments.

Considering the global environment is governed by institutions with agency to reshape goals and priorities, it would have seemed plausible to assume some sort of feedback loop. We theorized that if accountability tools were being adhered to but were not contributing to an improved environment, then adherence was not the main problem in environmental governance. Instead, as the empirical chapters of this collection bear out, outside the potential in the case of states in the UNFCCC, accountability processes, standards, and sanctions are not feeding back into the redesign of GEG procedures, precluding the opportunity to learn and adapt based on experience with implementation.

Addressing the Accountability Trap in Global Environmental Governance

This brings us back to the beginning of our volume and the trap that ignited the debate between our contributors: how do we explain the growing number of accountability mechanisms alongside the continued decline of the global environment? Is accountability indeed a necessary or sufficient condition for improving environmental outcomes? The case studies in this volume offered several responses.

Our response to the trap, which Gupta and van Asselt illustrate in the case of public accountability in the UNFCCC, is that accountability fails the environment when it is mainly focused on what we call Tier 2 governance concerns with implementation and what Gupta and Van Asselt call "ex post accountability." We contend that the scholarship and practice of accountability needs to shift its focus to who, what, and why questions of environmental action, which inform the design of interventions and underpin any subsequent effort of implementation.

The chapter by van der Ven, on private accountability, finds that in global value chains, accountability demands from consumers are reinterpreted by each producer in a long chain of communication that begins to resemble a game of broken telephone. Since none of these producers are actually accountable to the environment, the end product falls short of the original consumer signal. This explains why more accountability mechanisms, both up and down a global value chain, ultimately have limited effects on producing the desired environmental outcomes that consumers had in mind when they committed to voting with their wallets. In fact, the author suggests that maintaining a limited focus on using accountability to ensure compliance for narrow environmental goals will be counterproductive to environmental outcomes. This chapter shows that design decisions that require accountability do not just need to happen simply at the beginning of a process where a new product or intervention is being launched. Design decisions that require accountability happen all along a causal chain. Each time there is an implementation decision to be made there is a design opportunity for accountability to be realized.

Balboa's chapter, on voluntary accountability, advances another explanation to the trap of more accountability without better environmental outcomes. Proliferating accountability mechanisms within the ENGO sector run at cross-purposes with multiple conceptions of environmental protection. Hence, ENGOs are accounting for different ideas of nature and what is worth conserving, for whom, and why. This chapter highlights the impact of contested conservation values and goals within voluntary governance. Balboa traces the effects of unresolved fragmentation at the design stage, a period marked by the foundational question of problem definition, when rules of accountability (for what and to whom) are being constituted.

Widerberg, Pattberg, and Brower's chapter, on accountability in multistakeholder initiatives addressing climate change, Gulbrandsen and Auld's chapter, on governance of sustainable fisheries, and Elliott and Shaedla's chapter, on governance of illegal wildlife trade, all put into stark relief the opportunities and challenges for accountability in hybrid governance arrangements. And Balboa demonstrates that even within the voluntary sector alone, there is a great variation on ideas about conservation (which define what accountability will mean in practice).

However, these last three chapters, which comprise a mix of institutional actors, purposes, and stakeholders, exponentially increase the variation of ideas about the environment and complexity of responsibilities demanded, given, and owed in GEG. In such circumstances, who should be accountable to whom, and for what, becomes a central discussion regarding the demarcation of the political community for accountability. The absence of an agreement on these constitutive, or tier-one, governance questions results in a very uneven record of accountability and improved environmental outcomes.

Conclusion

We have noted throughout this last chapter that globalization has meant increasingly long chains of accountability, as well as shifting debts of accountability to different actors who form a political community. Is this a problem? Does fragmentation of action for governing the environment create incoherence and a conflict in goals? The chapter by van der Ven argues that it does. Balboa shows that globalization can exacerbate the slide into a MAD. Gulbrandsen and Auld's chapter also shows how globalization leads to an ever-shifting pattern of inclusion and exclusion of stakeholders who shape a political community that sets up the normative priorities around which accountability processes, standards, and sanctions will be formed. This might suggest a case for writing off accountability altogether as a potential tool of effective environmental governance.

However, as we think about the original promise and clear limits described in this volume for how accountability can help secure better environmental outcomes, we are encouraged by a metaphor that likens accountability to a meeting place where relationships of mutual obligation interact and must be negotiated. To use a comparison, Lehtonen, Sébastien, and Bauler (2016) assess the value of sustainability indicators in producing desired environmental policy outcomes and proposes that their main benefit is not in generating information for planners regarding proximity to preset targets of success. Instead, their value lies in their effect as instrumental, conceptual, and political tools. In accountability, we see a similar opportunity to act as a boundary object between institutional actors guided by different logics of action that can help negotiate the relationship between the human and nonhuman world. Accountability provides an actionable platform of engagement that is more concrete than higher order debates regarding legitimacy and democracy. Accountability can produce tangible outcomes that enable or curtail legitimate democratic governance.

Accountability is not a replacement for politics, as some of the scholarship and practice would tend to suggest, which focus primarily on functional requirements like monitoring and compliance. (Gupta and van Asselt 2017). Accountability on its own does not supplant trust between actors or impose a hierarchy of goals. It is not an end in itself, but rather a means to negotiate purposes and priorities. The functionally oriented approach to accountability, with a focus on implementation rather than design and learning, as described in these chapters, explains why accountability processes and constituent components like transparency end up simply mirroring existing conflicts between actors while amplifying power differentials.

In their conclusion to the 2017 article, Gupta and van Asselt hone in on this explicitly. They find that transparency and accountability reproduces politics. Their central claim is that

the scope and practices of existing transparency arrangements reflect ongoing disputes around responsibility, differentiation, and burden-sharing for climate action, and hence reflect key conflicts around who (which states) are to be held accountable, and for what. Instead of transparency mediating conflicts (as is the dominant assumption) and thereby facilitating accountability, our analysis suggests that existing UNFCCC systems of transparency mirror these disputes in their scope and design.

In chapter 2 of this volume, Gulbrandsen and Auld also conclude that

when the boundaries of a certification's global community are unclear and evolving, calls for more or deeper stakeholder participation… are unlikely to lessen the contested politics of accountability surrounding these governance institutions. Rather, they may only facilitate greater accountability to stakeholders that are already relatively influential—that is, stakeholders with whom a program has a dependent relationship due to the resources these stakeholders provide.

We have argued elsewhere (Kramarz and Park 2017, 8) that accountability is a "reflective surface of the underlying politics of choice that shape governance." Ultimately, this means that the presence of accountability mechanisms alone is not sufficient to guarantee either due process or effective problem solving. What we have pointed to is the prospect of using accountability, not just as a compliance tool, but as a means of exposing the underlying politics of choice, learning and reconstituting GEG to lead to better environmental outcomes.

References

Abbott, Kenneth W. The Transnational Regime Complex for Climate Change. *Environment and Planning. C, Government & Policy* 30 (4) (2012): 571–590.

Abbott, Kenneth W., and Duncan Snidal. The Governance Triangle: Regulatory Standards Institutions and the Shadow of the State. In *The Politics of Global Regulation*, ed. Walter Mattli and Ngaire Woods. 44–88. Princeton: Princeton University Press, 2009.

Abbott, Kenneth W., and Duncan Snidal. Strengthening International Regulation through Transnational New Governance: Overcoming the Orchestration Deficit. *Vanderbilt Journal of Transnational Law* 42 (2) (2009): 501–578.

Abessolo, Francois Kpwang, Tom Osborn, Paulinus Ngeh, and Martin Tadoum. The Africa Trade in Wildlife Information Exchange System. *Traffic Bulletin* 28 (2) (2016): 43.

Akhtar, Sandra. Environmental and Fishing Groups Unite to Push New Fishery Bill. States News Service, July 23, 1996.

Aldashev, Gani, and Thierry Verdier. Goodwill Bazaar: NGO Competition and Giving to Development. *Journal of Development Economics* 91 (1) (2010): 48–63.

Alter, Karen J., and Sophie Meunier. The Politics of International Regime Complexity. *Perspectives on Politics* 7 (1) (2009): 13–24.

Ammerman, N. T. (1992). *Bible believers: Fundamentalists in the modern world*. New Brunswick, NJ: Rutgers University Press.

Anton, Donald K., and Dinah L. Shelton. *Environmental Protection and Human Rights*. Cambridge: Cambridge University Press, 2011.

Armsworth, Paul R., Isla S. Fishburn, Zoe G. Davies, Jennifer Gilbert, Natasha Leaver, and Kevin J. Gaston. The Size, Concentration, and Growth of Biodiversity-Conservation Nonprofits. *Bioscience* 62 (3) (2012): 271–281.

Auld, Graeme. *Constructing Private Governance: The Rise and Evolution of Forest, Coffee, and Fisheries Certification*. New Haven, CT: Yale University Press, 2014.

Auld, Graeme, and Benjamin Cashore. Mixed Signals: NGO Campaigns and NSMD Governace in an Export-Oriented Country. *Canadian Public Policy* 39 (2) (2013): 143–156.

Auld, Graeme, and Lars H. Gulbrandsen. Transparency in Nonstate Certification: Consequences for Accountability and Legitimacy. *Global Environmental Politics* 10 (3) (2010): 97–119.

Auld, Graeme, and Stefan Renckens. Rule-Making Feedbacks through Intermediation and Evaluation in Transnational Private Governance. *Annals of the American Academy of Political and Social Science* 669 (2) (2017): 93–111.

Auld, Graeme, Stefan Renckens, and Benjamin Cashore. Transnational Private Governance between the Logics of Empowerment and Control. *Regulation & Governance* 9 (2) (2015): 108–124.

Babbie, E. (2012). *The Practice of Social Research* (13th ed.). Belmont, CA: Wadsworth.

Bäckstrand, Karin. Accountability of Networked Climate Governance: The Rise of Transnational Climate Partnerships. *Global Environmental Politics* 8 (3) (2008): 74–102.

Bäckstrand, Karin. Multi-stakeholder Partnerships for Sustainable Development: Rethinking Legitimacy, Accountability and Effectiveness. *European Environment* 16 (2006): 290–306.

Bäckstrand, Karin, Sabine Camp, Sander Chan, Ayşem Mert, and Marco Schäferhoff. Transnational Public-Private Partnerships. In *Global Environmental Governance Reconsidered*, ed. Frank Biermann and Philipp Pattberg. 123–148. Cambridge, MA: MIT Press, 2012.

Balboa, Cristina M. *The Paradox of Scale: How NGOs Build, Maintain, and Lose Authority in Global Environmental Governance*. Cambridge, MA: MIT Press, 2018.

Balboa, Cristina M. Mission Interference: How Competition Confounds Accountability for Environmental Nongovernmental Organizations. *Review of Policy Research* 34 (1) (2017): 110–131.

Balboa, Cristina M. The Accountability of Environmental Impact Bonds: The Future of Global Environmental Governance? *Global Environmental Politics* 16 (2) (2016): 33–41.

Balboa, Cristina M. The Accountability and Legitimacy of International NGOs. In *The NGO Challenge to International Relations Theory*, ed. William Demars and Dennis Djeuzkeul. 159–187. New York: Routledge, 2015.

Balboa, Cristina M. How Successful Transnational NGOs Set Themselves Up for Failure Abroad. *World Development* 54 (2014): 273–287.

Balboa, Cristina M. *When Non-governmental Organizations Govern: Accountability in Private Conservation Networks*. New Haven, CT: Yale University Press, 2009.

Balboa, Cristina M., Ava Berman, and Laurel Welton. *International Nongovernmental Organizations (INGOs) in New York City: A Comparative Study*. New York: Baruch College—CUNY School of Public Affairs' Center for Nonprofit Strategy and Management, 2015.

Banerjee, Subhabrata Bobby. Corporate Environmentalism: The Construct and Its Measurement. *Journal of Business Research* 55 (3) (2002): 177–191.

Bartley, Tim. Institutional Emergence in an Era of Globalization: The Rise of Transnational Private Regulation of Labor and Environmental Conditions. *American Journal of Sociology* 113 (2) (2007): 297–351.

Bartley, Tim, and Curtis Child. Shaming the Corporation: The Social Production of Targets and the Anti-Sweatshop Movement. *American Sociological Review* 79 (4) (2014): 653–679.

Bartley, Tim, and Curtis Child. Movements, Markets and Fields: The Effects of Anti-Sweatshop Campaigns on U.S. Firms, 1993-2000. *Social Forces* 90 (2) (2011): 425–451.

Bartley, Tim, and Shawna N. Smith. Communities of Practice as Cause and Consequence of Transnational Governance. In *Transnational Communities: Shaping Global Economic Governance*, ed. Marie-Laure Djelic and Sigrid Quack. 334–373. Cambridge: Cambridge University Press, 2010.

Behn, Robert D. *Rethinking Democratic Accountability*. Washington, DC: Brookings Institution Press, 2001.

Benner, Thorsten, Wolfgang Reinecke, and Jan Martin Witte. Multisectoral Networks in Global Governance: Towards a Pluralistic Systems of Accountability. In *Global Governance and Public Accountability*, ed. David Held and Mathias Koenig-Archibugi. 67–87. Oxford: Blackwell, 2004.

Bernstein, Steven. *The Compromise of Liberal Environmentalism*. New York: Columbia University Press, 2001.

Bernstein, Steven, and Benjamin Cashore. Can Non-state Global Governance Be Legitimate? An Analytical Framework. *Regulation & Governance* 1 (4) (2007): 347–371.

Bernstein, Steven, and Benjamin Cashore. Globalization, Four Paths of Internationalization and Domestic Policy Change: the Case of Ecoforestry in British Columbia,

Canada. *Canadian Journal of Political Science/Revue Canadienne de Science Politique* 33 (1) (2000): 67–99.

Biermann, Frank. *Earth Systems Governance: World Politics in the Anthropocene*. Cambridge, MA: MIT Press, 2014.

Biermann, Frank, and Aarti Gupta. Accountability and Legitimacy in Earth System Governance: A Research Framework. *Ecological Economics* 70 (2011): 1856–1864.

Biermann, Frank, and Philipp Pattberg. Global Environmental Governance Revisited. In *Global Environmental Governance Reconsidered*, ed. Frank Biermann and Philipp Pattberg. 1–24. Cambridge, MA: MIT Press, 2012.

Biermann, Frank, Philipp Pattberg, Harro van Asselt, and Fariborz Zelli. The Fragmentation of Global Governance Architectures: A Framework for Analysis. *Global Environmental Politics* 9 (4) (2009): 14–40.

Black, Julia. Constructing and Contesting Legitimacy and Accountability in Polycentric Regulatory Regimes. *Regulation & Governance* 2 (2) (2008): 137–164.

Blok, Kornelis, Niklas Höhne, Kees van der Leun, and Nicholas Harrison. Bridging the Greenhouse-Gas Emissions Gap. *Nature Climate Change* 2 (7) (2012): 471–474. doi:10.1038/nclimate1602.

Blok, Kornelius, and Kees Van Der Leun. Wedging the Gap. Ecofys, Netherlands, 2012. https://www.ecofys.com/en/info/wedging-the-gap.

Boiral, Olivier. Corporate Greening Through ISO 14001: A Rational Myth? *Organization Science* 18 (1) (2007): 127–146.

Boiral, Olivier, and Yves Gendron. Sustainable Development and Certification Practices: Lessons Learned and Prospects. *Business Strategy and the Environment* 20 (5) (2011): 331–347.

Börzel, Tanja A., Jana Hönke, and Christian R. Thauer. Does It Really Take the State? *Business and Politics* 14 (3) (2012): 1–34.

Boström, Magnus. Regulatory Credibility and Authority through Inclusiveness: Standardization Organizations in Cases of Eco-Labelling. *Organization* 13 (3) (2006): 345–367.

Bostrom, M., and C. Garsten, eds. *Organizing Transnational Accountability*. Cheltenham, UK: Edward Elgar, 2008.

Bowman, Marion. Personal communication on ARREST-related work. 2016.

Boyer, E. L. (1990). *Scholarship Reconsidered: Priorities of the Professoriate*. New York: Carnegie Foundation for the Advancement of Teaching.

Briner, Gregory, and Sara Moarif. *Enhancing Transparency of Climate Change Mitigation under the Paris Agreement: Lessons from Experience*. Paris: OECD, 2016.

Brooks, D. C., & Sandfort, J. R. (2013). Trial and Error: Iteratively Improving Research on Blended Learning. In A. G. Picciano, C. D. Dziuban, & C. R. Graham (Eds.), *Blended learning: Research perspectives*. Vol. 2, 141–149. New York: Routledge.

Brown, Dana L., Antje Vetterlein, and Anne Roemer-Mahler. Theorizing Transnational Corporations as Social Actors: An Analysis of Corporate Motivations. *Business and Politics* 12 (1) (2010): 1–37.

Brown, Simon, David J. Agnew, and Will Martin. On the Road to Fisheries Certification: The Value of the Objections Procedure in Achieving the MSC Sustainability Standard. *Fisheries Research* 182 (October 2016): 136–148.

Bulkeley, Harriet, Liliana B. Andonova, Michele Betsill, Daniel Compagnon, Thomas N. Hale, Matthew J. Hoffmann, et al. *Transnational Climate Change Governance*. New York: Cambridge University Press, 2014.

Büthe, Tim. Beyond Supply and Demand: A Political-Economy Conceptual Model. In *Governance by Indicators: Global Power through Quantification and Rankings*, ed. Kevin E. Davis, Angelina Fisher, Benedict Kingsbury, and Sally Engle Merry. 29–51. Oxford: Oxford University Press, 2012.

Büthe, Tim, and Walter Mattli. *The New Global Rulers: The Privatization of Regulation in the World Economy*. Princeton, NJ: Princeton University Press, 2011.

Caraiani, C., ed. *Green Accounting Initiatives and Strategies for Sustainable Development*. IGI Global, 2015.

Carroll, Archie B., Kenneth J. Lipartito, James E. Post, and Patricia H. Werhane. *Corporate Responsibility: The American Experience*, ed. Kenneth E . Goodpaster. Cambridge: Cambridge University Press, 2012.

Cashore, Benjamin. Legitimacy and the Privatization of Environmental Governance: How Non-State Market-Driven (NSMD) Governance Systems Gain Rule Making Authority. *Governance: An International Journal of Policy, Administration and Institutions* 15 (4) (2002): 503–529.

Cashore, Benjamin, Deanna Newsom, and Graeme Auld. *Governing Through Markets: Forest Certification and the Emergence of Non-State Authority*. New Haven, CT: Yale University Press, 2004.

Chan, Sander, Paula Ellinger, and Oscar Widerberg. Exploring National and Regional Orchestration of Non-State Action for a <1.5 °C World. *International Environmental Agreement: Politics, Law and Economics* 18 (1) (2018): 135–152.

Chan, Sander, and Philipp Pattberg. Private Rule-Making and the Politics of Accountability: Analyzing Global Forest Governance. *Global Environmental Politics* 8 (3) (2008): 103–121.

Chapin, Mac. A Challenge to Conservationists. *World Watch* 17 (6) (November/ December 2004): 17–31.

Charity Navigator. Giving Statistics. https://www.charitynavigator.org/index.cfm/ bay/content.view/cpid/42.

Charnovitz, Steve. Accountability of Non-governmental Organizations in Global Governance. In *NGO Accountability: Politics`, Principles and Innovation*, ed. Lisa Jordan and Peter van Tuijl. London: Earthscan, 2006.

Chen, Yu-Shan, and Ching-Hsun Chang. Greenwash and Green Trust: The Mediation Effects of Green Consumer Confusion and Green Perceived Risk. *Journal of Business Ethics* 114 (3) (2013): 489–500.

Chesterman, Simon. Globalization Rules: Accountability, Power, and the Prospects for Global Administrative Law. *Global Governance* 14 (2008): 39–52.

Christian, Claire, David Ainley, Megan Bailey, Paul Dayton, John Hocevar, Michael LeVine, et al. A Review of Formal Objections to Marine Stewardship Council Fisheries Certifications. *Biological Conservation* 161 (2013): 10–17.

Clapp, Christa, Jane Ellis, Julia Benn, and Jan Corfee-Morlot. *Tracking Climate Finance: What and How?* Paris: OECD, 2012.

Connekt. What Is Lean and Green? 2017. http://www.lean-green.nl/nl-NL/ algemeen/.

Conservation International. *2015 Impact Report*. Arlington, VA: Conservation International, 2015.

Conservation International. *2005 Annual Report*. Arlington, VA: Conservation International, 2005.

Convention on International Trade in Endangered Species (CITES) of Wild Fauna and Flora. Compliance and Enforcement. Resolution Conf. 11.3 (Rev CoP16), 2013.

Convention on International Trade in Endangered Species (CITES) of Wild Fauna and Flora. Enforcement Matters and the Development of a Global Seizures Database. CoP15 Inf. 37. Fifteenth Meeting of the Conference of the Parties Doha (Qatar), March 13–25, 2010.

Convention on International Trade in Endangered Species (CITES) of Wild Fauna and Flora. Enforcement Expert Group Report to the Fifty-eighth Meeting of the Standing Committee. SC58 Doc.23, Addendum, 2009.

Convention on International Trade in Endangered Species (CITES) of Wild Fauna and Flora. Submission of Enforcement-related Information by the Public and Nongovernmental Organizations to the CITES Secretariat. *Notification to the Parties*, No. 2004/078, December 9, 2004.

Convention on International Trade in Endangered Species (CITES) of Wild Fauna and Flora Secretariat. Implementation of Resolution Conf. 10.10 (Rev. CoP16) on Trade in Elephant Specimens. CoP17 Doc. 57.1., Seventeenth Meeting of the Conference of the Parties Johannesburg (South Africa), September 24 - October 5, 2016.

Convention on International Trade in Endangered Species (CITES) of Wild Fauna and Flora Secretariat. Interpretation and Implementation of the Convention: Compliance and Enforcement. CoP15 Doc.24, 15th Meeting of the Conference of Parties, Doha (Qatar), March 13–25, 2010.

Convention on International Trade in Endangered Species of Wild Fauna and Flora/ TRAFFIC. Memorandum of Understanding (MoU) between TRAFFIC International and the Secretariat of the Convention on International Trade in Endangered Species of Wild Fauna and Flora. November 1, 1999. https://cites.org/sites/default/files/common/disc/sec/CITES-TRAFFIC.pdf.

Cooley, Alexander, and James Ron. The NGO Scramble: Organizational Insecurity and the Political Economy of Transnational Action. *International Security* 27 (1) (2002): 5–39.

Creswell, J. W. (2013). *Research Design: Quantitative, Qualitative, and Mixed Methods Approaches* (4th ed.). Thousand Oaks, CA: Sage.

Da Fonseca, Gustavo A. Conservation Science and NGOs. *Conservation Biology* 17 (2) (2003): 345–347.

Dagnet, Yamide, Teng Fei, Cynthia Elliott, and Yin Qiu. *Improving Transparency and Accountability in the Post-2020 Climate Regime: A Fair Way Forward.* Washington, DC: World Resources Institute, 2014.

Dauvergne, Peter. *Environmentalism of the Rich.* Cambridge, MA: MIT Press, 2016.

Dauvergne, Peter, and Jane Lister. *Eco-Business: A Big-Brand Takeover of Sustainability.* Cambridge, MA: MIT Press, 2013.

Dauvergne, Peter, and Jane Lister. Big Brand Sustainability: Governance Prospects and Environmental Limits. *Global Environmental Change* 22 (1) (2012): 36–45.

Dauvergne, Peter, and Jane Lister. The Power of Big Box Retail in Global Environmental Governance: Bringing Commodity Chains Back into IR. *Millennium* 39 (1) (2010): 145–160.

Davenport, Eileen, and William Low. From Trust to Compliance: Accountability in the Fair Trade Movement. *Social Enterprise Journal* 9 (1) (2013): 88–101.

DeCarrio Voegele, J. (2016). Student Perspectives on Blended Learning through the Lens of Social, Teaching, and Cognitive Presence. In A. G. Picciano, C. D. Dziuban, & C. R. Graham (Eds.), *Blended Learning: Research Perspectives.* Vol. 2, 93–103. New York: Routledge.

Delmas, Magali A., and Venessa Cuerel Burbano. The Drivers of Greenwashing. *California Management Review* 54 (1) (2011): 64–87.

Dijkzeul, Dennis. Heart of Paradox: War, Rape, and NGOs in the DR Congo. In *The NGO Challenge for IR Theory*, ed. William Emile DeMars and Dennis Dijkzeul. New York: Routledge, 2015.

Deloffre, Maryam Z. Global Accountability Communities: NGO self-regulation in the Humanitarian Sector. *Review of International Studies* 42 (4) (October 2016): 724–747.

Deprez, Alexandra, Michel Colombier, and Thomas Spencer. *Transparency and the Paris Agreement: Driving Ambitious Action in the New Climate Regime*. Paris: Institut du développement durable et des relations internationals, 2015.

Dhume, Sadanand. Jurassic Showdown: It Feels Like the Most Ancient Place on Earth, but Komodo National Park Is Being Swept up in a Very Modern Debate: Is Private Better than Public When It Comes to Preserving Unique Habitats? *Far Eastern Economic Review* 165, (19) (May 16, 2002): 50–52.

Dingwerth, Klaus. Private Transnational Governance and the Developing World: A Comparative Perspective. *International Studies Quarterly* 52 (3) (2008): 607–634.

Doelle, Meinhard. Experience with the Facilitative and Enforcement Branches of the Kyoto Compliance System. In *Promoting Compliance in an Evolving Climate Regime*, ed. Jutta Brunnee, Meinhard Doelle and Lavanya Rajamani. 102–121. Cambridge: Cambridge University Press, 2012.

Dolnicar, Sara, Helen Irvine, and Katie Lazarevski. Mission or Money? Competitive Challenges Facing Public Sector Nonprofit Organizations in an Institutionalized Environment. *International Journal of Nonprofit and Voluntary Sector Marketing* 13 (2) (2008): 107–117.

Domanński, J. Competitiveness of Nongovernmental Organizations in Developing Countries: Evidence from Poland. *Nonprofit and Voluntary Sector Quarterly* 41 (1) (2012): 100–119.

Dowdle, Michael W. *Public Accountability: Designs, Dilemmas and Experiences*. Cambridge: Cambridge University Press, 2006.

Dowie, Mark. Conservation Refugees: When Protecting Nature Means Kicking People Out. *Orion Magazine* 24 (6) (November/December 2005): 16–27.

Dringus, L. P., & Seagull, A. B. (2016). A Five-Year Study of Sustaining Blended Learning Initiatives to Enhance Academic Engagement in Computer and Information Sciences Campus Courses. In A. G. Picciano, C. D. Dziuban, & C. R. Graham (Eds.), *Blended Learning: Research Perspectives*. Vol. 2, 122–140. New York: Routledge.

Dubash, Navroz K. Copenhagen: Climate of Mistrust. *Economic and Political Weekly* 44 (52) (2010): 8–11.

Dubnick Melvin, J., and H. George Frederickson. Introduction. In *Accountable Governance: Problems and Promises*, ed. Melvin J. Dubnick and H. George Frederickson, xi–xxx. Armonk, NY: M.E. Sharpe, 2011.

Dubnick, Melvin J., and Jonathan B. Justice. Accounting for Accountability. Paper read at American Political Science Association, September 2–5, 2004, at Chicago.

Dziuban, C. D., Picciano, A. G., Graham, C. R., & Moskal, P. D. (2016). *Conducting Research in Online and Blended Learning Environments: New Pedagogical Frontiers*. New York: Routledge/Taylor & Francis.

Ebrahim, Alnoor. Accountability Myopia: Losing Sight of Organizational Learning. *Nonprofit and Voluntary Sector Quarterly* 34 (1) (2005): 56–87.

Ebrahim, Alnoor. Accountability in Practice. Mechanisms for NGOs. *World Development* 31 (5) (2003): 813–829.

Ebrahim, Alnoor, and Edward Weisband. *Global Accountabilities: Participation, Pluralism and Public Ethics*. Cambridge: Cambridge University Press, 2007.

Eden, Sally, Christopher Bear, and Gordon Walker. Mucky Carrots and Other Proxies: Problematising the Knowledge-Fix for Sustainable and Ethical Consumption. *Geoforum* 39 (2) (March 2008): 1044–1057.

Elkington, John. *Cannibals with Forks: The Triple Bottom Line of 21st Century Business*. Gabriola Island, Canada: New Society Publishers, 1998.

Ellis, Jane, and Sara Moarif. *Identifying and Addressing Gaps in the UNFCCC Reporting Framework*. Paris: OECD, 2015.

Engels, Jens Ivo. Modern Environmentalism. In *The Turning Points of Environmental History*, ed. Frank Uekötter. 119–131. Pittsburgh: University of Pittsburgh Press, 2010.

Environmental Investigation Agency (EIA). *The Dirty Secrets of Japan's Illegal Ivory Trade*. Washington, DC: EIA US, 2016.

Environmental Investigation Agency (EIA). *Sin City: Illegal Wildlife Trade in Laos' Golden Triangle Special Economic Zone*. London: EIA, 2015.

Environmental Investigation Agency (EIA). *Organised Chaos: The Illicit Overland Timber Trade between Myanmar and China*. London: EIA, 2015.

Esty, Daniel C. Non-governmental Organizations at the World Trade Organization: Cooperation, Competition, or Exclusion. *Journal of International Economic Law* 1 (1) (March 1998): 123–147.

Falkner, Robert, Hannes Stephan, and John Vogler. International Climate Policy after Copenhagen: Towards a 'Building Blocks' Approach. *Global Policy* 1 (3) (2010): 252–262.

Finnemore, Martha, and Kathryn Sikkink. International Norm Dynamics and Political Change. *International Organization* 52 (4) (1998): 887–917.

Food and Agriculture Organization of the United Nations (FAO). *Free Prior and Informed Consent An Indigenous Peoples' Right and a Good Practice for Local Communities*. October 14, 2016. http://www.fao.org/3/a-i6190e.pdf.

Food and Agriculture Organization of the United Nations (FAO). *Guidelines for the Eco-labelling of Fish and Fisheries Products from Marine Capture Fisheries*. Rome, Italy: FAO, 2005.

Fowler, F. J. (2013). *Survey Research Methods* (5th ed.). Thousand Oaks, CA: Sage.

Freeland Foundation. ARREST Asia. 2016. http://www.freeland.org/stop-wildlife-trafficking/arrest-asia/.

Freeman, Jody. Extending Public Accountability through Privatization: From Public Law to Publicization. In *Public Accountability: Designs, Dilemmas and Experiences*, ed. Michael D. Dowdle. 83–114. Cambridge: Cambridge University Press, 2006.

Freeman, R. Edward. *Strategic Management: A Stakeholder Approach*. Boston: Pitman, 1984.

Freeman, R. Edward, Jessica Pierce, and Richard H. Dodd. *Environmentalism and the New Logic of Business: How Firms Can Be Profitable and Leave Our Children a Living Planet*. Oxford: Oxford University Press, 2000.

Foundation Center. Foundation Center Stats. 2014. http://data.foundationcenter.org/#/fc1000/subject:environment/all/top:recipients/list/2012.

Fowler, Alan. *Striking a Balance: A Guide to Enhancing the Effectiveness of Non-Governmental Organisations in International Development*. London: Earthscan, 1997.

Fowler, Penny, and Simon Heap. Bridging Troubled Waters: The Marine Stewardship Council. In *Terms of Endearment: Business, NGOs, and Sustainable Development*, ed. Jem Bendell. 135–148. Sheffield, UK: Greenleaf Publishing, 2000.

Fransen, Luc W., and Ans Kolk. Global Rule-Setting for Business: A Critical Analysis of Multi-stakeholder Standards. *Organization* 14 (5) (2007): 667–684.

Fransen, Luc W., Jelmer Schalk, and Graeme Auld. Work Ties Beget Community? Assessing Interactions among Transnational Private Governance Organizations in Sustainable Agriculture. *Global Networks* 16 (1) (2016): 45–67.

Gemmill, Barbara, and Abimbola Bamidele-Izu. The Role of NGOs and Civil Society in Global Environmental Governance. In *Global Environmental Governance: Options and Opportunities*, ed. Daniel C. Esty and Maria H. Ivanova. 77–100. New Haven, CT: Yale School of Forestry and Environmental Studies, 2002.

Gereffi, Gary, and Miguel Korzeniewicz. *Commodity Chains and Global Capitalism.* Westport, CT: Praeger, 1994.

Gibson, Robert B. In Full Retreat: The Canadian Government's New Environmental Assessment Law Undoes Decades of Progress. *Impact Assessment and Project Appraisal* 30 (3) (2012): 179–188.

Giving USA: The Annual Report on Philanthropy for the Year 2011. Chicago: Giving USA Foundation, 2012.

Grandia, Liza. 2004. Letter to the Editor Re: Mac Chapin. *World Watch Magazine.*

Grant, Ruth W., and Robert O. Keohane. Accountability and Abuses of Power in World Politics. *American Political Science Review* 99 (1) (2005): 29–43.

Green, Jessica F. *Rethinking Private Authority: Agents and Entrepreneurs in Global Environmental Governance.* Princeton, NJ: Princeton University Press, 2013.

Greenpeace. *Sanchi Oil Tanker Collision and Sinking—Greenpeace East Asia and Greenpeace Japan Factsheet.* January 15, 2018. http://www.greenpeace.org/eastasia/Page Files/299371/Sanchi%20oil%20tanker%20collision/Sanchi%20oil%20tanker%20 collision%20-%20Greenpeace%20East%20Asia%20factsheet.pdf.

Greenpeace. Where Do McDonalds Filet-O-Fish Sandwiches Come From? August 1, 2014 http://www.greenpeace.org/usa/mcdonalds-murkowski/.

Grieve, Chris. *Memo to MSC Certification Bodies, Fisheries Clients and Stakeholders.* London: Marine Stewardship Council, 2005.

Gulbrandsen, Lars H. *Transnational Environmental Governance: The Emergence and Effects of the Certification of Forests and Fisheries.* Cheltenham, UK: Edward Elgar, 2010.

Gulbrandsen, Lars H. Accountability Arrangements in Non-State Standards Organizations: Instrumental Design and Imitation. *Organization* 15 (4) (2008): 563–583.

Gulbrandsen, Lars H., and Graeme Auld. Contested Accountability Logics in Evolving Nonstate Certification for Fisheries Sustainability. *Global Environmental Politics* 16 (2) (2016): 42–60.

Gupta, Aarti. Transparency in Global Environmental Governance: A Coming of Age? *Global Environmental Politics* 10 (3) (2010): 1–9.

Gupta, Aarti. When Global is Local: Negotiating Safe Use of Biotechnology. In *Earthly Politics: Local and Global in Environmental Governance*, ed. Sheila Jasonoff and Marybeth Long-Martello. 127–148. Cambridge, MA: MIT Press, 2004.

Gupta, Aarti, and Harro van Asselt. Transparency in Multilateral Climate Politics: Furthering (or distracting from) Accountability? *Regulation & Governance* (July 26, 2017). In press.

Gutierrez, Alexis, and Thomas F. Thornton. Can Consumers Understand Sustainability through Seafood Eco-Labels? A U.S. and UK Case Study. *Sustainability* 6 (11) (2014): 8195–8217.

Gutierrez, Nicolas L., and David J. Agnew. MSC Objection Process Improves Fishery Certification Assessments: A Comment to Christian et al. (2013). *Biological Conservation* 165 (2013): 212–213.

Haedicke, Michael. *Organizing Organic: Conflict and Compromise in an Emerging Market.* Redwood City, CA: Stanford University Press, 2016.

Hale, Thomas N. All Hands on Deck: The Paris Agreement and Nonstate Climate Action. *Global Environmental Politics* 16 (3) (2016): 12–22.

Hale, Thomas N., David Held, and Kevin A. Young. *Gridlock: Why Global Cooperation Is Failing When We Need It Most.* Cambridge, MA: Polity Press, 2013.

Hall, R., and T. Biersteker. *The Emergence of Private Authority in Global Governance.* Cambridge: Cambridge University Press, 2002.

Halpern, Benjamin S., Christopher R. Pyke, Helen E. Fox, J. Chris Haney, Martin A. Schlaepfer, and Patricia Zaradic. Gaps and Mismatches between Global Conservation Priorities And Spending. *Conservation Biology* 20 (1) (2006): 56–64.

Hance, Jeremy. Has Big Conservation Gone Astray? *Mongabay*, April 26, 2016. https://news.mongabay.com/series/evolving-conservation/.

Hance, Jeremy. Conservation Today, the Old-fashioned Way. *Mongabay*, May 10, 2016. https://news.mongabay.com/2016/05/conservation-today-old-fashioned-way/.

Harbert, Tam. Ethics and the Supply Chain. *Sage Business Researcher.* April 25, 2016. http://businessresearcher.sagepub.com/sbr-1775-99621-2728048/20160425/ethics-and-the-supply-chain#NOTE[1].

Harrison, Kathryn. Racing to the Top or the Bottom? Industry Resistance to Eco-Labeling of Paper Products in Three Jurisdictions. *Environmental Politics* 8 (4) (1999): 110–136.

Held, David, and Mathias Koenig-Archibugi. *Global Governance and Public Accountability.* Oxford: Blackwell, 2005.

Herold, Anke. Experiences with Articles 5, 7, and 8 Defining the Monitoring, Reporting and Verification System under the Kyoto Protocol. In *Promoting Compliance in an Evolving Climate Regime*, ed. Jutta Brunnee, Meinhard Doelle and Lavanya Rajamani. 122–146. Cambridge: Cambridge University Press, 2012.

Highleyman, Scott, Amy Mathews Amos, and Hank Cauley. *An Independent Assessment of the Marine Stewardship Council*. Sandy River Pit, ME: Wildhavens, 2004.

Hoffmann, Matthew J. The Analytic Utility (and Practical Pitfalls) of Accountability. *Global Environmental Politics* 16 (2) (2016): 22–32.

Hoffmann, Matthew J. *Climate Governance at the Crossroads: Experimenting with a Global Response after Kyoto*. Oxford: Oxford University Press, 2011.

Holthus, Paul. *Peer Review of Cyanide Detection Testing Methods Employed in the Philippines*. Honolulu: Marine Aquarium Council, 1999.

Holmes, W. M. (2014). *Using propensity scores in quasi-experimental designs*. Thousand Oaks, CA: Sage.

Howell, J. T. (1972). *Hard living on Clay Street: Portraits of blue collar families*. Prospect Heights, IL: Waveland Press.

Houpt, Simon. Beyond the Bottle: Coke Trumpets Its Green Initiatives. *The Globe and Mail*, January 13, 2011. https://www.theglobeandmail.com/report-on-business/industry-news/marketing/beyond-the-bottle-coke-trumpets-its-green-initiatives/article569182/.

Howes, Rupert. Personal Interview with MSC Executive Director Rupert Howes by Lars H. Gulbrandsen, London, May 23, 2006 (on file with author).

Howlett, Michael. Beyond Legalism? Policy Ideas, Implementation Styles and Emulation-Based Convergence in Canadian and U.S. Environmental Policy. *Journal of Public Policy* 20 (3) (2000): 305–329.

Huggins, Anna. The Desirability of Depoliticization: Compliance in the International Climate Regime. *Transnational Environmental Law* 4 (1) (2015): 101–124.

Hurd, Ian. Legitimacy and Authority in International Politics. *International Organization* 53 (2) (1999): 379–408.

Intergovernmental Panel on Climate Change (IPCC). *Climate Change 2014: Synthesis Report. Contribution of Working Groups I, II and III to the Fifth Assessment Report of the IPCC on Climate Change*. Geneva, Switzerland: IPCC, 2015.

Intergovernmental Panel on Climate Change (IPCC). Summary for Policymakers. In *Climate Change 2014: Impacts, Adaptation, and Vulnerability. Part A: Global and Sectoral Aspects*. Contribution of Working Group II to the Fifth Assessment Report of the Intergovernmental Panel on Climate Change, 1–32. Cambridge: Cambridge University Press, 2014.

International Marinelife Alliance (IMA). *Response to the Review of the IMA Cyanide Testing Standard Operating Procedures Prepared by the Marine Aquarium Council*. Pasig City, the Philippines: IMA, 1999.

International Marinelife Alliance (IMA). *First Asia-Pacific Seminar/Workshop on the Live Reef Fish Trade*. First Asia-Pacific Seminar/Workshop on the Live Reef Fish Trade, Manila, Philippines, USAID, WRI, IMA, 1998.

IUCN/Institute for European Environmental Policy (IEEP). Biodiversity and Wildlife Trade. *Brussels in Brief*, Institute for European Environmental Policy, 2007.

Jacquet, Jennifer, Daniel Pauly, David Ainley, Sidney Holt, Paul Dayton, and Jeremy Jackson. Seafood Stewardship in Crisis. *Nature* 467 (September 2, 2010): 28–29.

Jasper, James. A Strategic Approach to Collective Action: Looking for Agency in Social-Movement Choices. *Mobilization: An International Quarterly (San Diego, Calif.)* 9 (1) (2004): 1–16.

Jepson, Paul. Governance and Accountability of Environmental NGOs. *Environmental Science & Policy* 8 (5) (2005): 515–524.

Jessop, Bob. *The Future of the Capitalist State*. Cambridge, MA: Polity Press, 2002.

Jiang, Ruihua Joy, and Pratima Bansal. Seeing the Need for ISO 14001. *Journal of Management Studies* 40 (4) (2003): 1047–1067.

Johnston, Alastair Iain. Treating International Institutions as Social Environments. *International Studies Quarterly* 45 (2001): 487–515.

Jordan, Lisa. Mechanisms for NGO Accountability. *GPPi Research Paper Series* no. 3. Berlin: Global Public Policy Institute, 2005.

Jordan, Lisa, and Peter van Tuijl. Rights and Responsibilities in the Political Landscape of NGO Accountability: Introduction and Overview. In *NGO Accountability: Politics, Principles and Innovation*, ed. Lisa Jordan and Peter van Tuijl. 3–20. London: Earthscan, 2006.

Karlsson-Vinkhuyzen, Sylvia, and Jeffrey McGee. Legitimacy in an Era of Fragmentation: The Case of Global Climate Governance. *Global Environmental Politics* 13 (3) (2013): 56–78.

Karlsson-Vinkhuyzen, Sylvia, and Harro van Asselt. *Strengthening Accountability under the 2015 Climate Change Agreement*. London: Climate Strat, 2015.

Kearns, Kevin P. *Managing for Accountability: Preserving the Public Trust in Public and Nonprofit Organizations*. San Francisco: Jossey-Bass, 1996.

Keck, Margaret E., and Kathryn Sikkink. *Activists Beyond Borders: Advocacy Networks in International Politics*. Ithaca, NY: Cornell University Press, 1998.

Keohane, Robert O. Global Governance and Democratic Accountability. In *Taming Globalization: Frontiers of Governance*, ed. David Held and Mathias Koenig-Archibugi. 130–159. Cambridge, MA: Polity Press, 2003.

Keohane, Robert O., and David G. Victor. The Regime Complex for Climate Change. *Perspectives on Politics* 9 (1) (2011): 7–23.

Koenig-Archibugi, Mathias, and Kate Macdonald. The Role of Beneficiaries in Transnational Regulatory Processes. *Annals of the American Academy of Political and Social Science* 670 (1) (March 2017): 36–57.

Kong, Xiangwen. Achieving Accountability in Climate Negotiations: Past Practices and Implications for the Post-2020 Agreement. *Chinese Journal of International Law* 14 (3) (2015): 545–565.

Kooiman, Jan, and Svein Jentoft. Meta-governance: Values, Norms, and Principles, and the Making of Hard Choices. *Public Administration* 87 (4) (December 2009): 818–836.

Koppell, Jonathan. The Legitimacy-Accountability Connection and Transnational Governance Organizations. Paper read at 2005 Annual Conference of the American Political Science Association, at Washington, DC

Koppell, Jonathan. Pathologies of Accountability: ICANN and the Challenge of "Multiple Accountabilities Disorder." *Public Administration Review* 65 (1) (2005): 94–108.

Korach, Hetty. Addressing Accountability at the Global Level: The Challenges Facing International NGOs. In *NGO Accountability: Politics, Principles and Innovation*, ed. Lisa Jordan and Peter van Tuijl. London: Earthscan, 2006.

Kothari, Ashish, and Manju Menon. *Participatory Conservation Gathers Momentum.* Gland, Switzerland: IUCN, 2000.

Kramarz, Teresa. Partnerships in Global Environmental Governance: The Growth of a Procedural Norm without Substance. In *Governing the Provision of Ecosystem Services*, ed. Roldan Muradian and Laura Rival. 47–65. New York: Springer, 2013.

Kramarz, Teresa, and Susan Park. Introduction: The Politics of Environmental Accountability. *Review of Policy Research* 34 (1) (2017): 4–9.

Kramarz, Teresa, and Susan Park. Accountability in Global Environmental Governance: A Meaningful Tool for Action? *Global Environmental Politics* 16 (2) (2016): 1–21.

Krueger, R., & Casey, M. A. (2008). *Focus groups: A practical guide for applied research* (4th ed.). Thousand Oaks, CA: Sage.

Kuyper, Jon, and Karin Bäckstrand. Accountability and Representation: Nonstate Actors in UN Climate Diplomacy. *Global Environmental Politics* 16 (2) (2016): 61–81.

Laird, Gordon. *The Price of a Bargain: The Quest for Cheap and the Death of Globalization.* Toronto: McClelland & Stewart, 2009.

Larrinaga-Gonzalez, Carlos, and Jan Bebbington. Accounting Change or Institutional Appropriation?—A Case Study of the Implementation of Environmental Accounting. *Critical Perspectives on Accounting* 12 (3) (2001): 269–292.

Leadbitter, Duncan, and Trevor Ward. Dispute Resolution and the MSC. In *Eco-labelling in Fisheries: What Is It All About?* ed. Bruce Phillips, Trevor Ward, and Chet Chaffee. 80–85. Oxford: Blackwell, 2003.

Lehtonen, Markku, Lea Sébastien, and Tom Bauler. The Multiple Roles of Sustainability Indicators in Informational Governance: Between Intended Use and Unanticipated Influence. *Current Opinion in Environmental Sustainability* 18 (2016): 1–9.

Liebenthal, Andres. *Promoting Environmental Sustainability in Development: An Evaluation of the World Bank's Performance.* Washington, DC: World Bank, 2002.

Like-Minded Developing Countries (LMDC). Submission on Elements of the 2015 Agreed Outcome. 2014. http://unfccc.int/files/documentation/submissions_from _parties/adp/application/pdf/adp_lmdc_ws1_20140309.pdf.

Like-Minded Developing Countries (LMDC). LMDC Views on Identification of Elements in ADP Workstream 1. November 18, 2013. https://unfccc.int/files/ documentation/submissions_from_parties/adp/application/pdf/adp2-3_lmdc _workstream_1_20131118.pdf.

Likert, R. (1932). A Technique for the Measurement of Attitudes. *Archives de Psychologie*, 140, 1–55.

Llopis, Glenn. Consumers Are No Longer Brand Loyal. *Forbes* (December 10) (2014). https://www.forbes.com/sites/glennllopis/2014/12/10/consumers-are-no-longer -brand-loyal.

LMMA Network. Locally Managed Marine Area Networks: the Voice of Communities. LMMANET.org. 2015.

Lober, David Bynum, Elizabeth Campbell, and Mary Jacques. The 100 Plus Corporate Environmental Report Study: A Survey of an Evolving Environmental Management Tool. *Business Strategy and the Environment* 6 (2) (1997): 57–73.

Lohmann, Larry. Toward a Different Debate in Environmental Accounting: The Cases of Carbon and Cost-benefit Accounting. *Organizações & Sociedade* 34 (3–4) (2009): 499–534.

Longhofer, Wesley, and Evan Schofer. National and Global Origins of Environmental Association. *American Sociological Review* 75 (4) (2010): 505–533.

MacDonald, Christine C. *Green, Inc.: An Environmental Insider Reveals How a Good Cause Has Gone Bad.* Guilford, CT: Lyons, 2008.

Maniates, Michael F. Individualization: Plant a Tree, Buy a Bike, Save the World? *Global Environmental Politics* 1 (3) (2001): 31–52.

March, James G., and Johan P. Olsen. The Logic of Appropriateness. In *The Oxford Handbook of Public Policy*, ed. Robert Goodin, Michael Moran, and Martin Rein. 687–706. New York: Oxford University Press, 2006.

Marine Stewardship Council (MSC). Final Determination on Echebastar Indian Ocean Tuna Fishery. *Marine Stewardship Council—News*, November 17, 2015. https://www.msc.org/newsroom/news/final-determination-on-echebastar-indian-ocean-tuna-fishery?fromsearch=1&isnewssearch=1.

Marine Stewardship Council (MSC). *Global Impacts Report Metadata*. 2015 ed. London: Marine Stewardship Council, 2015.

Marine Stewardship Council (MSC). 2014. Trustee's Report and Accounts for the Year Ended 31st March 2014. London: Marine Stewardship Council. https://www.msc.org/documents/institutional/finance/msc-accounts-2013-2014/view.

Marine Stewardship Council (MSC). *Marine Stewardship Council Fisheries Certification Methodology Version 6.1 (1 May 2010)*. London: Marine Stewardship Council, 2010.

Marine Stewardship Council (MSC). *TAB Directive 023: Revised Fisheries Certification Methodology Objections Procedure*. London: Marine Stewardship Council, 2010.

Marine Stewardship Council (MSC). *Annual Report 2008 / 09*. London: Marine Stewardship Council, 2009.

Marine Stewardship Council (MSC). *Marine Stewardship Council Fisheries Assessment Methodology and Guidance to Certification Bodies*. London: Marine Stewardship Council, 2008.

Marine Stewardship Council (MSC). *Leader in Fishery Certification and Eco-labelling Announces 100% Consistency with UN Guidelines*. London: Marine Stewardship Council, 2006.

Marine Stewardship Council (MSC). *MSC Quality and Consistency Project—Phase 1— Intent of MSC's Criteria Workshop Participant List*. London: Marine Stewardship Council, 2006.

Marine Stewardship Council (MSC). *The Quality and Consistency Project—Regional Workshops*. London: Marine Stewardship Council, 2006.

Marine Stewardship Council (MSC). *Improving Application of the Principles and Criteria for Sustainable Fishing: The Quality and Consistency Project—A Cornerstone of MSC's Reform Agenda*. London: Marine Stewardship Council, 2005.

Marine Stewardship Council (MSC). *Technical Advisory Board—Public Summary— Meeting No. 7, 6–7 June 2005*. London: Marine Stewardship Council, 2005.

Marine Stewardship Council (MSC). *Special Joint Session of the Stakeholder Council and the Technical Advisory Board—The MSC Claim of Sustainability*. London: Marine Stewardship Council, 2004.

Marine Stewardship Council (MSC). *Summary of MSC Board Meeting*. London: Marine Stewardship Council, 2004. https://www.msc.org/documents/governance/public

-summaries-of-board-meeting-minutes/Summary_February_2004_Board_meeting.
pdf.

Martín-López, Berta, Carlos Montes, and Javier Benayas. The Non-Economic Motives behind the Willingness to Pay for Biodiversity Conservation. *Biological Conservation* 139 (1–2) (2007): 67–82.

Marino, M. P. (2011). High School World History Textbooks: An Analysis of Content Focus and Chronological Approaches. *History Teacher*, 44 (3), 421–446.

Mashaw, Jerry Louis. Accountability in Institutional Design: Some Thoughts on the Grammar of Governance. In *Public Accountability: Designs, Dilemmas and Experiences*, ed. Michael D. Dowdle. Cambridge Studies in Law and Society, 115–156. Cambridge: Cambridge University Press, 2006.

Mason, Michael. The Governance of Transnational Environmental Harm: Addressing New Modes of Accountability/Responsibility. *Global Environmental Politics* 8 (3) (2008): 8–24.

Mason, Michael. *The New Accountability: Environmental Responsibility across Borders*. London: Earthscan, 2005.

Matthews, Adam. The Environmental Crisis in Your Closet. *Newsweek*, August 13, 2015. http://www.newsweek.com/2015/08/21/environmental-crisis-your-closet -362409.html.

Mattli, Walter, and Tim Büthe. Global Private Governance: Lessons from a National Model of Setting Standards in Accounting. *Law and Contemporary Problems* 68 (3/4) (2005): 225–262.

Mayer, Frederick, and Gary Gereffi. Regulation and Economic Globalization: Prospects and Limits of Private Governance. *Business and Politics* 12 (3) (2010): 1–25.

McDermott, Constance L., Lloyd C. Irland, and Pablo Pacheco. Forest Certification and Legality Initiatives in the Brazilian Amazon: Lessons for Effective and Equitable Forest Governance. *Forest Policy and Economics* 50 (2015): 134–142.

McLellan, Elisabeth, and Crawford Allan. Wildlife Crime Initiative Annual Update 2015. Gland: WWF and TRAFFIC, 2015.

Meidinger, Errol. The Administrative Law of Global Private-Public Regulation: The Case of Forestry. *European Journal of International Law* 17 (1) (2006): 47–87.

Miles, Edward L., Steinar Andresen, Elaine M. Carlin, Jon Birger Skjærseth, Arild Underdal, and Jørgen Wettestad. *Environmental Regime Effectiveness: Confronting Theory with Evidence*. Cambridge, MA: The MIT Press, 2001.

Milliken, Tom, Fiona M. Underwood, Robert W. Burn, and Louisa Sangalakula. *The Elephant Trade Information System (ETIS) and the Illicit Trade in Ivory*. Report to the

17th meeting of the Conference of the Parties to CITES, CoP17 Doc. 57.6 (Rev.1) Annex. May 27, 2016.

Minogue, Martin. The Internationalization of New Public Management. In *The Internationalization of New Public Management: Reinventing the Third World State*, ed. W. McCourt and M. Minogue. Cheltenham, UK: Edward Elgar, 2001.

Mitchell, George E., and Sarah S. Stroup. The Reputations of NGOs: Peer Evaluations of Effectiveness. *Review of International Organizations* 12 (3) (2017): 397–419.

Mitchell, Ronald B. *International Environmental Agreements (IEA) Database Project 2002–2015*. 2014.3 ver. https://iea.uoregon.edu/.

Mitchell, Ronald B. Transparency for Governance: The Mechanisms and Effectiveness of Disclosure-Based and Education-Based Transparency Policies. *Ecological Economics* 70 (11) (2011): 1882–1890.

Mol, Arthur P. J. The Environmental Nation State in Decline. *Environmental Politics* 25 (1) (2016): 48–68.

Morgan, Jennifer, Athena Ballesteros, Heather McGray, Kelly Levin, Florence Daviet, Fred Stolle, and Hilary McMahon. Reflections on the Cancun Agreements, Washington, DC: World Resources Institute. December 14, 2010. http://www.wri.org/blog/2010/12/reflections-cancun-agreements.

Mulgan, Richard. "Accountability": An Ever-Expanding Concept? *Public Administration* 78 (3) (2000): 555–573.

Mutersbaugh, Tad. Fighting Standards with Standards: Harmonization, Rents, and Social Accountability in Certified Agrofood Networks. *Environment & Planning A* 37 (11) (2005): 2033–2051.

Najam, Adil, and Mark Halle. *Sustainable Development Insights—Global Environmental Governance: The Challenge of Accountability. Sustainable Development Insights*. Boston: Boston University Frederick S. Pardee Center for the Study of the Longer-Range Future, 2010, http://www.iisd.org/publications/pub.aspx.

The Nature Conservancy. *Our World: 2015 Annual Report*. Arlington, VA: The Nature Conservancy, 2015.

The Nature Conservancy. *Conservation That Works: 2004 Annual Report*. Arlington, VA: The Nature Conservancy, 2004.

The Nature Conservancy. *Actions Taken by the Board of Governors*. Arlington, VA: The Nature Conservancy, 2003.

Nellemann, Christian, Ian Redmond and Johannes Refisch. *The Last Stand of the Gorilla—Environmental Crime and Conflict in the Congo Basin. A Rapid Response Assessment*. Arendal: GRID-Arendal/INTERPOL, 2010.

Nelson, Jane. *The Operation of Non-governmental Organizations (NGOs) in a World of Corporate and Other Codes of Conduct.* Cambridge, MA: John F. Kennedy School of Government, 2007.

Nielsen. *The Nielsen Global Survey of Corporate Social Responsibility and Sustainability— The Sustainability Imperative: New Insights on Consumer Expectations.* October 2015. http://www.nielsen.com/content/dam/nielsenglobal/dk/docs/global-sustainability-report-oct-2015.pdf.

Nielson, Daniel L., Michael J. Tierney, and Catherine E. Weaver. Bridging the Rationalist-Constructivist Divide: Re-engineering the Culture at the World Bank. *Journal of International Relations and Development* 9 (2) (2006): 107–139.

Newell, Peter. Civil Society, Corporate Accountability and the Politics of Climate Change. *Global Environmental Politics* 8 (3) (2008): 122–153.

Newell, P., and J. Wheeler, eds. *Rights, Resources and the Politics of Accountability.* London: Zed Books, 2006.

Obach, Brian K. *Organic Struggle: The Movement for Sustainable Agriculture in the United States.* Cambridge, MA: The MIT Press, 2015.

Oberthür, Sebastina. Options for a Compliance Mechanism in a 2015 Climate Agreement. *Climate Law* 4 (1–2) (2014): 30–49.

Okereke, Chukwumerije. Equity Norms in Global Environmental Governance. *Global Environmental Politics* 8 (3) (2008): 25–50.

Oliver, Christine. Strategic Responses to Institutional Processes. *Academy of Management Review* 16 (1) (1991): 145–179.

Ottaway, David B., and Joe Stephens. Nonprofit Land Bank Amasses Billions. *The Washington Post*, May 4, 2003, A01.

Paddison, Laura. WWF's President on Business Partnerships and Greenwashing. *The Guardian*, October 16, 2013. https://www.theguardian.com/sustainable-business/wwf-president-business-partnerships-greenwashing.

Pantel, Sandrine, and Noorainie Awang Anak. *A Preliminary Assessment of Pangolin Trade in Sabah.* Petaling Jaya, Malaysia: TRAFFIC Southeast Asia, 2010.

Park, Susan. *The World Bank Group and Environmentalists: Changing International Organisation Identities.* Manchester, UK: Manchester University Press, 2010.

Parker, Lee D. Social and Environmental Accountability Research: A View from the Commentary Box. *Accounting, Auditing & Accountability Journal* 18 (6) (2005): 842–860.

Pattberg, Philipp. The Forest Stewardship Council: Risks and Potential of Private Forest Governance. *Journal of Environment & Development* 14 (3) (2005): 356–374.

Pattberg, Philipp, and Oscar Widerberg. Transnational Multi-Stakeholder Partnerships for Sustainable Development: Conditions for Success. *Ambio* 45 (1) (2016): 42–51.

Pellizoni, Luigi, and Marja Ylönen. Responsibility in Uncertain Times: An Institutional Perspective on Precaution. *Global Environmental Politics* 8 (3) (2008): 51–73.

Porter, Michael, and Mark Kramer. Strategy and Society: The Link Between Competitive Advantage and Corporate Social Responsibility. *Harvard Business Review* 84 (12) (December 2006): 78–92.

Potoski, M., and A. Prakash, eds. *Voluntary Programs: A Club Theory Perspective*. Cambridge, MA: MIT Press, 2010.

Picciano, A. G. (2016). Qualitative Research in Online and Blended Learning. In C. D. Dziuban, A. G. Picciano, C. R. Graham, & P. D. Moskal (Eds.), *Conducting Research in Online and Blended Learning Environments: New Pedagogical Frontiers*. 84–96. New York: Routledge/Taylor & Francis.

Potoski, Matthew, and Aseem Prakash. Green Clubs and Voluntary Governance: ISO 14001 and Firms' Regulatory Compliance. *American Journal of Political Science* 49 (2) (2005): 235–248.

Power, Michael. *The Audit Society: Rituals of Verification*. Oxford: Oxford University Press, 1997.

Pratt, Vaughan R. *Establishment of Regional Network of Cyanide Detection Test (CDT) Laboratories in the Philippines, Vietnam, Sabah Malaysia*. Honolulu: International Marinelife Alliance, 2004.

Princen, Thomas, Michael Maniates, and Ken Conca. *Confronting Consumption*. Cambridge, MA: The MIT Press, 2002.

Pulles, Tinus. Did the UNFCCC Review Process Improve the National GHG Inventory Submissions? *Carbon Management* 8 (1) (2017): 1–13.

Raggo, Paloma. Leaders' Accounts: A Study of Transnational NGOs Leadership Views on Accountability. Doctoral dissertation, Syracuse University, 2014.

Rainforest Alliance. Our Work with Unilever. November 2014. https://www.rainforest-alliance.org/about/company-commitments/unilever.

Rajamani, Lavanya. Ambition and Differentiation in the 2015 Paris Agreement: Interpretive Possibilities and Underlying Politics. *International and Comparative Law Quarterly* 65 (2) (2016): 493–514.

Rajamani, Lavanya. Differentiation in the Emerging Climate Regime. *Theoretical Inquiries in Law* 14 (1) (2013): 151–171.

Raustiala, Kal. *Reporting and Review Institutions in 10 Multilateral Environmental Agreements*. Nairobi, Kenya: UNEP, 2001.

Raza, Rashid H., and Devendar S. Chauhan. *M. K. S. Pasha, and Samir Sinha. Illuminating the blind spot: A Study on Illegal Trade in Leopard Parts in India (2001–2010)*. New Delhi: TRAFFIC India/WWF India, 2012.

Ribot, Jesse C. *Democratic Decentralization of Natural Resources: Institutionalizing Popular Participation*. Washington, DC: World Resources Institute, 2002.

Risse, Thomas. Global Governance and Communicative Action. In *Global Governance and Public Accountability*, ed. David Held and Mathias Koenig-Archibugi. 164–189. Oxford: Blackwell, 2005.

Risse, Thomas, Stephen C. Ropp, and Kathryn Sikkink, eds. *The Power of Human Rights: International Norms and Domestic Change*. Cambridge: Cambridge University Press, 1999.

Romero, Filemon G., Laura Kadlecik, Aquilino A. Alvarez, Jr., and Vaughan R. Pratt. *CREST: Coral Reef Education for Students and Teachers Manual*. Manila, Philippines: International Marinelife Alliance, 1995.

Romzek, Barbara S., and Melvin J. Dubnick. Accountability in the Public Sector: Lessons from the Challenger Tragedy. *Public Administration Review* 47 (May/June 1987): 227–238.

Rosenau, James N. Change, Complexity, and Governance in Globalizing Space. In *Debating Governance: Authority, Steering, and Democracy*, ed. Jon Pierre. 167–200. Oxford: Oxford University Press, 2000.

Rosenberg, Andrew A., Jill H. Swasey, and Margaret Bowman. Rebuilding US Fisheries: Progress and Problems. *Frontiers in Ecology and the Environment* 4 (6) (2006): 303–308.

Rosenberg, Jonathan. More than a Question of Agency: Privatized Project Implementation, Accountabilities, and Global Environmental Governance. *Review of Policy Research* 34 (1) (2017): 10–30.

Roundtable on Sustainable Biomaterials (RSB). Certification | RSB Roundtable on Sustainable Biomaterials. *RSB*. 2016. http://rsb.org/certification/.

Roundtable on Sustainable Biomaterials (RSB). A Guide to RSB Certification: How to Get Your Operation Certified. *RSB*. 2017. http://rsb.org/wp-content/uploads/2017/04/RSB-Certification-Guide.pdf.

Rubec, Peter J. Testimony to U.S. Subcommittee on Fisheries Conservation, Wildlife, and Oceans Concerning House Resolution 87. Washington, DC, 1997. https://www.house.gov/resource/105cong/fishery/may06.97.rubec.htm.

Rubin, Edward. The Myth of Non-Bureaucratic Accountability and the Anti-Administrative Impulse. In *Public Accountability: Designs, Dilemmas and Experiences*, ed. Michael D. Dowdle. 52–82. Cambridge, MA: Cambridge University Press, 2006.

Ruggie, John Gerard. Reconstituting the Global Public Domain: Issues, Actors, and Practices. *European Journal of International Relations* 10 (4) (2004): 499–531.

Sacré, Vinciane. EU-TWIX: Ten Years of Information Exchange and Cooperation between Wildlife Law Enforcement Officials in Europe. In *Handbook of Transnational Environmental Crime*, ed. Lorraine Elliott and William H. Schaedla. 478–488. Cheltenham, UK: Edward Elgar Publishers, 2016.

Sapsford, R. (2006). *Survey Research* (2nd ed.). Thousand Oaks, CA: Sage.

Sawhill, John C. Mission Impossible?: Measuring Success in Nonprofit Organizations. *Nonprofit Management & Leadership* 11 (3) (2001): 371–386.

Schäferhoff, Marco, Sabine Campe, and Christopher Kaan. Transnational Public-Private Partnerships in International Relations: Making Sense of Concepts, Research Frameworks, and Results. *International Studies Review* 11 (3) (2009): 451–474.

Schank, R. (2011). *Teaching Minds: How Cognitive Science Can Save Our Schools*. New York: Teachers College Press.

Schillermans, Thomas, and Madalina Busuioc. Predicting Public Sector Accountability: From Agency Drift to Forum Drift. *Journal of Public Administration: Research and Theory* 25 (1) (2015): 191–215.

Schillemans, Thomas, and Remco Smulders. Learning from Accountability?! Whether, What, and When. *Public Performance & Management Review* 39 (1) (2015): 248–271.

Schimmelfennig, Frank. Strategic Calculation and International Socialisation: Membership Incentives, Party Constellations, and Sustained Compliance in Central and Eastern Europe. *International Organization* 59 (4) (2005): 827–860.

Searle, John. *The Construction of Social Reality*. New York: Free Press, 1995.

Shadish, W. R., Cook, T. D., & Campbell, D. T. (2001). *Experimental and Quasi-Experimental Designs for Generalized Causal Inference* (2nd ed.). Independence, KY: Cengage.

Shell, Ellen Ruppel. *Cheap: The High Cost of Discount Culture*. New York: Penguin Press, 2009.

Shore, Cris, and Susan Wright. Governing by Numbers: Audit Culture, Rankings and the New World Order. *Social Anthropology* 23 (1) (2015): 22–28.

Skibba, K. (2016). Choice Does Matter: Faculty Lessons Learned Teaching Adults in a Blended Program. In A. G. Picciano, C. D. Dziuban, & C. R. Graham (Eds.), *Blended learning: Research Perspectives*. Vol. 2, 203–212. New York: Routledge.

Smedley, Tim. Sustainable Sugar: Coca-Cola and BP Signed Up but Will It Go Mainstream? *The Guardian*, September 15, 2014. https://www.theguardian.com/sustainable-business/2014/sep/15/sustainable-sugar-can-coca-cola-bp-shell-bonsucro.

Smith, Lucy, and Katharina Klaas. *Networks and NGOs Relevant to Fighting Environmental Crime*. Berlin, Germany: Ecologic Institute, 2015.

Sommerer, Thomas, and Sijeong Lim. The Environmental State as a Model for the World? An Analysis of Policy Repertoires in 37 Countries. *Environmental Politics* 25 (1) (2016): 92–115.

South Africa. Ad Hoc Working Group on the Durban Platform for Enhanced Action. Design and Elements of the 2015 Agreement. Draft Submission by South Africa. 2014. http://unfccc.int/files/bodies/application/pdf/adp_elements_southafrica.pdf.

Stacey, Kiran. Shell Leaves Prince of Wales Climate Change Group amid Concerns. *Financial Times*, September 11, 2015. https://www.ft.com/cms/s/0/d63ea0c0-57dc-11e5-9846-de406ccb37f2.html.

Starobin, Shana, and Erika Weinthal. The Search for Credible Information in Social and Environmental Global Governance: The Kosher Label. *Business and Politics* 12 (3) (2010): 1–35.

Steele, Anne. Lumber Liquidators Settles Charges Related to Safety of Chinese-Made Laminate Flooring. *Wall Street Journal*, March 22, 2016. https://www.wsj.com/articles/lumber-liquidators-settles-charges-related-to-safety-of-chinese-made-laminate-flooring-1458665403.

Steiner, Achim. Accountability in a Globalized World. *World Conservation* (January 2007).

Stephens, Joe. The Nature Conservancy: Mixing with Business. *Washington Post*, May 6, 2003.

Stephens, Joe, and David B. Ottaway. $420,000 a Year and No-Strings Fund: Conservancy Underreported President's Pay and Perks of Office. *Washington Post*, May 4, 2003, A21.

Stephens, Joe, and David B. Ottaway. How a Bid to Save a Species Came to Grief. *Washington Post*, May 5, 2003, A01.

Stephens, Joe, and David B. Ottaway. Image Is a Sensitive Issue. *Washington Post*, May 4, 2003, A23.

Stephens, Joe, and David B. Ottaway. Landing a Big One: Preservation, Private Development. *Washington Post*, May 6, 2003, A09.

Stephens, Joe, and David B. Ottaway. Nonprofit Sells Scenic Acreage to Allies at a Loss: Buyers Gain Tax Breaks with Few Curbs on Land Use. *Washington Post*, May 6, 2003, A01.

Stephens, Joe, and David B. Ottaway. On Eastern Shore, For-profit 'Flagship' Hits Shoals. *Washington Post*, May 5, 2003, A11.

Stephens, Joe, and David B. Ottaway. Nature Conservancy Suspends Land Sales. *Washington Post*, May 13, 2003, A03.

Stephenson, Max, and Elisabeth Jr. Chaves. The Nature Conservancy, the Press, and Accountability. *Nonprofit and Voluntary Sector Quarterly* 35 (3) (2006): 345–366.

Stoner, Sarah S., and Natalia Pervushina. *Reduced to Skin and Bones Revisited: An Updated Analysis of Tiger Seizures from 12 Tiger Range Countries (2000–2012)*. Kuala Lumpur: TRAFFIC, 2013.

Suchman, Mark C. Managing Legitimacy: Strategic and Institutional Approaches. *Academy of Management Review* 20 (3) (1995): 571–610.

Sutherland, W. J., W. M. Adams, R. B. Aronson, R. Aveling, T. M. Blackburn, S. Broad, et al. One Hundred Questions of Importance to the Conservation of Global Biological Diversity. *Conservation Biology* 23 (3) (2009): 557–567.

Sutton, David. An Unsatisfactory Encounter with the MSC—A Conservation Perspective. In *Eco-labelling in Fisheries: What Is It All About?* ed. Bruce Phillips, Trevor Ward and Chet Chaffee. 114–119. Oxford: Blackwell Publishing, 2003.

Sutton, Michael. Marine Stewardship Council: An Appeal for Co-operation. *Samudra* 19 (1998): 26–30.

Tamang, Parshuram. An Overview of the Principle of Free, Prior and Informed Consent and Indigenous Peoples in International and Domestic Law and Practices. Presented at Workshop on Free, Prior, and Informed Consent and Indigenous Peoples, organized by the Secretariat of United Nations Permanent Forum on Indigenous Issues, 17–19 January 2005, United Nations Headquarter, New York, United States of America.

Terborgh, John. *Requiem for Nature*. Washington, DC: Shearwater Books, 1999.

Thauer, Christian R. *The Managerial Sources of Corporate Social Responsibility*. Cambridge, MA: Cambridge University Press, 2014.

Timmons, Roberts J., and Romain Weikmans. Postface: Fragmentation, Failing Trust, and Enduring Tensions over What Counts as Climate Finance. *International Environmental Agreement: Politics, Law, and Economics* 17 (1) (2017): 129–137.

TNO. Resultaat Toetsing TNO: Lean and Green Awards. December 29, 2015. http://www.lean-green.nl/uploads/2015/12/nieuw-assessmentformulier-v2.pdf.

Tokunaga, H. T. (2016). *Fundamental Statistics for the Social and Behavioral Sciences.* Thousand Oaks, CA: Sage.

TRAFFIC. *TRAFFIC's Engagement in the Fight against Illegal Trade in Elephant Ivory.* Cambridge, MA: TRAFFIC International, 2012.

TRAFFIC. EU-TWIX: Ten Years of Enforcement Assistance, *Press Release*, December 3, 2015. http://www.traffic.org/home/2015/12/3/eu-twix-ten-years-of-enforcement-assistance.html; accessed 28 November 2016.

TRAFFIC. Platform to Enhance Collaboration in Countering Illegal Wildlife Trade Launched in Central Africa. *Press Release*, February 16, 2016. http://www.traffic.org/home/2016/2/16/platform-to-enhance-collaboration-in-countering-illegal-wild.html.

Tuckman, Howard P. Competition, Commercialization, and the Evolution of Non-profit Organizational Structures. *Journal of Policy Analysis and Management* 17 (2) (1998): 175–194.

Underwood, Fiona M., Robert W. Burn, and Tom Milliken. Dissecting the Illegal Ivory Trade: An Analysis of Ivory Seizures Data. *PLoS ONE* 8 (10) (2013): 1–12.

United Nations Environment Programme Finance Initiative (UNEP FI). Portfolio Decarbonization Coalition: About. *Brochure.* 2016. http://unepfi.org/pdc/.

United Nations Environment Programme (UNEP). *The Emissions Gap Report 2015 – Executive Summary.* Nairobi: UNEP, 2015.

United Nations Environment Programme (UNEP). Global Environmental Outlook 5. 2012. https://www.unenvironment.org/resources/global-environment-outlook-5

United Nations Environment Programme Finance Initiative (UNEP FI). *The Portfolio Decarbonization Coalition: Mobilizing Financial Markets to Drive Economic Decarbonization.* Brochure, 2016.

United Nations Environment Programme Finance Initiative (UNEP FI), and CDP. *From Disclosure to Action: The First Annual Report of the Portfolio Decarbonization Coalition.* Geneva, Switzerland: UNEP FI: 2015. http://www.unepfi.org/fileadmin/documents/FromDisclosureToAction.pdf.

United Nations Framework Convention on Climate Change (UNFCCC). Submitted Biennial Update Reports (BURs) from Non Annex I Parties. Last updated on April 3, 2018. https://unfccc.int/national_reports/non-annex_i_natcom/reporting_on_climate_change/items/8722.php.

United Nations Framework Convention on Climate Change (UNFCCC). Ad-hoc Working Group on the Paris Agreement (APA), Second part of the First Session, Marrakech, 7–14 November 2016, Agenda Item 5—Modalities, Procedures, and Guidelines for the Transparency Framework for Action and Support Referred to in Article 13 of the Paris Agreement, Informal Note by the Co-Facilitators. UNFCCC, Bonn, Germany, 2016. http://unfccc.int/files/meetings/marrakech_nov_2016/in-session/application/pdf/apa_item_5_informal_note_v2.pdf.

United Nations Framework Convention on Climate Change (UNFCCC). *Parties' Views Regarding Modalities, Procedures and Guidelines for the Transparency Framework for Action and Support Referred to in Article 13 of the Paris Agreement. FCCC/APA/2016/INF.3*. Bonn, Germany: UNFCCC, 2016.

United Nations Framework Convention on Climate Change (UNFCCC). *Adoption of the Paris Agreement. Decision 1/CP.21*. Bonn, Germany: UNFCCC, 2015.

United Nations Framework Convention on Climate Change (UNFCCC). Guidelines for the Technical Review of Information Reported under the Convention Related to Greenhouse Gas Inventories, Biennial Reports and National Communications by Parties Included in Annex I to the Convention. Decision 13/CP.20. UNFCCC, Bonn, Germany, 2014.

United Nations Framework Convention on Climate Change (UNFCCC). Revision of the UNFCCC Reporting Guidelines on Annual Inventories for Parties Included in Annex I to the Convention. Decision 24/CP.19. UNFCCC, Bonn, Germany. 2013.

United Nations Framework Convention on Climate Change (UNFCCC). *Outcome of the Work of the Ad Hoc Working Group on Long-Term Cooperative Action under the Convention. Decision 2/CP.17*. Bonn, Germany: UNFCCC, 2011.

United Nations Framework Convention on Climate Change (UNFCCC). *Report of the In-depth Review of the Fifth National Communication of Canada. FCCC/IDR.5/CAN*. Bonn, Germany: UNFCCC, 2011.

United Nations Framework Convention on Climate Change (UNFCCC). *Submission from the African Group. FCCC/AWGLCA/2011/CRP.20*. Bonn, Germany: UNFCCC, 2011.

United Nations Framework Convention on Climate Change (UNFCCC). *Submissions from India. FCCC/AWGLCA/2011/CRP.11*. Bonn, Germany: UNFCCC, 2011.

United Nations Framework Convention on Climate Change (UNFCCC). *The Cancun Agreements: Outcome of the Work of the Ad Hoc Working Group on Long-term Cooperative Action under the Convention. Decision 1/CP.16*. Bonn, Germany: UNFCCC, 2010.

United Nations Framework Convention on Climate Change (UNFCCC). *Guidelines for the Preparation of the Information Required under Article 7 of the Kyoto Protocol. Decision 15/CMP.1*. Bonn, Germany: UNFCCC, 2005.

United Nations Framework Convention on Climate Change (UNFCCC). *Issues Relating to Adjustments under Article 5, Paragraph 2, of the Kyoto Protocol. Decision 22/CMP.1*. Bonn, Germany: UNFCCC, 2005.

United Nations Framework Convention on Climate Change (UNFCCC). *Procedures and Mechanisms Relating to Compliance under the Kyoto Protocol. Decision 27/CMP.1.* Bonn, Germany: UNFCCC, 2005.

United Nations Framework Convention on Climate Change (UNFCCC). Implementation of the Berlin Mandate: Additional Proposals from Parties. FCCC/AGBM/1997/MISC.1/Add.3. UNFCCC, Bonn, Germany, 1997. http://unfccc.int/cop5/resource/docs/1997/agbm/misc01a3.htm.

United States. U.S. Submission on the 2015 Agreement. October 17, 2013. https://unfccc.int/files/documentation/submissions_from_parties/adp/application/pdf/adp_usa_workstream_1_20131017.pdf.

UTZ. 2016. *UTZ Impact Report March 2016: Combining Insights from UTZ Monitoring Data with Findings from Impact Studies.* Amsterdam, The Netherlands: UTZ. https://www.utz.org/wp-content/uploads/2016/03/Impact-report-2016.pdf.

Van Asselt, H., J. Berseus, J. Gupta, C. Haug. *Nationally Appropriate Mitigation Actions (NAMAs) in Developing Countries: Challenges and Opportunities.* Bilthoven: Netherlands Environmental Assessment Agency, 2010.

Van Asselt, Harro, Weikmans Romain, Roberts Timmons, and Achala Abeysinghe. *Transparency of Action and Support under the Paris Agreement.* Oxford: European Capacity Building Initiative, 2016.

Vandermeer, John. *The Worship of Nature: Echoes of 19th Century Essentialism.* University of Michigan Department of Biology, 1994.

Van der Ven, Hamish. From Greenwash to Credible Governance: Explaining Industry Leadership in Sustainable Aquaculture Certification. Paper presented at the International Studies Association Annual Meeting, Atlanta, GA, March 18, 2016.

Van der Ven, Hamish. Correlates of Rigorous and Credible Transnational Governance: A Cross-Sectoral Analysis of Best Practice Compliance in Eco-Labeling. *Regulation & Governance* 9 (3) (2015): 276–293.

Van der Ven, Hamish. Gatekeeper Power: Understanding the Influence of Lead Firms over Transnational Sustainability Standards. *Review of International Political Economy.* Forthcoming.

Van der Ven, Hamish, Steven Bernstein, and Matthew Hoffmann. Valuing the Contributions of Non-State and Subnational Actors to Climate Governance. *Global Environmental Politics* 17 (1) (2017): 1–20.

Van der Ven, Hamish. Socializing the C-Suite: Why Some Big-Box Retailers Are "Greener" than Others. *Business and Politics* 16 (1) (2014): 31–63.

Victor, David G. *Global Warming Gridlock: Creating More Effective Strategies for Protecting the Planet.* Cambridge, MA: Cambridge University Press, 2011.

Vogel, David. Private Global Business Regulation. *Annual Review of Political Science* 11 (2008): 261–282.

Vogel, David. *The Market for Virtue: The Potential and Limits of Corporate Social Responsibility*. Washington, DC: Brookings Institution Press, 2007.

Wandesforde-Smith, Geoffrey. Looking for Law in All the Wrong Places? Dying Elephants, Evolving Treaties, and Empty Threats. *Journal of International Wildlife Law and Policy* 19 (4) (2016): 365–381.

Warner, Rosalind. *Discourses of Global Environmental Governance from Colonialism to the 21st Century*. Toronto: York University, 2005.

White, Rob. NGO Engagement in Environmental Law Enforcement: Critical Reflections. *Australasian Policing* 4 (1) (2012): 7–11.

Widerberg, Oscar, and Philipp Pattberg. Accountability Challenges in the Transnational Regime Complex for Climate Change. *Review of Policy Research* 34 (1) (2017): 68–87.

Widerberg, Oscar, and Johannes Stripple. The Expanding Field of Cooperative Initiatives for Decarbonization: A Review of Five Databases. *Wiley Interdisciplinary Reviews: Climate Change* 7 (4) (2016): 486–500.

Widerberg, Oscar, Philipp Pattberg, and Kristian Kristensen. *Technical Paper*. vol. 2. Mapping the Institutional Architecture of Global Climate Change Governance. Amsterdam: Institute for Environmental Studies, 2016. http://fragmentation.eu/wp-content/uploads/2016/06/Technical-report-Climate-change-R16-02-FINAL.pdf.

Wildlife Alliance. Wildlife Rapid Rescue Team, 2016. http://www.wildlifealliance.org/page/view/82/wildlife/wildlife-rapid-rescue-team.

Wildlife Conservation Society (WCS). WCS to Collaborate with World Customs Organization on Illegal Wildlife Trade. *Press Release*, January 7, 2016. https://newsroom.wcs.org/News-Releases/articleType/ArticleView/articleId/8474/WCS-to-Collaborate-with-World-Customs-Organization-on-Illegal-Wildlife-Trade.aspx.

Wilshusen, Peter R., Steven R. Brechin, Crystal L. Fortwangler, and Patrick C. West. Reinventing a Square Wheel: Critique of a Resurgent Protection Paradigm in International Biodiversity Conservation. *Society & Natural Resources* 15 (1) (2002): 17–40.

World Bank Inspection Panel. *Democratic Republic of Congo: Transitional Support for Economic Recovery Grant (TSERO)*. Investigation Report. Online. Washington, DC: World Bank, 2018. http://siteresources.worldbank.org/EXTINSPECTIONPANEL/Resources/FINALINVREPwhole.pdf.

World Customs Organization. WCO and TRAFFIC Sign MoU to Build the Enforcement Capabilities of Customs Frontline Officers in the Fight against Illicit Trafficking in Wild Fauna and Flora. *Press Release*, October 21, 2013. http://www.wcoomd.org/en/media/newsroom/2013/october/wco-and-traffic-sign-mou.aspx.

World Wildlife Fund (WWF). Market Transformation Initiative Strategy. 2012. http://assets.panda.org/downloads/how_the_wwf_markets_transformation_initiative_works.pdf.

World Wildlife Fund (WWF). A promising future for rhinos in Nepal's Chitwan Park. *Focus* 30, no. 4 (July/August 2008): 1, 7.

World Wildlife Fund (WWF). *2005 Annual Report*. Gland, Switzerland: Andrew White Creative Communications, 2005.

Yamin, Farhana, and Joanna Depledge. *The International Climate Change Regime: A Guide to Rules, Institutions, and Procedures*. Cambridge: Cambridge University Press, 2004.

Yin, Robert K. *Case Study Research: Design and Methods*. 5th ed. Thousand Oaks, CA: SAGE Publications, 2014.

Zahar, Alexander. *International Climate Change Law and State Compliance*. London: Routledge, 2015.

Contributors

Graeme Auld is Associate Professor and Director of the School of Public Policy and Administration at Carleton University, Canada. He holds a cross appointment in the Institute of Political Economy, and he is a Research Fellow with the Carleton Centre for Community Innovation and a Faculty Associate at the Governance, Environment, and Markets Initiative at Yale University. He has broad interests in comparative environmental politics and global environmental governance. His main research interest focuses on the emergence, evolution, and impacts of transnational private governance regimes across sectors of the global economy. He also studies natural resource policy, climate change policy, and information disclosure and transparency policies. He is coauthor (with Benjamin Cashore and Deanna Newsom) of *Governing Through Markets: Forest Certification and the Emergence of Non-state Authority* (Yale University Press, 2004), and the author of *Constructing Private Governance: The Rise and Evolution of Forest, Coffee, and Fisheries Certification* (Yale University Press, 2014).

Cristina Balboa is an Associate Professor at the Marxe School of Public and International Affairs, Baruch College—CUNY. Her research incorporates international relations, comparative policy, and organization theory to demonstrate the relationship between an organization's internal characteristics (like structure, capacity) and its external accountability, legitimacy, and efficacy. Her book *The Paradox of Scale: How NGOs Build, Maintain, and Lose Authority in Environmental Governance* is available from MIT Press. Other publications include "How Successful Transnational NGOs Set Themselves up for Failure on the Ground" in *World Development* (2014); "Policymaking in the Global Context: Training Students to Build Effective Strategic Partnerships" (with Deloffre, 2015) in the *Journal of Public Affairs Education;*

and "Environmental Impact Bonds: The Future of Environmental Governance?" in *Global Environmental Politics* (2016).

Lieke Brouwer has a BSc in Psychology, with a minor in Social Psychology, and an MA in Criminology from Utrecht University. This is complemented by courses on environmental law and policy and public policy challenges of the 21st century. Throughout her master's work, she has immersed herself in green criminological issues with a focus on climate and analyzed various aspects and perspectives. Lieke carried out her master's thesis at the Institute for Environmental Studies (IVM) at the Vrije Universiteit Amsterdam, studying global climate policy and mechanisms of accountability and compliance in cooperative climate governance initiatives.

Lorraine Elliott is Professor Emerita in the Department of International Relations and ANU Public Policy Fellow in the Bell School of Asia Pacific Affairs at The Australian National University. She has published extensively on global and regional (Asia Pacific) environmental governance and ethics, human security, climate change and migration, transnational environmental crime, and Australian foreign policy. Her research on global environmental governance has been funded by the Australian Research Council, the Academy of the Social Sciences in Australia, the Royal Netherlands Academy of Arts and Sciences, and the Japan Foundation. Professor Elliott is Lead Faculty with the Earth System Governance program and holds a nonresident Senior Fellowship with the Institute for Asia and Pacific Studies at the University of Nottingham. From 2015 to 2018 she is Chair of the Academic Council on the United Nations System.

Lars H. Gulbrandsen is a Research Professor and the Deputy Director at the Fridtjof Nansen Institute in Oslo, Norway, where he also served as director of the research program on global environmental governance (2010–2016). His main research interests are within the fields of global environmental politics and international political economy, with a particular focus on transnational private governance programs, international forest politics, climate and energy policy, carbon markets, and protected areas management. He is the author of *Transnational Environmental Governance: The Emergence and Effects of the Certification of Forests and Fisheries* (Edward Elgar, 2010), coauthor (with Jon Birger Skjærseth, Per Ove Eikeland, and Torbjørg

Jevnaker) of *Linking EU Climate and Energy Policies* (Edward Elgar, 2016), and coeditor (with Jørgen Wettestad) of *The Evolution of Carbon Markets: Design and Diffusion* (Routledge, 2018).

Aarti Gupta is Associate Professor with the Environmental Policy Group at the Department of Social Sciences in Wageningen University, the Netherlands. Her research focuses on global environmental governance, including anticipatory governance of novel technologies and the role of science and knowledge therein, as well as questions of transparency and accountability, with an empirical focus on climate, forests, biodiversity, and biosafety. Publications include guest-edited special issues in Ecological Economics and Global Environmental Politics, and the coedited volume Transparency in Global Environmental Governance: Critical Perspectives (MIT Press, 2014). She holds a PhD from Yale University, and has been a Postdoctoral Fellow with Columbia University's Center for Science, Policy and Outcomes (CSPO) and a Global Environmental Assessment Fellow at Harvard University. She is Associate Editor of the journal Global Environmental Politics, and Lead Faculty of the international Earth System Governance Research Project, as well as cofounder of the interdisciplinary REDD@WUR network.

Teresa Kramarz is Associate Professor at the Munk School of Global Affairs in the University of Toronto. She directs the Munk One undergraduate program, codirects the Environmental Governance Lab, and is the co-convener with Dr. Susan Park of the Accountability in Global Environmental Governance Task Force of the Earth System Governance network. Her work examines the impact of the World Bank's public-private partnerships on democracy, innovation, and financially sustainable conservation governance, the legitimacy of the World Bank as a global knowledge actor, democratic accountability in environmental politics, and extractivism in Latin America. Recent publications appear in *Global Environmental Politics, Environmental Policy and Governance, and Review of Policy Research*. Teresa is a Research Associate in the Munk School of Global Affairs, and a Senior Research Fellow of the Earth System Governance. She brings to her scholarship extensive professional experience in developmnent, monitoring, and evaluation of international organizations' projects and initiatives throughout Latin America. Teresa worked for ten years on sustainable development programs with the World Bank, the United Nations Development

Programme, the Food and Agricultural Organization, and the Canadian International Development Agency.

Susan Park is an Associate Professor in International Relations at the University of Sydney. She focuses on how state and nonstate actors use formal and informal influence to make the Multilateral Development Banks (MDBs) greener and more accountable. Susan has published in numerous journals, most recently in the *Review of International Political Economy*. Her textbook, *International Organisations and Global Problems: Theories and Explanations* was published in 2018 (Cambridge University Press). She published *The World Bank Group and Environmentalists: Changing International Organisation Identities* in 2010 (Manchester University Press). Susan has coedited with Antje Vetterlein, *Owning Development* (Cambridge University Press, 2010) and with Jonathan Strand, *Global Economic Governance and the Development Practices of the Other Multilateral Development Banks* (Routledge, 2015). Susan is an associate editor of the journal *Global Environmental Politics* and is co-convener with Teresa Kramarz (at the University of Toronto) of the Earth Systems Governance (ESG) Task Force on "Accountability in Global Environmental Governance." Susan was the chair of the Environmental Studies Section of the ISA from 2015 to 2017. She is a Senior Research Fellow of the ESG, an affiliated faculty member of the Munk School's Environmental Governance Lab at the University of Toronto, an External Associate of the Centre for the Study of Globalisation and Regionalisation at Warwick University, and a research affiliate of the Sydney Environment Institute at the University of Sydney.

Philipp Pattberg is Professor of transnational environmental governance and policy and head of department for Environmental Policy Analysis, Institute for Environmental Studies at VU University, Amsterdam, the Netherlands. He is also the general director of the Netherlands Research School for Socioeconomic and Natural Sciences of the Environment (SENSE). Pattberg specializes in the study of global environmental politics, with a focus on climate change governance, biodiversity, forest and marine governance, transnational relations, public-private partnerships, network theory, and institutional analysis. Pattberg's current research scrutinizes institutional complexity, functional overlaps, and fragmentation across environmental domains (http://fragmentation.eu). Pattberg's most recent book publication is the Encyclopedia of Global Environmental Governance and Politics (coedited with Fariborz Zelli, Edward Elgar 2015).

William H. Schaedla is an environmental specialist with over 30 years of experience in management, policy, research, and teaching. He holds a PhD in ecology and evolutionary biology from Arizona State University. His professional background includes conservation science and natural resources activities in the United States, Latin America, and Asia. He was Deputy Chief of Party to the Association of Southeast Asian Nations Wildlife Enforcement Network (ASEAN-WEN) Support Program. He served as WWF Country Director in Thailand and as Southeast Asia Regional Director for TRAFFIC, the wildlife trade monitoring network. He is presently an instructor with the United States Bureau of Indian Education, where he is a collaborator on National Science Foundation (NSF) and National Institutes of Health (NIH) supported research projects. He has held visiting appointments at the Australian National University and the Thailand Institute of Scientific and Technical Research and sits on the advisory board for the Journal of International Wildlife Law and Policy. He is also the manager of Ecolloquium, a nongovernmental forum for environmental problem solving. His work has been published in scientific journals, UN reports, media commentary, and consultancy reports. He is the coeditor of (and author of contributions to) the *Handbook on Transnational Environmental Crime* (Edward Elgar Publishing, 2016).

Harro van Asselt is Professor of Climate Law and Policy at the University of Eastern Finland Law School, and Senior Research Fellow at the Stockholm Environment Institute. He is author of *The Fragmentation of Global Climate Governance* (Edward Elgar, 2014) and coeditor of *Climate Change Policy in the European Union* (Cambridge University Press, 2010). He has published extensively on issues related to global climate governance in edited books and journals, including *Global Environmental Politics, Climate Policy, Law & Policy,* and *Nature Climate Change.* He is editor of the *Review of European, Comparative and International Environmental Law* (RECIEL), and also serves as Associate Editor of the *Carbon and Climate Law Review.*

Hamish van der Ven is an Assistant Professor in the School of Environment and the Department of Political Science at McGill University. He is also affiliated with the Governance, Environment, and Markets Initiative at Yale University, the Environmental Governance Lab at the University of Toronto, and the Earth System Governance Project. His research examines the growing role of nonstate actors in transnational environmental governance. He holds a PhD in Political Science (2015) from the University of Toronto, an MA in Political Science (2006), and a BA in History from the University of British Columbia.

Oscar Widerberg is an Assistant Professor at the Institute for Environmental Studies (IVM) at the Vrije Universiteit Amsterdam. His research focuses on global environmental governance, primarily on the interactions between international, transnational, national, and local climate governance. He also teaches master and bachelor courses in environmental policy, climate governance, and research methods. Oscar is an Earth System Governance Project research fellow and member of several climate governance policy and research networks. He has published book chapters and articles on global climate governance in journals such as *WIREs Climate Change*, *Millennium*, and *Global Policy*. Before joining the IVM, Oscar worked in various consultancies, carrying out assignments on climate change and environment and energy policy for international public institutions such as the European Commission and the World Bank.

Index

www.ingramcontent.com/pod-product-compliance
Lightning Source LLC
Chambersburg PA
CBHW031415270326
41929CB00010BA/1458